Stilling
the Storm

The Vital Worship, Healthy Congregations Series
John D. Witvliet, Series Editor

Published by the Alban Institute in cooperation with the
Calvin Institute of Christian Worship

BOOKS IN THE SERIES

C. Michael Hawn
One Bread, One Body:
Exploring Cultural Diversity in Worship

Norma deWaal Malefyt and Howard Vanderwell
Designing Worship Together:
Models and Strategies for Worship Planning

Craig A. Satterlee
When God Speaks through Change:
Preaching in Times of Congregational Transition

Peter Bush and Christine O'Reilly
Where 20 or 30 Are Gathered:
Leading Worship in the Small Church

Robert P. Glick
With All Thy Mind:
Worship That Honors the Way God Made Us

Kathleen S. Smith
Stilling the Storm:
Worship and Congregational Leadership in Difficult Times

Stilling the Storm

Worship and Congregational Leadership in Difficult Times

Kathleen S. Smith

THE
ALBAN
INSTITUTE
Herndon, Virginia
www.alban.org

The Alban Institute
2121 Cooperative Way, Suite 100
Herndon, VA 20171

Unless otherwise noted, scripture quotations are from the New Revised Standard Version, © 1989, Division of Christian Education of the National Council of Churches of Christ in the United States of America. Published by Thomas Nelson, Inc. Used by permission of the National Council of Churches of Christ in the United States of America.

Scripture quotations marked NIV are taken from the Holy Bible, New International Version. Copyright © 1973, 1978, 1984 by International Bible Society. Used by permission of Zondervan. All rights reserved.

Cover design by Wendy Ronga, Hampton Design Group.

Library of Congress Cataloging-in-Publication Data

Smith, Kathleen S.
  Stilling the storm : worship and congregational leadership in difficult times / Kathleen S. Smith ; foreword by Arthur Paul Boers.
    p. cm. -- (The vital worship, healthy congregations series)
  Includes bibliographical references.
  ISBN-13: 978-1-56699-327-2
  ISBN-10: 1-56699-327-X
  1. Worship. 2. Suffering--Religious aspects--Christianity. 3. Change--Religious aspects--Christianity. I. Title.

  BV15.S49 2006
  264--dc22
                                        2006028444

    10 09 08 07 06   UG   I 2 3 4 5

To my mother, Elaine Ryskamp Hofman, who worshiped
and worked beside her pastor husband for 56 years,
both in difficult times and through many good years.
On the date of her death, August 24, 2005.

Contents

Editor's Foreword

Healthy Congregations

Christianity is a "first-person plural" religion, where communal worship, service, fellowship, and learning are indispensable for grounding and forming individual faith. The strength of Christianity in North America depends on the presence of healthy, spiritually nourishing, well-functioning congregations. Congregations are the cradle of Christian faith, the communities in which children of all ages are supported, encouraged, and formed for lives of service. Congregations are the habitat in which the practices of the Christian life can flourish.

As living organisms, congregations are by definition in a constant state of change. Whether the changes are in membership, pastoral leadership, lay leadership, the needs of the community, or the broader culture, a crucial mark of healthy congregations is their ability to deal creatively and positively with change. The fast pace of change in contemporary culture, with its bias toward, not against, change only makes the challenge of negotiating change all the more pressing for congregations.

Vital Worship

At the center of many discussions about change in churches today is the topic of worship. This is not surprising, for worship is at the center of congregational life. To "go to church" means, for most members of congregations, "to go to worship." In *How Do We Worship?*, Mark Chaves begins his analysis with the simple assertion, "Worship is the most central and public activity engaged in by American religious congregations" (Alban Institute, 1999, p. 1). Worship styles are one of the most significant reasons that people choose to join a given congregation. Correspondingly, they are central to the identity of most congregations.

Worship is also central on a much deeper level. Worship is the locus of what several Christian traditions identify as the nourishing center of congregational life: preaching, common prayer, and the celebration of ordinances or sacraments. Significantly, what many traditions elevate to the status of "the means of grace" or even the "marks of the church" are essentially liturgical actions. Worship is central, most significantly, for theological reasons. Worship both reflects and shapes a community's faith. It expresses a congregation's view of God and enacts a congregation's relationship with God and each other.

We can identify several specific factors that contribute to spiritually vital worship and thereby strengthen congregational life.

- Congregations, and the leaders that serve them, need a shared vision for worship that is grounded in more than personal aesthetic tastes. This vision must draw on the deep theological resources of Scripture, the Christian tradition, and the unique history of the congregation.
- Congregational worship should be integrated with the whole life of the congregation. It can serve as the "source and summit" from which all the practices of the Christian life flow. Worship both reflects and shapes the life of the church in education, pastoral care, community service, fellowship, justice, hospitality, and every other aspect of church life.
- The best worship practices feature not only good worship "content," such as discerning sermons, honest prayers, creative artistic contributions, celebrative and meaningful rituals for baptism and the Lord's Supper. They also arise out of good process, involving meaningful contributions from participants, thoughtful leadership, honest evaluation, and healthy communication among leaders.

Vital Worship, Healthy Congregations Series

The Vital Worship, Healthy Congregations Series is designed to reflect the kind of vibrant, creative energy and patient reflection that will promote worship that is both relevant and profound. It is designed to invite congregations to rediscover a common vision for worship, to sense how worship is related to all aspects of congregational life, and to imagine better ways of preparing both better "content" and better "process" related to the worship life of their own congregations.

It is important to note that strengthening congregational life through worship renewal is a delicate and challenging task precisely because of the uniqueness of each congregation. This book series is not designed to represent a single denomination, Christian tradition, or type of congregation. Nor is it designed to serve as arbiter of theological disputes about worship. Books in the series will note the significance of theological claims about worship, but they may, in fact, represent quite different theological visions from each other, or from our work at the Calvin Institute of Christian Worship. That is, the series is designed to call attention to instructive examples of congregational life and to explore these examples in ways that allow readers in very different communities to compare and contrast these examples with their own practice. The models described in any given book may for some readers be instructive as examples to follow. For others, a given example may remind them of something they are already doing well, or something they will choose not to follow because of theological commitments or community history.

In the first volume in our series, *One Bread, One Body: Exploring Cultural Diversity in Worship,* Michael Hawn poses the poignant question "is there room for my neighbor at the table?" and explores what four multicultural congregations have to teach us about hospitality and the virtues of cross-cultural worship. His work helps us step back and reflect on the core identity of our congregations.

In our second volume, *Designing Worship Together: Models and Strategies for Worship Planning,* Norma deWaal Malefyt and Howard Vanderwell enter the trenches of weekly congregational life. They give us helpful insights into the process of how services are planned and led. It is hard to overstate the significance of this topic. For without a thoughtful, discerning, collaborative worship planning process, all manner of worship books, conferences, and renewal programs are likely either to make no inroads into the life of a given congregation or, when they do, to damage rather than renew congregational life.

In the third volume, *When God Speaks through Change: Preaching in Times of Congregational Transition,* Craig Satterlee addresses the question of how worship (and particularly preaching) might best respond to times of significant congregational transition. The vast majority of published perspectives and resources for preaching and worship unwittingly assume a level of constancy in congregational life, taking for granted that the congregation will have the resources (emotional and otherwise) to absorb some significant new message or practice. However, on any given Sunday, a strikingly large number of churches are simply trying to cope with a significant transition in community life or leadership. These transitions do limit what preachers and worship leaders can do on Sunday, but they also present unparalleled opportunities for the reception of the gospel. For congregations in transition, this book provides a useful and necessary frame for viewing almost all other advice and resources about what should happen in public worship.

In the fourth volume, *Where 20 or 30 Are Gathered: Leading Worship in the Small Church,* Peter Bush and Christine O'Reilly probe a topic that is instructive not only for small congregations, but also for large ones. When representatives of small congregations attend worship conferences or read books about worship they are frequently confronted with practices and resources that are entirely impractical for their purposes, requiring time and money that simply aren't available. Yet, as Bush and O'Reilly demonstrate, "small" certainly does not mean "deficient." In fact, smaller congregations have the potential to achieve participation, flexibility, and intimacy that larger congregations find much harder to achieve. In the upside-down world of the kingdom of God, could it be that those of us from larger congregations should be attending conferences in smaller congregations, rather than just the other way around?

In our fifth volume, *With All Thy Mind: Worship That Honors the Way God Made Us,* Robert Glick turns our attention to the people who gather for worship. As alert pastors know so well, when worshipers assemble they bring with them remarkable differences in aptitude, temperament, and preferences. For leaders who eagerly desire that their congregations participate in worship in knowing and engaged ways, coming to terms with this diversity is essential. It is otherwise too tempting for preachers to prepare sermons and musicians to prepare music for people who are just like themselves. Recent writers have given us several ways to understand the diversity of persons who worship: personality type indicators, theories of multiple intelligences, and right-brain/left-brain differences. Glick works with the latter approach to help us understand that some differences among us can't be resolved by simply asserting our own point of view more loudly.

By now, readers can sense an important pattern in this series. Our goal is to probe several pastoral realities that many books about worship often ignore. This is especially true of this volume, Kathy Smith's *Stilling the Storm: Worship and Congregational Leadership in Difficult Times*. Moments of crisis, transition, and conflict are those in which congregations most need well-grounded, vibrant worship practices. Yet they are precisely the times in which the leadership capacity of many congregations is most threatened.

This is particularly true when worship itself is the source of conflict. We feel out of balance precisely when we most need pastoral poise. Yet worship experts in many traditions continue to offer advice mostly for periods of stability, growth, and resource expansion, ignoring the simple fact that pastoral ministry is more often practiced in the messiness of uncertain and challenging circumstances. Rev. Smith begins to fill this lacuna here, drawing on her years of experience as pastor, teacher, administrator, and leader. As she suggests, it is during times of uncertainty that we learn the habits of trust, vulnerability, and patience that are so fundamental to a vital Christian life and, ultimately, to worship itself. Indeed, in the surprising upside-down world of the gospel, worship is yet one more place where to lose our life is to find it. May this book not only instruct many of us to prepare for difficult times, but also buoy those who are caught in the middle of them.

By promoting encounters with instructive examples from various parts of the body of Christ, we pray that these volumes will help leaders make good judgments about worship in their congregations and that, by the power of God's Spirit, these congregations will flourish.

John D. Witvliet
Calvin Institute of Christian Worship

Foreword

I must begin with an embarrassing confession: it took me an awfully long time to appreciate the importance of worship for Christian life and congregations. I was a pastor for a number of years before I recognized the centrality of worship. I was preoccupied with all kinds of good things—devotional life of congregants, pastoral care, Bible study, social action—but failed for a long while to see the primary rootedness of all these Christian practices in what happened on Sundays with the gathered community. Happily, the congregations I served set me straight and worship gained a prominent place in my imagination and has been central to my ministry ever since.

Worship is the venue where we bring and lift up our most important longings and yearnings. Here we name what matters most to us. Here we uncover, recover, and discover our true identity in God. Here we are swept up into God's salvation story. How I could have missed the primacy of worship for so long leaves me baffled even now.

Of course, worship itself often misses the mark and falls short, and it becomes easy for us to misunderstand or misconstrue it. While at times our highest hopes are fulfilled there, at other times we experience our deepest disappointments there too. While at times we come with expectations of renewal, other times we leave feeling drained. One of the most troubling realities of church worship is that all too often it does not address the disruptions and dislocations of day-to-day life. If here creature and Creator do not meet, if God remains abstracted from our world and struggles, or if we do not embody God's love, redemption and call, then worship becomes worse than meaningless.

Kathleen Smith is mindful of the importance of Christian worship addressing us in the very places where we hurt, suffer, and experience difficulty. Church bodies—not to mention the bodies who attend and participate in church life—are particularly vulnerable during crises, transitions, and conflicts. What church has not known the trauma of tragic death, fire, natural catastrophe, conflict, schism, difficult transitions, loss of beloved members or leaders, change, or worship wars? And how many churches know how to address any of these forthrightly and with appropriate sensitivity on Sunday? Ironically, our congregations get a bad reputation when we avoid, smooth over, or ignore such realities and perform our worship "as normal," as if nothing else is wrong. Even more troubling, worship life is affected by those troubles whether we ignore them or not. And to add one more complicated wrinkle, worship itself can often be a lightning rod for intense dissatisfaction and grievances.

Thus it is best to face into the situation directly and name dynamics at work. But all too few resources are available for us to know how to do this. Thus stymied by both our own anxiety and our paucity of ideas, we often do nothing. Kathy Smith offers a remedy for both problems. Her approach is compassionate, responsive to real needs, and missional—addressing some of the most pressing challenges to church life and witness today.

This book is filled with useful insights, whether for pastors, elders, other church leaders, seminarians, or seminary professors. Smith handily introduces us to family systems and its implications. She explores why change is difficult. She alerts us to pay attention to the unexpected. She honors the importance of lament in Biblical traditions. She teaches us about the various wrinkles of four kinds of frequent transitions (leadership, space, membership, vision). She explores the possibilities of appreciative inquiry. She lowers the anxiety on facing conflict in the congregation. She alerts us to people who may easily be alienated or overlooked in worship: newcomers, children, youth, and folks who are hurting. She shows us how to embody both clarity and hospitality. She offers examples, as well, of liturgical elements and approaches that can be employed during congregational worship. She succinctly instructs us in what it means to be a Christian leader in the face of such challenges. All of this is set in the context of clear-sighted theological reflection, told alongside stories and case studies that will sound all too familiar to most readers. Smith writes with passion and a pastor's heart for the well-being of the wider church and all those within it.

I envy Kathy because she is obviously way ahead of me on the importance and possibilities of Christian worship. She knew long ago that worship is the congregation's main event. She did not need to be converted by congregations she served. Rather, she has been in conversation with many churches for many years about the rich possibilities of worship in the most difficult circumstances. Her engagement has not just yielded the good stories and rich examples that abound in the text but helped her think systematically and theologically about the issues at stake. Kathy does not fall into the trap of turning worship into a means for pastoral care, conflict transformation, or whatever. Rather, she helps us name worship's healing potential and take seriously the hope and priority of orienting ourselves to and before God. One reason that she does this so well is that she is grounded in clear theological thinking and priorities. One expects no less, of course, from a disciplined Reformed thinker.

I have known Kathy for some years. I deeply respect her work and involvements in teaching ministry and worship in various settings throughout the church, and I am in awe of her quiet-spoken pioneering as one of the first women ordained in her denomination. Thus when I first heard of her project, I was sure that it would be fresh, intriguing, and fruitful. As a latecomer to the priority of worship in Christian life, I feel indebted to her for teaching me a lot. Because of her work here and in her other ministries, I am deeply hopeful about the church's ongoing ability to worship meaningfully, faithfully, and with integrity even in the hardest of situations. With her pastoral approach, worship can be an avenue of pastoral care and healing, a means of grace.

Arthur Paul Boers
Associated Mennonite Biblical Seminary

Preface

This project began with a question: "Are any liturgical resources available for churches going through difficult times?" The question came to our staff at the Calvin Institute of Christian Worship from a pastor working in a denominational ministry for pastor-church relations. We explored the inquiry by brainstorming about the difficult times that churches experience and imagining how they might be addressed in worship. I researched denominational hymnals, service books, and Web sites, and found that liturgical resources are indeed available for times of transition in congregations—pastoral retirements, building additions, congregational closings, and the like. But these liturgies still need to be contextualized for a particular situation. To be effective, they need to be nuanced to fit the congregation and the specific transition it is experiencing.

As we discussed these issues further, we realized that providing a compilation of worship services or even an annotated list of resources would be an inadequate way of addressing the original question. We discovered that before liturgies can be chosen or designed for worship in a difficult time, certain basic questions must be asked about the nature of congregations, worship, and leadership. All of these must be considered in planning worship for a difficult time.

My assignment as part of the discussion group was to research the topic and to write a paper summarizing the questions and issues that needed to be addressed for worship in a congregation's difficult times. That summary also served as a paper for a course in my Master of Theology (Th.M.) degree program and later became an article in a theme issue on "Worship in Difficult Times" in

Reformed Worship.[1] The discussions with the advisory council of
Reformed Worship and the Calvin Institute of Christian Worship
(CICW) were influential in that writing. Subsequently, the paper
became my Th.M. thesis and was accepted by the Alban Institute
as a proposal for this book in the CICW book series the institute
publishes.

This book arose out of that original conversation about liturgical resources for difficult times, as well as many conversations
about particular congregations and the difficulties they have faced.
In fact, as I reflected on my own life and ministry, I realized that
many of the situations in our discussions had happened in one or
another of the churches in which I had grown up or served.

To research the matter further, I surveyed a number of pastors who were likely to have dealt with congregations in difficult
circumstances, including all the regional and interim pastors of
the Christian Reformed Church in North America and its general
secretary emeritus, Leonard J. Hofman (my father). Furthermore,
I discussed the topic with pastors and church leaders in the context
of workshops that I led on this subject in Langley, British Columbia, in November 2004, and at the 2005 Calvin Symposium on
Worship in Grand Rapids, Michigan.

I also consulted with several pastors, professors, and congregational consultants with specific expertise to offer. These included
Craig Barnes, Meneilly Professor of Leadership and Ministry at
Pittsburgh Theological Seminary and pastor of the Shadyside Presbyterian Church in Pittsburgh, Pennsylvania; Richard Blackburn,
director of the Lombard Mennonite Peace Center in Lombard, Illinois; Robert DeVries, professor of church education at Calvin
Theological Seminary in Grand Rapids, Michigan; Jaco Hamman,
associate professor of pastoral care and counseling at Western
Theological Seminary in Holland, Michigan; Ron Nydam, professor of pastoral care at Calvin Theological Seminary; Robb Red-
man, author of *The Great Worship Awakening* and pastor of a
Presbyterian congregation in Texas; Gilbert Rendle, senior consultant with the Alban Institute and United Methodist pastor; and
Joseph Smith, Presbyterian pastor and rural-ministry consultant
at Oak Hills Fellowship in Bemidji, Minnesota. Each of them pro-

vided insights into the issues and pointed me toward resources and readings.

Finally, I participated in a pastors' consultation in Chicago that led to the publication of another book in the CICW/Alban Institute's Vital Worship, Healthy Congregations Series, by Professor Craig Satterlee of Lutheran School of Theology at Chicago, titled *When God Speaks through Change: Preaching in Times of Congregational Transition.*[2] These pastors and priests, and especially my small-group members at that event—Christian Reformed pastor Mary Hulst of Champaign, Illinois, and Rabbi Ken Chasen of Los Angeles, California—provided many stories and insights for my thinking on this topic. And I had several discussions with pastors Norm Thomasma and Duane Visser of the Christian Reformed Pastor–Church Relations office, who had first asked the question.

The thesis of this book: *When congregations go through difficult times, those difficulties will affect the worship life of the congregation, and the practice of worship will itself be a key part of the congregation's healing process.*

Chapter 1 sets the stage for understanding difficult times and their impact on worship through the stories of six congregations and the difficulties they faced. Though the stories are real, the names of the churches have been changed to protect their identities and to indicate that these situations can and do arise in many locations. The congregational stories offer two examples each of the three categories of difficult times discussed in this book: crisis, transition, and conflict. The chapter introduces some of the questions raised about worship in each of these difficult times.

Chapter 2 offers more examples of difficult times and explains the congregational dynamics that accompany such times. In doing so, the chapter looks at the congregation as a living system and considers how it will react to the stress of difficult situations. Learning how congregations typically respond to change will help church leaders to deal with the changes that come along, whether planned and carefully carried out, or sudden and disturbing. Understanding these changes and the likely congregational reactions will also help worship leaders and planners to offer appropriate help in worship. The basis for the material in this chapter can be found in family systems theory as it is applied to congregations and in a biblical ecclesiology of the church. The chapter also looks at three main types of difficulty that congregations can face—times of crisis, transition, and conflict—and considers their differences and similarities and their implications for worship. Most difficulties that congregations experience fall into these three categories, although there is some overlap. For instance, a crisis can lead to a conflict or a transitional period, a poorly handled transition can result in conflict, and a conflict can intensify and lead to a crisis. This chapter also explores the transitional nature of all congregational life—congregations are always changing or responding to some kind of issue or dilemma.

Chapter 3 takes a closer look at worship itself to consider its meaning and purpose and its function in congregational life. Better understanding of the role of worship helps to clarify how it is affected by changing times in general, as well as by difficult times in particular congregations. This chapter reviews some basic principles of worship and applies those principles to worship in difficult times. It looks at the formative aspect of worship—the way the unique moments and regular habits of worship shape the congregation and its members. It also reveals the potential of worship to be a means of healing and a primary occasion for the congregation both to stop to lament, and then to move through and beyond the turbulence of the difficulty. Worship leaders are provided with questions and case studies for coping in crisis, taking time for transitions, and keeping calm in conflict. Specific examples are given for accomplishing these tasks in subsequent chapters.

Chapter 4 looks more specifically at the effects of crisis on congregations. It explores the role of worship as pastoral care in crisis, and especially the important function of lament in worship to express the sadness and anger that come with a crisis. In addition to lament, the chapter suggests some other important themes for congregations and their worship planners to pursue after a crisis, and offers a sampling of liturgical resources for such times, making suggestions for the various elements of the liturgy.

Chapter 5 does the same for worship in times of transition, especially transitions of congregational leadership, space, membership, or vision. Major topics in this chapter include fittingness and discernment, appreciative inquiry, and practices of worship, with a list of suggested liturgical resources.

Chapter 6 considers worship in times of conflict, with an emphasis on confession and reconciliation. The consequences of changes in congregations that affect worship are explored, as well as situations in which worship is the focus of the change and the conflict.

These three chapters give a sampling of resources for use in worship, but not an exhaustive list. They are intended to guide worship planners and worship leaders in thinking about how to help the congregation respond to difficult times in worship.

Chapter 7 offers specific advice for pastors and church leaders in difficult times—worship leaders as well as leaders who serve in governing or staff positions in the church; those employed by the church in leadership roles, as well as volunteers selected by the congregation to supervise the ministry of the church (the board, council, session, or vestry, depending on the organization and terminology of the congregation). The need for planners and leaders of worship to be in close connection with those who govern or supervise the congregation is explored, and suggestions are offered for doing this effectively.

The peculiar nature of leadership in a congregational setting is considered from the understanding that a congregation is a unique organization because of its relationship with God, and this reality has implications for how leaders and followers relate to one another. Here again we draw on a systems perspective, which recognizes the reciprocal nature of leadership. Not only are followers necessary if leaders are to lead; the leadership that results is a function of the relationship between the leader and the followers—the dynamic system of the entire group. Suggestions are offered to leaders for dealing with their own stress while leading a congregation through a difficult time.

This book is intended to apply to all congregations, regardless of their historical and theological traditions. As a pastor in the Christian Reformed Church in North America, I belong to an evangelical Protestant denomination with roots in the Calvinist traditions of Switzerland, France, and especially the Netherlands.

However, the biblical theology and understanding of worship, leadership, and congregational issues advocated here go far beyond any particular tradition. In fact, they have been embraced by many churches. Furthermore, the systems-based understanding of leadership and group dynamics endorsed here has been influential in many organizations, both religious and nonreligious. It is my hope that this book will help educate leaders and congregations about the worship we offer to God in all times and situations, and serve as a resource for congregations when they encounter difficult times.

Acknowledgments

I wish to express my deep gratitude to a number of people who have supported me in the effort to research and write this book.

First of all, I thank Dr. John D. Witvliet, director of the Calvin Institute of Christian Worship, and Dr. Henry De Moor, vice president for academic affairs at Calvin Theological Seminary, for their encouragement to embark on this project and for providing many resources and insights, as well as occasional time away from my regular work as director of continuing education for the institute and the seminary. I also thank the staff of the continuing education office—Elizabeth Steele Halstead, Fiona Baker, Rachel Klompmaker, and Rebecca Ochsner—for managing the office well to allow me time to write. Special thanks go to Rachel for her research assistance, and to Emily Cooper for securing copyright permissions for the many hymns and prayers included in this book.

I also thank all the pastors and professors who have told me their stories and helped me to understand a greater variety of difficult congregational times. And I thank Beth Ann Gaede, editor for the Alban Institute, for editing drafts of this book with a keen eye and a pastor's heart, and Jean Caffey Lyles for her expert copyediting.

I am grateful to my husband, Doug, and my daughters, Melissa, Jacqueline, and Nichole, for their patience when I was preoccupied with this project, and their support of my ongoing education in so many ways.

Finally, I thank God for providing this opportunity to continue learning and integrating theology and ministry practice in a way that provides a helpful resource for the church.

Chapter One

Stories of Crisis, Transition, and Conflict

The congregation of Resurrection Life Church discovers on a Tuesday morning that a fire has destroyed most of its church facility, leaving just the badly damaged sanctuary standing. Devastated by the loss of their building but gathering strength from calm leaders who pull them together, the members look for a place to worship together. Amid several offers from community organizations and local businesses, they decide to return to the local school gymnasium that they used at the beginning of their history—before the small group of people forming a new congregation even had a building. In an act of faith that will communicate to all observing this church in crisis, they string across the front of their charred church a banner displaying the words of Romans 8:28: "We know that all things work together for good for those who love God."

A second congregation, at Faith Community Church, is grieving along with its pastor the tragic death of his daughter in an accident on a wintry Saturday. Congregational leaders initially deal with the crisis by making some last-minute changes for the next morning's worship and later make more significant adjustments when the pastor is given a leave of absence for several months. But now that he has returned and more months have gone by, they are trying to decide how to observe the various services of the liturgical year with appropriate sensitivity to those who are grieving, and especially through a grieving worship leader. As winter approaches again, they wonder how long they will stay in the "longing" of Advent, and if they will ever be able to sing Christmas carols with joy again.

A third congregation, First Presbyterian, is facing the loss of a large portion of its membership to a new church established nearby, and therefore the loss of many volunteers who had used their gifts in the church, especially in worship. They are slowly sorting through logistical frustrations. They don't have enough people to perform various roles, and not enough of them know exactly how to do their tasks. Beyond that difficulty, they also face feelings of resentment toward the new church that "stole" too many of their "sheep," and lingering sadness about the loss of a pastor who wasn't able to keep them together. They wish she had been a better preacher or a stronger leader, but despite those weaknesses her departure has, all the same, left them grieving.

A fourth congregation, Unity in Christ Church, is adjusting to a merger—the consolidation of a smaller congregation into its membership and its leadership. Suddenly, new people are in the pews and new leaders in the board room, and the older congregation—the mother church of this homecoming daughter—wonders what this merger will do to the family. The leaders had undertaken this change willingly to help out the smaller group that had struggled to remain viable in its location on an out-of-the-way city block. The members were happy to gather them into their spacious main-street facility. But they wonder what other kinds of changes will result. In fact, their greatest fear is that the smaller, more conservative congregation will move them backward on issues like worship style and evangelistic outreach. Members of the smaller congregation have their own concerns—about getting lost in the crowd, and being accepted and finding a niche for their gifts—even as they grieve the loss of their own church and their congregational identity.

Fifth, the congregation at Peace Lutheran Church is struggling to keep together factions that have polarized over changes in worship. The members have been caught in the "worship wars," but they realize that other issues also underlie the debate—issues of direction and mission. They tried holding two worship services of different styles, "traditional" and "contemporary," but the people didn't like being separated. So even before the end of the six-month trial period, they have gone back to one service. Now they are trying to figure out how to do "blended" worship, but they face a lot of hurt feelings and accusations about lack of good process. They are no longer trying to please all of the people all of the time; they wonder if it's possible to please *any* of the people at *any* time!

And finally, the congregation of the Independent Church of God is dealing with a major conflict between the pastor and the elders. The disagreement centers on leadership style and who has the authority to make important decisions. Can the pastor decide to change the worship style and hire staff members to support that style without consulting the elders? Can the elders make counter decisions at meetings called in the pastor's absence? Who is in charge? Who really runs the church? And how can this congregation avoid becoming a house divided?

These examples represent just a few of the difficult times that congregations can face. Many others could be listed, from natural disasters to planned building additions or relocations to major staff changes—both arrivals and departures. Furthermore, the uniqueness of each congregation multiplies the variety of difficulties that may arise. Just as each person and every family is unique, so too congregations with particular histories and makeup of membership have their own idiosyncratic ways of communicating with each other, showing appreciation or admonition to members, and dealing with change in their lives. In fact, transitional times tend to magnify a congregation's characteristics, quirks, and distinctive habits.

But though difficult times have a different shape and impact in each congregation, some factors are always in play in these situations. One is that no matter what the difficulty, it is certain to have an impact on the worship life of the congregation. Trying times affect various aspects of a congregation's life, but they especially affect its worship life. Even if the difficulty is not directly worship-related, it will affect the worship services in one way or another because the worshipers themselves are affected by it. The effects may be noticed in the decreased availability of volunteers for planning or participating in the service, or in an uncomfortable tone to the worship services owing to tensions in the congregation, or in the adoption of a new venue for the worship service, or in different people leading the worship service.

Worship is affected even in congregations that are not dealing with specifically worship-related challenges because it is in worship, more than at any other time, that the congregation gathers and expresses its identity as a community. The weekly worship service is the time when most of the members are together, so it is the "main event" in terms of presence and participation. But it is also central because in the act of worship a congregation expresses its identity as the people of God. There the congregants act out the relationship with God that defines who they are—a people chosen by God and set apart for receiving God's blessing and extending God's peace to the world. A congregation may engage in many activities, but if worship is not one of them, and a central one, it cannot truly be considered a congregation.

Worship is somewhat like the holiday dinner, when everyone in the family comes home. These people are together because they have a family relationship with one another, and such relationships are usually more important than any others. "You can choose your friends, but not your relatives," we often joke. But it is true. Families are important, and that's why we go home for Christmas, Thanksgiving, and other holidays. Such occasions can be joyful or painful, depending on the circumstances. A family may celebrate a new in-law at the table or a new baby in the high chair, sigh over the empty space left by a family member who has died or divorced, or struggle with tension between members who have argued but not reconciled. Like biological or adoptive families, faith communities are shaped by the various changes and difficulties that the congregation faces, and these changes affect us as we come to worship, as we gather around God's table.

That shaping includes the stretching and pushing and pulling that congregations experience as difficult times. Such difficulties raise the level of anxiety in the congregation, and this unease will be apparent in worship. These are some of the questions that arise from a look at congregations in difficult times:

- If a congregation is dealing with a crisis, a transition, or an ongoing conflict, what effect will this have on worship?
- How can congregations plan worship thoughtfully and meaningfully through the difficult time?
- How *can* congregations worship in difficult times?
- How can worship assist a congregation in the process of healing?
- And how can God work in these congregations through worship in a challenging time?

This book seeks to show how difficult times in the lives of congregations affect worship, and how worship can both reflect and affect the issues causing difficulty. Ultimately, I hope to show how worship can be part of a healthy process for a church dealing with a trying time.

Understanding how congregations tend to be affected by difficulties and determining a healthy process for dealing with them in worship will require much discernment on the part of congregations and their leaders. But the task must be undertaken because worship is the central aspect of congregational life, and ultimately, worship is the element of congregational life that offers the greatest potential for healing a congregation. Though most difficulties cannot be predicted, congregations can prepare for them to a certain extent by learning how changes will affect them and their worship. As a result, they can prepare for such changes when they face minor dilemmas, and will find themselves better able to deal with major turbulence in the future. Congregations can work today to develop healthy practices that will serve them well as future challenges arise.

We approach this possibility with confidence and joy because we worship the One who stills the storms of crises, transitions, and conflicts. To be sure, the gospel accounts of Jesus's nature miracles are about his encounters with natural forces rather than the human storms of crises, transitions, and conflicts. But the New Testament also teaches us that the church—Christ's body—is a place of healing, reconciliation, and forgiveness. So as congregational leaders navigate carefully to the other side of their particular stormy waters, they can have faith in the One who brings peace to our world and our churches. And then, in turn, they can instill calm in turbulent situations by keeping on with the practices Jesus commanded—gathering, preaching, praying, celebrating sacraments, and going out to serve as a powerful witness to the enduring peace of Christ in all times and places. Leaders must remember that at the end of the day, all their efforts will be for nothing without the power of God to still the storms in our hearts and in our congregations.

Chapter Two

Congregational Dynamics in Difficult Times

The congregational stories of difficult times told in chapter 1 fall into three main categories. The congregations stricken by the sudden loss of their church facility to fire and by the loss of a member of the pastor's family in an accident were in *crisis* situations. The churches experiencing a major decline in membership and a merger of one congregation into another were facing *transitions*. And the ones dealing with strained relationships between the pastor and the elders, or between factions within the congregation, were in the category of *conflict*. Most of the difficult times congregations will face fall into these three categories, although there is some overlap. A crisis can lead to a conflict or a transitional period; a mismanaged transition can lead to conflict; and poor handling of a conflict can lead to a crisis.

Refined by Fire

After the fire at Resurrection Life Church, the congregation moved into crisis mode, activating the prayer chain and notifying church members of the calamity. Leaders immediately recognized the need for the congregation to gather for worship, and an on-site prayer service was held just two days after the fire. Like those who both grieve and rejoice at a funeral or committal service, members faced the reality of their church's destruction but also put their hope in the God who would carry them through the fire—and perhaps even refine them with it. The next step for dealing with the crisis was to design a new process for communication among leaders. Since their congregational mailboxes were burned in the fire and they now had no central gathering place, they quickly developed e-mail and telephone messaging systems. Temporary facilities were needed, and nearby hotels and churches offered the use of their space. The leaders realized that corporate decision-making about what to do next would require face-to-face meetings and discussions and could not be accomplished electronically. They also wanted to act quickly to avoid an interruption in their ministries—from worship services to children's programs to adult Bible studies.

Congregational leaders decided to go "back to school"—back to the elementary school building where they had first gathered when their church began, a place that was familiar and had some history for many of them. A familiar landmark in the community, it provided one main location for their worship, educational, and outreach ministries. While they found it helpful to have a space to gather and worship, they sorely missed their own sanctuary, their "church home." Many of them had been involved in its original construction, or had spent their lives growing up in it.

Perhaps related to the discomfort of this change was the mild conflict that arose over the time of the Sunday morning worship service. The congregation had been accustomed to holding two identical services in its regular facility because of a lack of sanctuary and parking space. In the large school gymnasium, there was room for everyone in one service, and it was easier for setup and takedown crews to have only one service. But the leaders had to decide on a time—would they go with the hour of one service or the other, or would they compromise with a time halfway between? The church council met and, under severe time pressure, made a decision without a lot of process or polling. The council chose the time of the earlier service, and of course that decision did not please everyone. So, despite the initial cooperation after the fire, people did resist somewhat when they were forced to make changes in their own worship patterns—involving both time and space.

After weathering the initial crisis, this congregation moved into a transitional phase, and leaders and members began to plan for rebuilding. They received insurance and construction advice, and then had to decide whether to clean up the damaged sanctuary and build a new educational wing to replace the one that had burned, or to demolish the sanctuary and start over with a new building that would give them complete flexibility in planning and design.

This time leaders instituted a process of discussion and reflection. Had they not been able to agree on a direction, conflict could have led to a new crisis—if, for example, a segment of the congregation had decided to leave over the conflict. Thankfully, they were able to come to consensus and decided to build a whole new church at the same location. In fact, with the new building they were able to worship all together in one service on Sunday mornings, a practice they had learned to enjoy again in the post-fire days in the school gymnasium. So Resurrection Life Church had moved from crisis through transition while avoiding major conflict, and was able to rise from the ashes of the fire and rebuild its facility on the foundation of a healthy congregation.

Learning through Difficulties

Although the three categories of difficulty I have identified can overlap and congregations may move from one to another, distinct issues arise with each one. Varying leadership responses and approaches to worship are required by each type of difficulty as well. Sometimes quick decisions and implementation are called for. In other situations, careful planning and collaborative decision making will be more effective. Church leaders will need discernment to know which leadership and worship approaches are appropriate in which situations.

In a certain sense, all congregational life is in transition. That is, there will always be a transitional aspect to congregational life, because congregations are living, growing, changing organizations. In fact, congregations need to change and grow to be healthy. Despite the transitional nature of all congregational life, however, certain situations go beyond the normal ups and downs of congregational life and have long-term effects on the congregation.

These major challenges and long-term effects are not always bad. Difficult times often lead to great growth for congregations, and such situations can be gifts of God. Just as individuals who go through tough times often speak of their personal growth and learning—learning that would not have occurred without the challenge—congregations can respond to testing the same way, whether it comes in the form of a crisis, a transition, or a conflict. A recent *Leadership* journal survey of pastors found that while 95 percent of them reported that their congregations had experienced conflict, 94 percent of them also reported some positive results.[1] A congregation's heightened awareness of its identity and struggles can lead, for example, to important and lasting adjustments to its sense of mission and ways of worshiping and ministering together.

The potential for learning through difficulty is an opportunity that is simply not present at other times. Congregations in these situations are more aware of the issues to be dealt with, and have a heightened desire to act. At the very least, their curiosity is aroused. In most cases, the symptoms of the difficult time—anxiety, increased conversations, and activity around the presenting issue; worry about the church; and so forth—are evidence of how much people care about their church. And the people who truly care are often the ones who are most open to learning and best able to bring the church to a new level of understanding and functioning. The congregation may not always experience this process as learning, because it usually involves some pain, but leaders can help members and participants understand both the normality of what they're going through and the opportunity it brings to grow in their life in Christ.

A Congregation Is a Living Being

One issue a congregation can learn about through a difficult time is how congregations work, and that learning will serve leaders and members well in all times. Before looking at particular difficulties and their characteristics in congregations, some basic features of congregations need to be understood as well. And the first issue to notice is that the congregation is an organism—not just an inanimate object or organization, but a living being. In fact, because the congregation is the manifestation of Christ's presence and work in this world, it's a very special organism. The church is the body of Christ. A congregation has all the necessary parts and gifts of an active living body, but it also differs from other organizations in the world because of its identity in Christ. The mission and purpose of a congregation is to represent Jesus Christ in the world, to carry out his redemptive purpose for the world, and to gather people into his fellowship. Congregations are living and growing—growing in the grace and knowledge of the Lord and growing as they gather God's people to express their identity in Christ.

Try to imagine a congregation as a living being—not as a group of individuals. If a congregation could be described as a person, what kind of person would it be? A young, naive teenager eager to try lots of things, but reluctant to stick with any of them for long? A motherly protector of those who aren't accepted elsewhere; one who tolerates unusual speech, actions, and even appearances in the interest of keeping people in the family? An inexpressive businessman who loves order and discipline and despises displays of emotion? Imagining the characteristics that would describe a congregation if it were a person may begin to explain how the living system of a church works—how it has its own peculiar "personality."

The truth from Scripture is that the church is a living being— the body of Christ. Paul emphasized the functioning of this body in 1 Corinthians 12, describing how the church has many interconnected parts, all of which are important though gifted in various ways. As this image relates to worship, some parts of the body are singers, others dancers, still others readers, and so on. The dancer needs the choreographer to design movement, who needs the service planner to determine the flow of the service, who needs the pastor to connect the theme for the service to the Scripture readings, who needs the congregation to discern the Scripture and themes needed at this time.

The point is that the parts of the body need each other. The human body is an interdependent system of many parts. And while the brain and the heart are examples of important parts, other less noticeable parts are also necessary. Think of the important functions of certain glands and lymph nodes in the body. Think of how difficult it is to walk if a small thing like a big toe is injured. Living bodies need all these various parts. Big toes are important, as are little ones. The quiet church member who spends Sunday afternoons writing encouragement cards may be as important as the Sunday morning liturgist in influencing the congregation toward praise and gratitude to God.

Just as the various parts of the body are themselves important, so also are the body's processes of healing and adjusting to
change. Think how the body adjusts to temperature changes by
sweating or shivering—reactions to changing conditions that help
it to be comfortable and to thrive. Similar adjustments are needed
in a congregational system—sometimes it needs to "sweat," and
sometimes it needs to "shiver." Most people can imagine times in
congregations that felt like sweating or shivering—probably times
of crisis. Watching fire destroy one's church building can create an
inward anxiety that is similar to the outward sweating from the
heat of the flames. The jolt of a sudden death in the congregation
can lead to a cold shock that renders members numb or shivering,
unable at first to believe that a beloved church member is gone.
Sweating and shivering are essential to the well-being of the body.

The important thing for a congregation to learn in preparation for situations that bring sudden change is that just as it is
normal for human bodies to adjust to temperature changes, so it
is normal for congregations to adjust to changes in their environment by exhibiting behaviors that are the equivalent of sweating
or shivering. Congregations can even be described as being "cold"
to new ideas, or as having a "hotbed" of conflict or criticism. The
challenge for church leaders and members is to remember that
these reactions are all part of a normal process for a living being.
Shivering and sweating are ways in which the body both responds
to crisis and maintains its health. Now, certainly a congregation
at times gets too hot or too cold to be healthy, and that's when
outside help may be needed. Congregational or denominational
consultants and pastors with specialized training can provide di-
agnostic help and pastoral care that will restore stability and more
"normal" temperatures.

Responding to Change in the Congregational System

Another key to remember is that in any system, each part affects
the whole system, and every part is affected by the actions of any
other part. In a congregation, each person is part of the system

and what he or she says or does will affect the whole system, just as he or she will be affected by the behavior of others. When a congregation is in distress, it may seem that certain individuals are either causing the difficulty or making the situation worse by how they react to it. The truth, however, is that the difficulty is always a function of the entire system. A few people who are outspoken and highly critical of a change going on in the congregation—such as a transition to a new style of worship, or the introduction of a new hymnal, or the use of presentational technology in the worship service—are part of an entire congregation that reacts or responds to their critique. The congregation may react out of fear that confronting these people will alienate them and force them to leave, or it may quickly capitulate to their strong opinions. A congregation that reacts out of fear of the rumblings in one part of the system is held hostage when it allows a small number to control the rest of the group.

In less mature or more chronically anxious congregations, the most reactive people are given the most attention and are allowed to influence decisions, often raising the level of anxiety, slowing down the process of transition, and creating other difficulties along the way. In a healthy, mature congregation, members do not *react;* rather, they thoughtfully and dispassionately *respond.* Critics are reminded of the congregation's purpose in making the transition, and their anxiety is not allowed to raise the anxiety of the entire system. Leaders listen to the concerns expressed out of a genuine desire to be open to all points of view and to learn from the conversation, as well as to show appreciation for the people who are concerned about the church. But they graciously resist making changes simply because the critics demand them, knowing that they would be encouraging such demands and actually elevating the stress level of the system. Effective leaders are also humble enough to learn from criticism. They sometimes discern even more pointed and helpful suggestions than the critics themselves were able to formulate.

Even though changes are essential to the well-being of all living things, including congregations, they do heighten tension and anxiety—because change involves loss, and people become anxious when they experience loss and grief. Any time there's a change, there is also a loss. The anxiety that bubbles up is a signal that the person or the system is recognizing and working through the loss. Of course, the anxiety usually presents itself as resistance to change, so leaders are tempted to take it personally and to react in a defensive way. But by doing so, they may be shutting down or short-circuiting the important process of dealing with the change.

Therapists know that when people start to get upset or angry, their reactions are often a sign that the most productive time in their treatment is imminent. Congregations too must be helped to see that anxiety in the system is a sign of engagement—a sign that the group is dealing with an issue that it cares deeply about, and that, by God's grace, they will work it out. Congregations need not run from or fear the chaos and anxiety that come with change and difficult times. They need to expect change and to learn to trust God and one another as they go through it.

Learning from Biology

Changes and transitions and trying times actually make us stronger and more mature. This is true for individuals as well as for congregations. Living things need to be challenged to grow and be healthy. Pastor and author John Ortberg tells of an experiment conducted at the University of California at Davis in which the perfect conditions were created for an amoeba—a microscopic organism—to survive. Perfect levels of moisture, temperature, and nourishment were provided so that researchers could expect to have a happy little amoeba on their hands. But instead of thriving, the amoeba died! The conclusion of the experimenters was that living things need to be challenged in order to survive.[2] Seemingly perfect conditions aren't enough; it is the changing of conditions and the adjusting of organisms to those changes that provide the strength to survive conditions that are not so ideal.

Another illustration from the world of biology clarifies the point. "Biosphere 2" in Oracle, Arizona, was an artificial ecological system used to test whether people could live in a closed biosphere while performing scientific experiments. Peter Steinke, church consultant and expert in systems theory, tells how in one of the biosphere's experiments with plants grown under supposedly perfect conditions, fruit trees were dropping their fruit too soon, because the stems weren't strong enough to hold them. Why not? Because there was no wind in the biosphere: therefore no resistance was created, and without the necessity to adjust to the wind, the plants didn't grow as strong.[3] Living things need to be challenged, and they need to adjust to changes in their environment to be strong and healthy.

Just as living organisms grow stronger by adjusting to imperfect and changing conditions and tree branches are strengthened by storms and wind, so congregations that have lived through a few difficult times are generally stronger ones—more able to deal with adversity in healthy, mature ways. The functioning of living systems is greatly affected by their level of maturity and ability to deal with anxiety, according to authors Jim Herrington, Robert Creech, and Trisha Taylor. They compare a congregation's level of maturity to a reservoir, and its level of anxiety to the water level in that reservoir. If a congregation has a deep reservoir of maturity, then the normal rising of anxiety in a turbulent time will not overflow the system and flood the area. However, a congregation that does not have such depth, but exhibits a pattern of overreacting to adverse situations, will not be able to absorb that anxiety and transition through the difficult time nearly as well. Its anxiety will overflow and spill out into the community.[4]

Leading through Change

It becomes obvious then that difficult times of crisis, transition, and conflict require church leaders to pay careful attention to congregational dynamics—the functioning of the living organism. These situations increase stress on the congregational system, producing a variety of symptoms. Church leaders must learn to expect and recognize the symptoms of anxiety in the congregation, no matter what the source of the challenging time, and understand that people will react or respond in different ways. Some church members will withdraw, unable to face the pain. Others may try to solve the problem too soon, unable to live with its uncertainties.

Still others may complain about seemingly unrelated matters in an unconscious attempt to avoid the issue and to divert the attention of the leaders. If the leaders seem to be functioning at a lower level than usual, especially in a crisis, some members may cause trouble for them by lighting another fire somewhere in the congregation's life, thereby forcing the leaders to react, instead of allowing them time to consider and craft a careful response. But leaders who consistently respond carefully in difficult times will promote healthy growth and maturity in the congregation. They will help to deepen the reservoir of congregational maturity. Though no congregation will be able to avoid all future crises and transitions, discerning leaders can help congregations to build up a measure of immunity and stability as difficulties approach.

Those who lead a congregation through change need to keep in mind that because change involves loss and grief, grieving people tend to resist further change—and loss. Therefore, they tend to hang onto familiar things even more than usual. So whereas trying out a lot of new songs at any other time might not be a major issue, during a difficult time, it may be a volatile move. Leaders should be prepared for the hostility and passive aggressiveness that may come from frustrated people. They need to remain as calm as possible, absorbing some of the anxiety of the system and providing immunity to the congregational body.

One way for leaders to remain calm is to remember that it is Christ's church, and ultimately, Christ will lead the church as it relies on the promises of God and the guidance of the Holy Spirit. Leaders must be humble enough to know that the outcome depends more on God's plan than on theirs. But they must also be wise enough to know that careful listening and learning in difficult times will serve Christ's church well and help it to flourish.

The opportunity for learning and growing exists no matter what the source of a congregation's pain. A closer look at the three categories of difficulty introduced above will explain their impact on the congregation and the learning that will help it get through the difficult time. Even though the three categories of difficulty identified in this book share some characteristics, distinct issues arise with each one. Varying leadership responses and approaches to worship are required by each type of difficulty, as will be seen in the next few chapters. Sometimes quick decisions and implementation are called for. In other situations, careful discussion and collaborative decision making will be more effective. Church leaders will need to discern which leadership and worship approaches are appropriate in which situations. Understanding the characteristics of each category can help begin that discernment process.

Crisis

A crisis is a sudden change that creates a great amount of tension and upheaval for the people affected. Examples of congregational crises include the sudden death of, or a serious accident involving, a leader or church member; the unexpected suspension or resignation of a pastor or staff member; a natural disaster that damages the church facilities or community; or a national or international incident that affects the members of the congregation. In a crisis frequent, accurate, and effective communication is paramount. The following questions and issues need to be addressed:

- How should leaders respond to the crisis, both publicly and within the congregation?
- What methods should be used to communicate the crisis and subsequent developments? What confidentiality issues need to be addressed?
- Which individuals and groups will need special care and attention during this crisis?
- What adjustments in schedule, personnel, and assignments will be needed?

Crises will bring on busy times—times that don't allow for a lot of reflection—so it is important for leaders to be grounded in the understanding of the church explained above as the living body of Christ. They need to operate with a clear understanding of congregational dynamics as well as a strong faith in Christ to lead the church through the crisis. They also need to be aware of and ready to use available denominational resources and procedures. It is also crucial for them to stay as calm as possible to keep the church stable in the immediate aftermath of the crisis. The congregational boat may be rocking quite a bit, but leaders who can manage their own anxiety in the midst of a tempest will be most successful in guiding their congregations through the storm.

When the pastor's daughter died suddenly on a wintry Saturday, the staff and elders of Faith Community Church stepped in quickly to make arrangements for the care of the pastor and his family, as well as for the worship services the next day. They lined up a guest preacher, chose different hymns for the service, and activated the telephone prayer chain to inform the congregation of the tragedy and to enlist members' help in prayer. As time went on, they secured an interim pastor to fill in while their grief-stricken leader was given a leave of absence.

Whether or not a crisis involves a death in the congregation, the loss inherent in any type of change, including a crisis, will result in a period of grieving—for a person, a building, a way of life, or even a congregational identity. The character of the grieving depends on the nature of the crisis, but grieving usually involves phases of anger, sadness, fear, and guilt. Although church members do not usually recognize that a crisis leads to grieving, the reality is that a loss has occurred and will need to be mourned. The typical stages of grief that individuals experience also apply to congregations dealing with loss—shock, denial, anger, bargaining, and eventually, acceptance.

Of course, the way grieving individuals—or grieving congregations—express themselves varies, but these main patterns are to be expected. The manner in which a particular congregation deals with crisis will also reflect its idiosyncratic ways of dealing with other difficult situations. A congregation that dealt with its last pastoral transition well will be better equipped for the sudden death or departure of the next pastor. A congregation that has healthy patterns of communication will respond more effectively to a community event or natural disaster. If the congregational reservoir is deep, that maturity will help it through when another crisis comes along.

The crisis then leads to a time of transition, or in some cases, a time of conflict. So the issues for leaders and worship planners do not quickly go away after a crisis. How leaders respond will have long-term effects on the health and well-being of the congregation and may have great influence in the next chapter of the congregation's life—particularly determining whether the congregation will move into a transition or a more turbulent conflict.

Transition

A transition can be defined as the process of changing from one form, state, activity, or place to another. The most common transitions that occur in congregations are changes in pastoral leadership or church staff. Other major transitions include building additions and relocations, joining or leaving a denomination, development of new worship services or other major programs or directions, mergers of two or more congregations, and consolidations of one congregation into another.

As opposed to a time of crisis, when decisions must be made quickly and people who see the need to do certain things often just step in and do them, in a transitional time more opportunity is afforded for careful planning. But, as in a time of crisis, there are important questions to ask:

- Does this situation amount to more than the normal ebb and flow of congregational life, and does it therefore need more careful planning?
- What issues lie behind the transition? What is motivating this change?
- How can church leaders steer through the transitional time while taking care of those who have been hurt by the change?
- How can the congregation find the way God is leading through this difficult time?

When Unity in Christ Church was going through a consolidation that gathered up the members of a struggling daughter congregation and enfolded them back into the mother's nest, leaders had to ask even more specific questions:

- How will we welcome these people back into the church family of their grandparents, acknowledge their presence

in worship, and invite them to serve as worship leaders—
as musicians, lectors, assisting ministers, and so forth?

- How will we also acknowledge that together we become a
  new "us"—that each congregation involved in the consolidation is changing?
- How will we help these new members through the grief
  of losing their own identity (and even their building and
  many of their ways)?
- How can the gifts and practices of both congregations be
  honored? Even a tiny congregation absorbed by a large
  congregation has gifts to offer the new entity.
- How do we recognize the loss of the building where the
  congregation that moved formerly worshiped? What can
  they bring with them—perhaps even literally carry from
  one location to another, ritualizing the transition?
- Consolidations are often most difficult for the group that
  must adapt to a new space; it's as if the people who know
  the location of all the light switches control everything.
  How might we initiate the new folks to all the light-switch
  locations as a humorous way to acknowledge and address
  the issue? How might we share with them the "secrets"
  of our church—how to find hidden rooms and resources,
  whom to ask about what, and so on?

While this consolidation was obviously a huge transition for
the congregation, all church life is transitional and church leaders
are always dealing with change and transition. What is it, then,
that qualifies a transition for mention here as a "difficulty"? Perhaps a transition has become a difficulty when leaders and members begin to say, "Our church is going through _____." If the
blank can be filled in with a specific word or phrase, then it is a
specific transition—or maybe several interconnected issues—that
should be addressed.

Transitions often have multiple aspects and are actually a
constellation of changes. Often these things go together: facility
changes along with staff changes and location changes. In the
complexity of transitional situations, congregations often make
the mistake of trying to hurry the transition along, rather than
being patient through the adversity and asking what God may be

teaching them through this process. While this feat is difficult to pull off, congregations need to take their time as they go through a transition, because it is an opportunity for growth, and a rushed transition could lead to further difficulties.

New Community Church went through a merger, a relocation, and a building project all at once. Two historic urban congregations, both struggling to survive, decided to merge and relocate as a new congregation with a vision to "develop a regional church with multiple ministries and worship opportunities that meet the spiritual needs of our growing community." Together, these congregations built a new facility on the outer edge of the suburbs. Their new building had an open style of architecture with space for visual arts in the sanctuary and a large community gathering area. To help worshipers remember and stay visually connected to their history, the beautiful stained-glass windows from one of the urban sanctuaries were incorporated into the design of the new suburban church. The result was a stunning octagon-shaped sanctuary, with six 25-foot-high windows, three on each side of the chancel area. Other sections of the old stained glass were installed in the wall separating the sanctuary from the narthex, as a way of looking through "who we were" to see "who we are now." Representing memories of the old church, these windows now came as visual art along with the people to the new "wide and spacious place" where God had brought them.

New Community Church came through the transitional time well, because members and leaders listened carefully and worked at honoring the past even as they moved into the future. They took the time needed to mull over their losses and their dreams, and found visible, concrete ways to express them. So those church members who felt the losses of the transition most acutely found the history of the church affirmed every time they walked into the new facility. And in that affirmation they were also comforted in their loss. The transitional time resulted in new growth for this congregation which had the vision to enter a new chapter in its history as it answered God's call to extend its ministry to a new place.

The multiple aspects of the transition of New Community Church involved a long process of learning and changing. In *Managing Transitions: Making the Most of Change,* William Bridges explains that a transition is "a three-phase process that people go through as they internalize and come to terms with the details of the new situation that the change brings about." He calls the first phase the *ending*—"Letting go of the old ways and the old identity people had." This is the time to help people deal with losses. The second phase is the *neutral zone* in which "the old is gone but the new isn't fully operational." This is the time to help people create new patterns. The third phase is *making a new beginning,* the time to help people develop their new identity with a new energy and sense of purpose. As Bridges puts it, "transition starts with an ending and ends with a beginning." He notes that organizations tend to overlook the importance of the first phase and the losses that need to be addressed. Skipping that phase will "nearly guarantee that the transition will be mismanaged and that, as a result, the change will go badly."[5]

The second phase, the neutral zone, can be a time of uncertainty, one requiring steady leadership. Organizations tend to rush through it or try to escape it, but that short-circuits the process and the learning. Since this is the time when people are most open to creativity and innovation, congregations that rush through it miss great opportunities. Making a new beginning refers to the gradual acceptance of the change, probably nuanced and shaped by the very folk who had originally resisted the change. Being aware of these phases will help congregations as they find their way down the path of transition. One can hope that this awareness will also help them avoid detouring into the thickets of conflict.

Conflict

A conflict is a prolonged controversy or disagreement between opposing forces. Church conflicts can center on a variety of issues, from style of worship to style of leadership to style of interior decorating. They may develop out of an unresolved or poorly handled crisis. They may begin with a sharp disagreement or with a quiet dispute that grows into a heated discussion. Even in the heat of the moment, leaders have to think carefully about whether their actions fan the flame or douse it. Conflicts often serve as evidence of deeper disagreements or hurts within the congregational culture. Maybe a disagreement at a public meeting was never resolved between the affected parties, or the departure of a pastor was never acknowledged in a way that allowed people to express their regret, or even relief. Sometimes healing has been needed but not nurtured for a long time, and the conflict surfaces as a symptom of a much deeper issue that is causing anxiety in the congregation.

It is important to recognize that almost all churches deal with conflict at some point or another. As noted above, a recent *Leadership* survey found that 95 percent of churches reported having experienced conflict. Congregations need to learn that it is a normal part of congregational life and that often the results, in terms of learning for the congregation, are positive ones. As *Leadership* editor Marshall Shelley writes, "healthy conflict" may seem like an oxymoron,[6] but it is true that healthy churches will experience conflict at some point and will learn and grow from those situations. In fact, lack of conflict may be a sign of lack of health. As noted preacher and author Haddon Robinson has been known to say, "Congregations with no problems have *big* problems!" A congregation that seems to be running incredibly smoothly may be a congregation that is coasting, and one that needs a prophetic challenge in some area of its life to better fulfill the demands of the gospel. Or it may be a sign that the congregational culture has tacit rules that don't allow creativity or diversity of opinions and that stifle new ideas, thereby maintaining the status quo with an iron fist. Conflict in such a setting could be a sign of healthy questioning that will begin to loosen the grip of traditionalism.

In times of conflict, leaders should ask questions like these:

- Who is involved in the conflict and what seems to be the source of the conflict?
- What underlying causes may there be for this conflict? What history, if any, does this congregation have with this type of conflict?
- What pastoral care needs exist as a result of this conflict?
- What pace is needed in resolving the conflict? Will a quick resolution be detrimental to the learning of the congregation?

- Is the conflict keeping people from worship? From fellowship with one another?
- Should the conflict be directly named in worship, or addressed indirectly through prayers and biblical themes?
- Should forgiveness and reconciliation be strongly encouraged, or nurtured along?

Church conflicts vary greatly because of the variety of possible conflicting parties. A conflict can involve the pastor and other staff, or the pastor and other leaders, such as the governing board or council. Or, the conflict can pit the congregation against the leaders. Or there can even be conflict between two congregations, or between the congregation and the regional or denominational judicatory, or between the congregation and a group in the community. Conflict could also arise between factions within the church, involving a variety of issues. Or it could be an interfamilial or interpersonal conflict that affects the whole church because of its severity, because those involved are key members, or because the topic of the conflict itself is related to the congregation. All these variations will influence the effect of the conflict on the congregation and its worship, and will determine some of the choices leaders make, such as whether to address the conflict directly in the worship service.

The congregation of Peace Lutheran Church tried to resolve conflicting views on worship by holding two very different services on Sunday morning. They expected that those who preferred to worship in their accustomed style would be content with an earlier service of time-honored liturgies, and that those who had been pushing for change and a more innovative style—something to engage and hold the young people—would be happy to attend the later, more upbeat service. But they were wrong. It seemed that no one was happy—about the service styles or the service times. The people didn't like being separated, and they didn't like the new times, and they didn't even follow the expectations of the leaders about which age groups would prefer which service. Their church name notwithstanding, "peace" did not describe this chapter of church life. There was much grumbling by some, and silence among others who gradually slipped away from the conflict—and the church.

One thing leaders need to understand is a congregation's unique way of dealing with conflict. Most congregations tend to repeat a pattern of dealing with conflict in a certain way that can then be predicted. Some are unlikely to talk about the conflict, and certainly not in angry voices, but are prone to sweep it under the rug. Others are vocal about their disagreements, but able to set aside opinions and remain friends while disagreeing agreeably. Still others tacitly assign conflicting roles to certain members and watch the conflict play out in front of them, feeding it with their own anxious grumbling.

Alban Institute consultant Speed Leas has written an overview of conflict management that identifies the levels of conflict and their characteristics in a helpful way and suggests the skills and people needed to deal with those conflict levels.[7] He explains that in a healthy conflict, church members understand that conflict is inevitable and see it as an opportunity to learn and grow. They can see the difference between the people and the problems and don't mix them by personalizing the issues. They keep open lines of communication, speaking directly to one another and making sure that everyone has the same information. They keep a short list of issues at hand, and refrain from bringing up things that happened months or years ago. They allow for an exchange of ideas in a spirit of cooperation and openness, and they listen carefully to one another. They accept the fact that a problem needs solving, but they are willing to allow as much time as needed to go through the journey together, experience the pain, and come out together on the other side.

On the other hand, in an unhealthy conflict church members see conflict as wrong or sinful. They quickly mix people and problems and assume that by changing or eliminating the people involved, the problem will also go away. They don't communicate directly, but speak only to individuals with whom they already agree and use third parties or letters to carry messages. They have long lists of grievances that have collected over time. Rather than talking and reasoning with one another, they become reactive and touchy, firing back unpleasant responses. They tend to ignore the real problems and deny what is going on, and at the same time, try to solve problems too quickly. They want to avoid the pain of conflict by saying "Let's get it over with," an approach that also allows them to avoid the pain of identifying and working out the real issues.

There is no quick fix to a conflict; it takes careful sorting out, listening to one another, and working to identify the real issues. When conflict is dealt with in a healthy way, learning can happen that will result in growth and strength for the church. Acts 6 and 15 show examples of the New Testament church dealing with conflict—in one case over the care of widows, and in the other about the acceptance of Gentile members. In those situations the conflict was discussed, the issues were addressed, and solutions were found. And it all happened through the guidance of the Holy Spirit. In Acts 15:28 Paul reports what "seemed good to the Holy Spirit and to us": they came to a way of moving forward by accepting Gentiles into the church but not requiring them to become Jewish. As congregations today deal with conflict over various issues—including accepting visitors who are a bit different from most of their church members—they must also listen intently to what the Holy Spirit may be teaching them as they discuss and discern their way through a conflict. It is one thing to come to a decision that is supported by most of the congregation. It is an even better thing to make a decision that has been shaped and guided by Christ through his Spirit.

One issue frequently related to conflict in congregations is that of changes in worship style. Churches make such changes for a variety of reasons, but often get hung up in the process. Is it possible for congregations polarized over changes in worship style to find a way forward that seems good to the Holy Spirit and to them? Yes, if they recognize that the main issue is not ultimately about projectors and screens, or songs and instruments, but about their identity as a congregation and what God is calling them to be and to do at this time in their history. Understanding the nature of Christian worship and how it functions in times of congregational difficulty is our next topic.

Chapter Three

Worship in Difficult Times

Intending to attract new people to their church, the pastor and a few members of the Main Street United Methodist Church in a rural midwestern town gradually introduced some innovations in worship, but found them consistently to meet with resistance. One year the group purchased copies of the newly revised denominational hymnal and placed them in the pew racks, but other members built new book holders and attached them beneath the seats in order to retain the old hymnals. Over the next few years, the resisters regularly complained to the pastor that he did not choose enough songs from the old hymnal.

Several years later, the innovators tried installing a projection system to put song lyrics, sermon outlines, and visual images on screens to aid in worship and to communicate a more up-to-date atmosphere to any visitors who might stop in. But the same members who had resisted the new hymnal became so incensed about this development that they threatened to leave the church and take their financial contributions with them. A shouting match erupted in the board meeting at which the matter was discussed, and the leaders polarized, taking sides for and against the pastor. That division spread through the small congregation as members heard about the conflict and also took sides. The tension was felt by all in the Sunday worship services, and the outreach-minded group began to wonder if they wanted visitors to come after all, lest they be drawn into the conflict.

Worship and Change

The words "worship" and "change" are a familiar pair these days, but the juxtaposition may be positive or negative, depending on one's perspective. Some churches are still "dying for change," as Leith Anderson, pastor of Wooddale Church in Eden Prairie, Minnesota, put it several years ago in his book of that title.[1] Others are dying *from* change—the process of changing worship has been so turbulent and destructive that some churches don't survive it.

It is true that in some settings, worship has changed much in recent years. United Methodist Bishop William Willimon notes, "There is more writing, thought, and change in Christian worship today than there has been in the past hundred years of church history."[2] Congregations that have gone through a difficult time over changes in worship are not hard to find. In fact, few churches make such changes without some difficulty. When I ask a group of pastors if they have seen changes in worship in the past five years, all hands go up. If I then ask how many of them experienced smooth, easy changes in worship, the hands drop quickly. As noted in a previous chapter, change always brings resistance because loss is involved. That is certainly true of worship. Changing to new patterns, rituals, songs, or spaces means the loss of familiar things and ways for many in the congregation.

While some people are eager for innovation in worship, many in the church are less enthusiastic about change. Instead of looking forward to new ideas with excitement and interest, they dread them and quote the familiar hymn "Abide with Me": "Change and decay in all around I see. . . ." Even people who welcome change in other areas of life—such as the doctor's office—can be reluctant to embrace change in the church. They want their physicians to be up on the latest diagnoses and treatments, but they aren't so eager for their pastors and worship leaders to prescribe new songs and worship styles.

Why are so many in the church resistant to change? Is it because they face change in so much of life that they want the comfort of sameness at least in church? Is it because in most areas of life, they have to accept and adapt to change beyond their choosing, but in church they feel they can control some of it? Or is it because matters of faith are tied so closely to what they do in worship that changing worship seems like questioning their beliefs? Is that why they often would rather abide with the God "who changes not" and try to create a church that "changes not" too?

Of course, for others, change is good, and "new and improved" is always better. Or even just new—some churches have been so eager to do what's new that they haven't been very discerning about changes from theological and biblical perspectives. Sometimes those who push for change argue that the congregation needs to adapt to what "the young people want," but that claim is often made without actually asking the young people. Their preferences are not so easy to identify, and certainly not all of them appreciate the same worship style. In fact, in some regions the young people are the strongest proponents of worship styles that go deep into the history of the church.

Basic Truths about Worship

Conversations about worship and change usually have to do with style and preferences, but that may not be the most productive way to begin. In fact, starting with a basic understanding and theology of worship is as important for this discussion as it is for any worship planning meeting, whether the congregation is responding to some broader transition or not.

In considering worship, its real audience must be identified. And that leads to the humble realization that worship is first about God, not the worshipers. Michael Lindvall, senior pastor of Brick Presbyterian Church in New York City, refers to the Sunday worship service as "weekly practice at not being God."[3] Alcoholics Anonymous (AA) is one organization that understands this concept well; in fact, a historical account of its early days is entitled *Not God.*[4] AA's genius is the recognition that sobriety comes only if you acknowledge a power greater than yourself. To recover, you have to recognize that you're *not God.* According to Lindvall, every time we go to church for a worship service, we also acknowledge that we are not God.

The ultimate goal of worship should be to bring glory to God— not to ourselves, either as leaders or worshipers. In the midst of all the change going on in worship these days, we must keep this basic purpose in mind. As Lindvall writes in his book on the Christian life, the common inquiry "What did you get out of that service?" is

the wrong question to ask at any time, and certainly in the context
of a difficult transition in a congregation. "The better question
might be: What did you lose in that service? What burden did
you drop at the foot of the cross? What pride did you shed? What
gnawing anger are you going home without? What lie do you no
longer believe?"[5]

In this book, worship is generally referred to as congregations
gathering on Sunday to listen and respond to God. While it is certainly true that the term "worship" can more narrowly refer to an
individual experience or more broadly to all of life lived before
the face of God, worship is presented here as the public event that
takes place when a community gathers in Christ's name to glorify
God. To understand how worship functions in transitional and
difficult times, a few basic principles about worship follow that
come as wonderful resources from the Christian tradition. Using
these common criteria will help to emphasize values that are essential to the practice of worship and make it at once more profound and also more hospitable. Thoughtful worship planning in
all times should include these aspects of worship.[6]

First, worship that is *biblical* is based on the Bible as the source
of knowledge about God and is fitting to the Scripture's instruction both about God and about the proper attitudes and practices
of worship. Biblical worship focuses on revealing the plan of redemption in Jesus Christ. In difficult times, the Bible's narratives
and instruction help interpret the experience of the congregation.
Scripture will reflect their pain and frustration as well as guide
them into an understanding of the current situation within the
greater story of God's plan for redeeming the world. Their main
guide for interpreting events and responding appropriately will be
the Bible itself.

Second, worship that is *dialogic* reflects the conversation
between God and God's people. In worship, God speaks words
of comfort and challenge, but also listens to praises and confessions—and all of the people's responses. They in turn also speak
and listen in worship, aware of the reality that God is the primary
partner in this conversation—God is the One who calls them to
worship. It is not that they come to worship and ask God to show
up. God invites *them*. In fact, God invites people to join in the

worship that is ongoing among the angels in heaven and the creatures of this world. They respond to the invitation with praise for God's greatness and nearness, confession of their inadequacy and brokenness, and dedication of their lives to grateful service.

In difficult times, it is especially important to think about the character of this dialogue. What questions need to be voiced? In what ways should a congregation be listening to God at this point in its congregational life? How do worshipers know when to confess, when to lament, and when to let the difficult matter rest a while? How does worship reflect both the needs of the people and the Word of the Lord? How can worshipers acknowledge the difficulties between them, or the differences in their attitudes regarding the difficulty facing the congregation? Should they have more spoken laments, confessions, and testimonies, or more times of silence? Should they employ richer uses of visual arts to express that which is difficult to put into words? Should they repeat Scripture readings, songs, and hymns that are familiar and comforting, or try new ones—especially those that speak particularly well to this unique point in their life together? Answering these and other questions will help guide the dialogue through difficult times.

Third, when this worship dialogue takes place in the context of a relationship based on promises between parties who attend to and care about one another, the *covenantal* nature of biblical worship is affirmed. For that reason, in worship people remember the promises of God to be with them and bless them, and they rehearse their promises by recommitting their lives to God and responding in gratitude for this wonderful covenant relationship. Especially in times of difficulty, these promises become important. Worshipers need to believe that God will not abandon them but will remain with them through thick and thin. It is critical to remember that God is a loving God, not one who requires compensation from people in order to bless them. So, even as they go through difficult times, they know that God is *for* them and will certainly keep the promises made to them. Their inability to keep their lives in order or to control completely the effects of crisis and chaos is not going to nullify the covenant. Actually, the covenant becomes even more significant in difficult times, bringing stability in times of uncertainty.

Fourth, the best example of a promise-fulfilling relationship of love and caring is found in the triune God, so worship that reflects this relationship is *trinitarian*. God as Father, Son, and Holy Spirit exemplifies a perfect relationship. *Trinitarian* worship then acknowledges that God calls the congregation into worship and hears the people's responses, God perfects and mediates their praise and petitions, and God helps them comprehend what they hear and prompts them to respond. Especially in times of distress, they need to trust in the love of God, the One who created and sustains us and everything in this world. They need to remember that they have been saved by Jesus Christ—that none of them is without sin, and all are in need of forgiveness at the cross. And it gives them great joy and peace to know that the Holy Spirit is not only comforting them in their sorrows, but also shaping them into a sanctified, holy people through this very difficulty. Trinitarian worship brings balance to their off-kilter days and steadies their souls when they are swamped with anxieties.

Fifth, while it is possible to worship as individuals, Scripture makes it clear that the gospel was proclaimed into a community and that worship is intended to express that *communal* identity of the church. Even though the church is made up of a variety of individuals, the beauty of worship is increased and more fully expressed by the gathered community, which in turn expresses the unity of the body of Christ. Of course, in difficult times, unity may be threatened, but that gives all the more reason to come together in worship. Worship services then must be designed with all parts of the congregation in mind, aware of various worshipers' concerns and needs. Worship must also encourage honest expression of both praise and lament to God. Enacting the practices of worship during a difficult time is as important to a congregation's health as eating regular meals is to the nourishment of a grieving individual for whom food does not seem important at all.

Sixth, worship that is *hospitable, caring, and welcoming* will not create an exclusive club, but will always be open to the guests who are invited to the Lord's banquet. Emphasizing hospitality will naturally result in serving others and inviting them into worship. Sometimes worship and evangelism are viewed as separate matters—mutually exclusive tasks of the church—and congregations facing difficulty may be inclined to turn inward and avoid the calling of the church to invite others to join. But separating worship and evangelism during turbulent times prevents the community from displaying the grace of God to the world—showing how the gospel both comforts and disturbs the congregation in ways that lead to healing as well as action. Unbelievers, seekers, and new believers should always be welcomed into worship and encouraged to experience the presence of God, since all are graciously called into God's presence. And difficult times could be the best times for visitors truly to see how the congregation functions and whether it is committed to befriending and enfolding new people into the community no matter what else is going on.

Seventh, worship that is *"in but not of" the world* will reflect the context and culture out of which it arises as well as the congregation's unique patterns of using time, space, music, speech, and movement. Since the difficult time is also part of the church's current context, it should not be ignored in worship. But worship must not be a slave to its context and history—whether that refers to a time long ago or last week. Authentic worship must challenge any patterns that are not true to Scripture. Like the people of God in this world, worship ought to be *in the world, but not of it.* So, just as a congregation that is not hospitable to visitors needs to be challenged by God's word, so a congregation that allows conflict to prevent worship from taking place or the sacraments from being administered is denying the work of Christ in and through the church. Similarly, worship that pretends nothing is going on and avoids addressing the difficulty is not honest worship. One congregation felt deep pain as members adjusted to the news that their pastor was slowly succumbing to cancer. Their pain was increased by his stoic refusal to acknowledge his condition in worship, and their grief at his death was acute. When the new pastor arrived a year later, he knew that to heal, the members needed an opportunity to work through their grief. He certainly did not expect to contract cancer himself, but he did, and God used his illness and recovery to bring healing to the entire congregation as members worked through it together.

Finally, worship proceeds as a *generous and excellent outpouring of ourselves before God.* Whether church members express praise or lament, they do so through their best offerings given in sincere worship that attends fully to God. Excellent worship means offering their best to God no matter how difficult the circumstances may seem. They don't automatically put special service plans on hold during difficult times, and they don't lower the quality of readings, music, prayers, and sermons. Rather, they bring their best to worship out of faith in the ongoing promises of God to give marvelous gifts to the people. Continuing to bring their best offerings to God even in difficult times will communicate strength and comfort to the congregation.

Worship as Formation

Congregations will learn and grow as they worship through difficult times and are formed by God as a community of faith. As they weather a crisis or transition or endure a conflict, they can pull together in ways that overcome their factions and move into a new chapter in their formation as a living, growing body of Christ. The following anecdotes show some of the wonderful and unexpected benefits of such growth.

- A historic urban congregation endured a summer sanctuary renovation by meeting outdoors under the shade trees along the edge of its parking lot and as a result found a renewed interest in its neighborhood. Church members came to see the neighborhood as the primary context of worship, once it was no longer separated from them by stained-glass windows.
- Another congregation learned the power of lament in worship after the tragic accidental death of a member's child. Members realized how limited their expression of human emotion had been and how much richer their experience of God became as they incorporated the many psalms of lament into their services in addition to the praise songs they had been singing.
- A rural congregation that launched a program to affirm its artists and craftspersons by forming groups to create visual arts for worship on various biblical themes found an unexpected benefit from the Holy Spirit. While members were

planning a program to involve as many people as possible in the arts, they discovered that God was executing a program that taught them to love one another more deeply as they encountered each other in new ways.

- Forced by a building expansion project to temporarily merge groups that had been worshiping separately with different styles of worship, one congregation learned the beauty of combining elements of various styles in a way that was enriching to all. The merging of the services provided the extra benefit of helping the previously separated groups to better understand and appreciate each other.

- A young church embroiled in conflict over leadership issues learned the importance of confession in worship by holding a service of reconciliation to acknowledge the hurts they had inflicted on one another, to confess those particular sins, and to seek forgiveness from God and one another. They also came to realize that the service of confession (which they had eliminated from their weekly worship so as not to put off visitors) was actually a powerful message to newcomers about their dependence on God. Those seeking a church were attracted by their vulnerability more than by their previous upbeat and polished services.

The formative aspect of worship—the way it forms people of faith both individually and corporately—may be more noticeable in difficult times than in ordinary ones. How church members talk about their faith in worship, how and what they sing, how they pray—these words, actions, and rituals are all critical to the development of their faith in God and their knowledge of Jesus Christ through a process that is led and guided by the Holy Spirit. Worship gives them the language of faith and the habits through which they practice their faith.

Practicing the habits of worship is always important, but especially so in difficult times. Repeating the historic language of faith gives assurance in uncertainty, and hearing and meditating on the language of Scripture carries people through arduous times. They may find words for their anger and frustration, as well as words of comfort and reassurance. Some people may really hear God's

Word for the first time, precisely *because* of the difficult moment, a time that heightens their sensitivity and openness to the way God works in and through people in good times and bad.

When considering the formational aspect of worship, the children and young people in the congregation must especially be remembered. Not only are they forming patterns and practices that will likely last throughout their lives; in addition they are especially astute when it comes to difficult times. Children are quick to notice tense words, especially in the church—a place where kindness is supposed to rule. (How many parents encourage their children to use their "church voices" in the sanctuary!) They will be watching closely to see how the congregation responds to a crisis or conflict, wondering if all those instructions they had been taught about "loving one another" will be followed by the adults around them. They will be curious to discover whether the emotions of anger and fear can be expressed in worship in grim times. Worship services experienced in these times are likely to create memories that will last for years.

Because young people are watching and learning so much from the congregation's response to the difficulty, it is important to watch the words and tone of voice used around them. Adults also must take care to explain the difficulty to them in words they can understand. One associate pastor masterfully assured his congregation's children in the Sunday morning children's message that even though their senior pastor had left for another position, God would not leave them but would provide another shepherd for them. His simple, compelling words captured the children's hearts and brought as much comfort to the adults in the pews as to the children on the chancel steps.

Moments and Habits

One way to think about the formational aspect of worship is to see it as a combination of "moments and habits."[7] The moments occur when there is a confluence—a coming together of an occasion and a theme with participants and leaders engaged in the spirit of the worship in a deeply significant way. Such moments are made possible by habits built up through the regular practice of the rituals and actions of worship. Moments are gifts and cannot be engineered. However, they may not happen without the kind of careful planning and sensitivity that makes space for them. Just as jazz music works only if musicians begin with some basic chord progressions as a spine that then allows for infinite variation, so moments in worship are most likely to happen when careful planning and ongoing practices provide the skeleton or backbone behind the variation. The spine is especially important when a congregation is experiencing the intense variations of crises, transitions, and conflicts. Those who have nurtured the habits of faith in regular practices of worship are more likely to adjust to the times of difficulty and more likely to carry these habits through with them.

In times of difficulty, it is more important than ever to be grounded in these habits. They are what sustains the relationship with God that is remembered and celebrated in worship. Just as a marriage requires wives and husbands habitually to show love to one another on a long-term basis, since love cannot be sustained during difficult days simply by remembering moments of ecstasy, so too the covenant relationship between people and God cannot be sustained by mountaintop religious experiences—which certainly don't happen every Sunday for every worshiper. On some Sundays worshipers feel more as though they're walking through the valley of the shadow of death, but even then, by going through the rituals of worship they can be sustained and strengthened as they endure a grueling time. By gathering for worship every Sunday, congregations create opportunities for moments to happen and establish the stability that can see a congregation through a challenging chapter in its history.

Some of the special moments that occur in worship are more poignant than celebratory, but they still generate meaningful times of worship that will be long remembered by those present. They will generate comments such as, "I'll never forget Pastor Miller's prayer the morning after 9/11," and "I'll always remember the sermon she preached on Psalm 46 that day." These are moments that happen *because of* the difficult time. Worship leaders need to be especially aware of the significance and memory-making potential of services held in difficult times, as well as the variations in worship patterns that develop during those times.

When the congregation of Resurrection Life Church started worshiping in the school gymnasium after a church fire, members found the congregation changed by this new situation. People sat in different places in relation to one another and struck up new acquaintances. They felt less reserved and were given to childlike chatter during the prelude. The new variations in the practice of gathering for worship resulted in less formality and greater fellowship, even when they eventually returned to their rebuilt sanctuary. And the novelty of the worship space also encouraged new, livelier patterns of worshiping and relating to one another.

Sometimes the liturgy literally keeps the congregation going in a difficult time. When an elderly church member fell ill and collapsed in the middle of Grace Church's annual Advent Service of Lessons and Carols, the choir director could tell what was happening in the congregation behind her by looking at the tear-filled eyes of her choir members, especially the stricken man's granddaughter. Between lessons she allowed time for the pastor to offer a prayer for the man and the medical personnel attending to him. His prayer sensitively recognized the crisis and the feelings it evoked in the congregation and gently led the people back to the service of Scripture readings and songs. He concluded with words appropriate to a poignant worship moment: "We know that your Word is important to Henry, as is your Advent promise that our Savior will come again, so help us to focus on your Word and your will once again, even as we entrust our dear friend to your care."

Lament in Worship

Difficult times of crisis and conflict often call for lament in the liturgy, an element that is too seldom practiced on a regular basis. While 21st century North American churches tend to avoid it, lament is an integral part of the worship and speech of God's children in Scripture and certainly is emphasized greatly in churches that face persecution in parts of our world. Congregations facing other difficulties can learn from their example. The psalms present good models for lament that can be easily translated into worship as readings, prayers, and songs. They boldly voice the most painful human questions with angry words, confessing belief in God as well as doubts about God's providence. Some church members may be uneasy asking such daring questions of God but will be reassured by knowing that these are the words of the Bible itself. Those who look to the church for answers in the aftermath of a natural disaster or tragedy will value the opportunity to ask hard questions of God within the crucible of the congregation.

Words that express doubt are actually statements of faith in God, declarations that expect to be heard and answered. John D. Witvliet, director of the Calvin Institute of Christian Worship, notes that prayers of lament "end with expressions of hope, confidence, and trust; however muted they might be by the present situation. Lament is eschatological prayer. It always looks to the future."[8] Lament in worship helps us to face the pain of this broken life, but to do so in the safety of God's care and in the confidence that one day all things will be made new and there will be "no more death or mourning or crying or pain" (Rev. 21:4 [NIV]).

Responding in Worship to Crisis, Transition, and Conflict

Lament is just one of the responses appropriate in worship through a difficult time. Others include confession, penitence, and reconciliation, as well as remembering, healing, and looking ahead in hope. These responses are appropriate in worship in more normal times, of course, but they can be highlighted in turbulent congregational times in meaningful ways. More specific responses to crisis, transition, and conflict in worship depend on the particular incident that the congregation is facing. In various circumstances, crisis may call for lament as well as comfort; transition may require persistent faith and hope in the transforming power of God; conflict may necessitate confession and reconciliation.

Coping in Crisis

When a *crisis* hits, worship leaders should be prepared to ask questions like these:

- What will we say to the people on Sunday morning, and who will say it?
- How will we tell the news in a way that makes it possible for us still to worship?
- If the pastor or worship leader is absent because of the crisis, who will lead the service and preach the sermon?
- How can the liturgy provide comfort and stability while acknowledging the crisis?
- Which parts, if any, of the planned music will need to be changed?
- How might other parts of the liturgy be adjusted— the prayers or readings, or the way in which they are presented?
- In churches that do not follow a set liturgy, how might the order of worship itself be reformulated to allow room for responding to the crisis? Should we scrap the planned liturgy completely and simply start over?
- Who is going to make these decisions?

Immediately after the accidental death of the pastor's daughter at Faith Community Church, several church leaders stepped in to help, since the accident happened on a Saturday, and Sunday's services had to be adjusted quickly. A staff member made phone calls to find substitute preachers. An elder went through the hymnal and picked out new songs for the service that changed the focus from praise to lament, and the organist selected more appropriate service music for the prelude, offertory, and postlude. The church prayer chain was activated, so that many members of the congregation received the news on Saturday evening and immediately began to pray for the pastor's family and the congregation in the time of crisis. Still, enough members showed up on Sunday morning without having heard the information that an elder needed to make the difficult announcement at the beginning of the service to explain the pastor's absence. The first hymn sung in the service was "Come, You Disconsolate," an appeal to the believers to bring their wounded hearts to the throne of God. The hymn concludes the first verse with the phrase: "Earth has no sorrows that heaven cannot heal," words that greatly comforted the congregation. The guest preacher for the morning brought a message from Mark 5 on Jesus's healing of the little girl who had died and pointed the congregation to the hope of the resurrection.

Another congregation experienced the sudden absence of its pastor after charges of sexual abuse were brought against him. That announcement was also made at the very beginning of the Sunday morning worship service. This time, the news came as a shock to all in attendance. Stunned, they may not have heard every word of the sermon delivered by a neighboring pastor with much experience in pastoral care. But later many recalled her effective message about the Aaronic blessing in Numbers 6:22–27 and remembered the comforting words of those verses. They were assured that even in adversity, God would continue to bless and keep them. As time went on and the pastor was suspended, members of the congregation felt hurt and betrayed but expressed those feelings in different ways. Some members withdrew and others became angry, taking sides either for or against the pastor. Unable to accept the possibility of his guilt, some either denied the truth of the allegations or blamed the victim for the situation.

Soon an interim pastor was appointed to provide pulpit supply and pastoral care to help the congregation through the crisis. In addition to the regular duties of preaching and visiting, he listened to those most hurt by the situation, and planned and led an optional service of healing on a weeknight several months after the initial announcement. All the members were invited to this service of healing, and those who came were encouraged to voice their concerns and their pain. The service was framed by psalms, beginning with a sung version of Psalm 6, "Lord, Chasten Not in Anger." The pastor described it as "a mournful song sung by people who wonder what God is up to but who dare to ask God too for a healing word in a time of deep pain." The congregation broke into small clusters of three or four to share their feelings, listen to one another respectfully, and pray together. Then they returned to the sanctuary for a reading of Psalm 62 and a meditation on finding rest in God alone.

Taking Time for Transitions

The examples above show how two congregations lived through crises in their congregational worship life. Many of the same questions can be asked in times of *transition*, though the time pressure is not as great and the anxiety level may not be as high. Some of those questions follow:

- How will information and updates about the transition be provided?
- What kind of language will we use to talk about the transition and influence how people think about it? For example, we can either talk about our congregation's vacancy when a pastor leaves, or about our preparation for the next shepherd God will send us.
- To what extent should the transition change our worship? Is it only a matter to remember in prayer? Or will it influence the choices of themes and texts?
- In churches that follow the lectionary, how can the transition be addressed using prescribed texts?
- Will the transition require changes in worship leadership? In worship space? In worship planning processes?
- In a leadership transition, how will we say goodbyes and hellos, while keeping the focus of worship on God?
- If a congregation has an extended time of guest leaders or preachers, how can laypeople be used to bring continuity to the services?
- In a building or location transition, how can the comings and goings be acknowledged within the ritual of the liturgy?
- When introducing a new mission of the congregation, how can that direction be tied to Scripture and celebrated in the liturgy?
- In a transition to a new style or form of worship, how can new aspects be introduced meaningfully and with a careful pace?

In some ways, more complicated situations occur when the transition that affects worship is a result of a change in the practice of worship itself. An example of a transition that many congregations face at some point in their history—and one that can easily lead to conflict—is the introduction of a new hymnal or songbook in the worship service. Heritage Baptist Church experienced a strident reaction to a new hymnal—mostly from members who were upset that their favorite hymns had been changed, or worse, eliminated. This change was part of a larger conversation and disagreement about worship style and whether to update the musical language of worship, a common point of contention these days. What happened when the new hymnal was introduced? People complained about what was *not* there and what *was* there. The older generation missed some of their gospel favorites and militaristic hymns, and they didn't like the new global music and praise songs. Others accepted the new songs and enjoyed learning them but questioned the wisdom of spending money on new books when so much music is available to project on a screen—not realizing that the costs of licenses or permission fees come into play even with projected lyrics or music.

While the fight seemed to be about preferences, it really was a deeply theological conversation. As senior Alban Institute consultant Gil Rendle observes, "Arguments about style are one of the cultural ways we have the conversation about meaning." We are well trained by our culture and all the product marketing forces to be aware of our preferences. Rendle explains, "We have deep preferential language but shallow theological language. We need habits to deepen our theological language, so a discussion of preferences when it comes to songs and hymns may be one of the most spiritual and theological conversations a congregation can have."[9]

The members of Heritage Baptist Church complained that they didn't like the new hymnal, not realizing exactly why. They needed help to understand that hymns with military metaphors like "Onward, Christian Soldiers" and "Lead On, O King Eternal" didn't communicate the same way to generations X and Y as they did to "the greatest generation" of the World War II era.[10] Instead of singing about conquering people for Christ, they were now asked to learn the indigenous songs of some of the peoples they had fought against! Unable to perceive and appreciate the global cultural and theological shifts, they could only complain at the loss of their music. Regardless of the reasons for the resistance, the introduction of a hymnal, a songbook, or a set of songs projected on a screen is an important time to slow down for the theological conversation that people need to have. A time of transition such as this is an opportunity for education, for teaching a language about worship that goes beyond preferences.

Another common congregational transition is that of a change in pastoral leadership. When pastors retire or leave for another calling, congregations tend to want to replace them as soon as possible. But often, though a quick substitution relieves the immediate anxiety of being seemingly leaderless, it doesn't allow the congregation sufficient time to grieve the loss of the former pastor and to go through the learning process that will lead them to seek the best kind of pastor for their church's next chapter. Worship services that acknowledge the ending of a pastorate are extremely important to the future health of the congregation.

One pastor humbly and stubbornly refused to have a fuss made over him when he retired after a 20-year stay in a small congregation. So there was no farewell service, no retirement party; the pastor simply left quietly. Seven years later the same congregation was embroiled in conflict with that pastor's successor, requiring intervention by a church consultant. The "diagnosis" of the consultant was that the congregation had not accepted and worked through the loss of their beloved former pastor, so they actually brought him back and did the farewell service after all those years!

Calm in Conflict

In a time of *conflict,* wisdom is needed to discern how best to acknowledge the disagreement and how to work toward resolution. Leaders will struggle over when and how to address the conflict and, if they're wise, they will consider how the conflict affects their worship time. They should ask questions such as these:

- What themes do we need to emphasize in worship in a conflicted time?
- When and how should we "name" the conflict in worship?
- How will we know when it is time to speak words of confession to one another? What is the best way to do that?

- How can we encourage confession without forcing acts of contrition that are not genuine?
- How can we involve members who are on different "sides" of the conflict, and use them as worship leaders?
- How can worship build hope in the congregation that "this too will pass" and that our Lord has better things in store for us?

Conflict can be extremely challenging to deal with in worship. In a crisis, people step in of necessity and do what needs to be done, with the goal of sustaining the congregation. In a transition, people also step in to help, but leaders have more time to discern and decide what needs to be done. In a conflict, when the situation is emotionally loaded and tensions are high, people may be eager to step in, but not always to help. They may demand that decisions go a certain way, or want to prevent something from happening. Wisdom is called for on the part of church leaders, so that they do not allow a faction to control worship in a way that intensifies the conflict instead of calming it.

Leaders will also need to discern whether the conflict should be addressed privately or publicly. The tendency is to avoid any public announcements for fear of scaring visitors away. But perhaps the real motivation is an unwillingness to admit that the church is not perfect and really does need the grace of God. When a church is dealing with a conflict, many eyes will be watching closely—and it won't be just the children's eyes. Simply because of the public nature of worship services, it may be impossible to hide some of the difficulty. But it may be more meaningful and a better witness to guests to show how the congregation is working the conflict out. Often people can observe the conflict blowing up, but they don't see the careful work planned behind the scenes to move toward healing.

Worship offers an opportunity for members and guests alike to see the congregation at work and in God's care. There are both risks and benefits to deciding not to shroud conflict from view. Depending on the nature of the conflict, some aspects may need to remain confidential and not be acknowledged publicly. Leaders must take care to honor the privacy of the individuals involved and ought to gain their permission before issuing any public statements that affect them personally. At the same time, being as open as possible will serve to decrease the anxiety the congregation experiences over the conflict. Uncertainty and lack of accurate information make for nervous congregations that will subsequently be even more reactive, losing their ability to stay calm and to respond thoughtfully.

Central Avenue Church's new pastor launched a contemporary service using presentational technology in worship and was stunned by the conflict that ensued between members who were all for the innovation and others who couldn't stand "that off-the-wall music." She was especially surprised because the pastoral search committee had led her to believe that the entire congregation was eager for such changes. Despite her attempts to please the burgeoning factions, the congregation polarized into groups—the "traditional" people and the "contemporary" people. They characterized themselves as "those who were interested in evangelism and the future of the church" and "those who wanted to preserve and honor the past as long as members continue to attend." The new pastor became the scapegoat and, convinced that she had failed to accomplish what the congregation wanted, resigned under pressure. No one—not the pastor, church leaders, or members—ever acknowledged that the real issue was not the music and words being projected, but the difficulty of accepting the loss of a previous beloved pastor and becoming accustomed to a new pastor. Even though they encouraged her to help them change, they were not ready to do it. It was their lack of readiness for more change when they were already dealing with a leadership change that led to the conflict, not the innovations of the new pastor.

Such signs of conflict, as noted in chapter 2, may be signs that the congregation is dealing with an important issue—something they care about deeply and need to work through. By resigning, the new pastor may have short-circuited the learning process. Willimon reminds pastors that resistance is not about them; it's about the issue facing the congregation. So resistance "may not be a sign of pastoral failure; it may be an indication of pastoral success!"[11]

Some symptoms of conflict may be healthy signs of a congregation struggling to deal with vital issues.

The challenge for leaders is to avoid taking the resistance personally and reacting in a way that makes the conflict worse. As Harvard leadership expert Ronald Heifetz likes to point out, they need to remember that in a football game the players don't chase and tackle the quarterback because they dislike him. They do it because he's carrying the football.[12] Similarly, congregational leaders need to remind themselves often that they are carrying the ball as they sort out a conflict, and that therefore they will become the focus of the congregation's anxiety. It takes great personal strength to remain calm and to absorb some of that anxiety rather than being hurt or angered by it. Leaders have to remember that the resistance is focused not on them, but on the "football."

It also takes great wisdom to speak on behalf of the congregation about the conflict. Worship based on the biblical principles outlined earlier in this chapter will require honest confession and, in time, reconciliation of the conflict. In most worship services, parishioners acknowledge their personal shortcomings in prayer and seek God's forgiveness and the washing away of their sins. Such personal confession needs to be expressed corporately when the conflict involves several people and perhaps the entire congregation. Wise leaders will call the congregation to confession while honestly acknowledging their inability to agree on this matter, and perhaps the difficulty they are having in disagreeing agreeably as well.

Confessing the uncharitable things that have been thought and said on both sides of the conflict can be a good starting point. There is usually plenty of blame to go around. But rather than trying to place blame, it is better to acknowledge the human tendency toward wickedness before God and to request forgiveness for all. A congregation should not be defined by its conflict and by the people who are either for or against an issue. All members of the congregation are part of Christ's body and need to move into God's will while traveling together in the same direction.

Church consultant Norman Shawchuck tells the story of a pastor who was asked to consult with a neighboring congregation that suffered from a seemingly irreversible conflict.[13] Church members had disagreed over the vision of the pastor and had allowed the fight to divide the congregation. Long after the exasperated pastor left, the congregation continued to be paralyzed in conflict. Shouting matches and name-calling were common as longtime members dwindled away. The consulting pastor helped them face the choice between reconciliation or fighting to the death—of the congregation. He addressed the conflict in a worship service that included a sermon on Acts 15, followed by the sacrament of the Lord's Supper. In his message he first addressed the reality of conflict in the New Testament churches—in Galatia, Corinth, and Philippi, as well as in Jerusalem, as recorded in Acts 15. Second, he pointed out that conflict is usually not a result of "sin in the camp" but of differences of opinion between individuals and groups—just as this congregation had differences about the pastor's ideas and whether he should stay or go. Third, he showed how sin enters church conflicts when we use other people as tools to be manipulated or sandpiles to be bulldozed, when we ignore people and refuse to talk with them or listen to their ideas, and when we play God and pretend that we alone know the truth.

Instead of moving directly from the sermon to the sacrament, the pastor asked all those who had been involved in the church conflict to join in a brief time of congregational self-examination in the fellowship hall. Gradually the church members followed him into the hall until the sanctuary was empty. Then he explained that the purpose of this session was to begin to seek reconciliation so that they could sit down at the table of the Lord as a community experiencing healing. He proceeded to name the conflict—the opposing views regarding the previous pastor—and asked the people to physically take sides by moving into three groups: those who had supported the pastor, those who had opposed him, and those who had remained neutral. The groups were asked to make lists of the sins they felt had been committed against them and the ways in which they had been hurt by the conflict. The pastor gathered the lists and read them aloud.

Then he read from Matthew 5:24 and said, "Those who would come to the table of the Lord to celebrate the Lord's Supper must be reconciled to their brothers and sisters. You have come to the table, you have had your memories refreshed that your brothers and sisters have something against you, and you have heard the desire of the Lord that you be reconciled by going to your brother or sister. The time is *now*. Will you go?" After some tense moments and silent stares across the room, they suddenly were all moving to find each other to ask forgiveness and be reconciled. After about 10 minutes, while the impromptu ritual was still going on, the pastor announced that it was time to celebrate together; the communion feast was at hand. They returned to the sanctuary and broke bread and shared the cup together, sang a hymn of unity, and received God's blessing. The refreshment time that followed the service was a continuation of the conversation and led to further confession and reconciliation. Not every church conflict will require the sort of intervention described in this story, but each one will require a discerning balance of grace and truth in an environment that calls for and honors both. Worship is certainly a context that does so.

Worship Brings Healing

Difficult times of crisis, transition, and conflict require church leaders to pay careful attention to congregational and interpersonal dynamics. Often the most thorny issues will be focused on worship, the major corporate activity of the church. Worship can become the congregational lightning rod, because it involves the greatest portion of the congregation all at once and because the worship experience is tied so closely to people's faith and feelings. Moreover, the claim that a church is in a "worship war" has become so common that it is almost expected by church members. It could even become the smokescreen that conceals the real underlying problems of the congregation. So, paying careful attention to worship is all the more important in difficult times.

In chapter 2 the congregation was compared to a human body—a living being made up of many parts, as Paul describes the church in 1 Corinthians 12. Another biblical metaphor for the gifts of the church and its web of relationships is a horticultural one. In John 15 Jesus says, "I am the true vine, and my Father is the vine-grower. He removes every branch in me that bears no fruit. Every branch that bears fruit he prunes to make it bear more fruit." Both images are helpful in understanding what happens to a congregation in a difficult time and how the difficulty is expressed. When a person has a sore tooth, her whole head can hurt. If her eyes are blind, the activity of her entire body is affected. When a branch is pruned or shocked by frost, the plant will react by working harder to heal the broken parts. Or it may shed them.

Similar reactions can be found in the church. The members of Faith Community Church initially pulled out all the stops to care for their grief-stricken pastor and his family. The family's grief was the pain of the whole congregation. Church members brought meals; the young people's group painted a mural in the youth room to memorialize their lost friend; the church staff worked overtime to accomplish the administrative tasks that normally fell to the pastor. People helped in every way possible to allow the pastor time to heal. But some of their care and patience wore thin when months went by and the pastor was still unable to function fully in his work. While some parishioners were long-suffering, others were eager to move on and frustrated with the slow pace. Gradually they became more critical of the pastor, and eventually he was the one who moved on—to another ministry and a fresh start, away from the painful reminders of the family's loss.

As more churches understand the dynamics of change and difficult times, they will be able to come through such situations with healing. Worship can be the greenhouse or the nursery in which suffering plants are brought back to health, the rehabilitation unit in which broken bodies become whole again through nutrition and physical therapy. The life-giving Word and Spirit of God bring sustenance through the habits and actions of the liturgy. In worship God's people learn again to abide in the Vine—both by hearing the Word of God and by reenacting its stories through the rituals of worship. In worship, they are also nourished by the water, bread, and wine of the sacraments. They remember who they are as baptized persons, and they celebrate their redemption at Christ's supper, where they receive the nutrients that feed their souls and give them life. In worship they recall God's faithfulness and seek to bear the Spirit's fruit. Like plants that take in oxygen and put out carbon dioxide in the process of photosynthesis, so in worship they engage in dialogue, a reciprocal relationship between the creatures and the Creator. In the next chapter, we will examine the various elements of this liturgy to see how they can be part of the healing process in a difficult time.

Chapter Four

Worship in Times of Crisis

Worship is so essential to the church that it is rarely cancelled. Even when a church suffers from a fire, an alternative location for worship is almost always found quickly. The members of the worshiping body want to be together in times of crisis to comfort one another. Whether out of strong desire or simple habit, their first impulse is to be present with one another and with God. Even congregations that experience severe conflict in the wake of a crisis usually still meet for worship, because it is in worship that the most appropriate venue for healing and reconciliation is found. In worship church members recognize that they need to abide together and abide in Christ, offering pastoral care to one another.

Many stories can be told of congregations that pulled together in remarkable ways through a time of crisis and were able to celebrate that outcome in worship. Presbyterian pastor and author Jill Hudson writes that "worship is the heart of Christian life." She observes that for congregations experiencing trauma, "using the experience of being together in the presence of God for prayer, to hear the Word preached, to share at Christ's table, and to lay out all our emotions is one of the most effective ways of helping a congregation to cope with the reality of what has happened."[1] So worship is not only the natural impulse of congregations in distress; it is also where healing begins to take place.

United Methodist pastor and author Carol M. Norén explains how worship functions in crises, and how it can help congregations through them. She writes: "Worship reminds those who are present of the Lord's faithfulness in the past, invokes the Spirit's sustenance in the present, and looks forward to God's unfolding purpose."[2] This trinitarian approach to worship will serve congregations in crisis well, and will provide for the learning of the congregation in the process. As Norén notes, "In crisis as well as in sorrow, worship should include instruction and preparation of the saints for the challenges that lie ahead. Questions and anguish should not be suppressed but offered up to God reverently and honestly." In the safety of worship—among friends and with God—the wounds of crisis can be cleansed and soothed with balm, and the healing process will begin.

This chapter will include a closer look at worship as pastoral care in the healing process that follows a crisis and specific ways to help congregations through the challenges of worshiping in times of crisis. Subsequent chapters will do the same for congregations going through transition or conflict.

Worship as Pastoral Care in Crisis

Congregations find their way through crises as they worship. Acting out the habits and familiar rituals of worship helps parishioners manage their feelings of shock, regret, and grief following a crisis. Just as the rituals of a funeral service and the surrounding times of visitation provide structure for grieving family members and friends, so also worship services can provide that structure for congregations experiencing the acute pain and loss of a crisis. Pastors may want to turn to a funeral manual for ideas and guidance for worship in a crisis, because whether or not an actual death has occurred, there has been a loss—of safety, of facilities, of relationships, or of persons.

Worship functions as a way to come to terms with the trauma and loss of a crisis, not only for church members but also for members of the community. People are drawn to the church by a tragedy. They want assurance, answers, and comfort. They instinctively look to God—or to the church that claims to speak for God—to find some hope in a seemingly hopeless situation. On the eve of the Gulf War in January 1991, numerous churches in the United States planned prayer services and advertised them on television and radio. With only a few hours' notice, churches in many cities were filled with people pleading for peaceful solutions that would avoid the need for war. The churches provided a place for people to express their fears and their hopes.

On September 11, 2001, and in the days that followed the terrorist attacks on the United States, churches opened their doors for prayer, not even waiting to plan services in every case. Impromptu ecumenical gatherings took place in churches throughout the country where people gathered to pray for the families of the dead and the missing, and to ask God to protect the country from further harm. Worship services soon followed to give form to the prayers and to bring a word from the Lord into a desperate and fearful situation.

Norén points out two pastoral concerns for leaders involved in ministry to those experiencing loss and grief: "clarity and hospitality."[3] These two topics are also ways that worship can meet people's pastoral needs. People are looking for understanding and for comfort, and they look to the church for both. The need for clarity among those in crisis becomes an opportunity to proclaim the gospel. In addition to the need for accurate information is the broader reality that despite the horrors of terrorist attack, war, tragic death, or natural disaster, God is still with us and ministers to us through the Spirit of Christ. This is as true for worship services following tragedies as it is for funerals. And those worship services ought to be characterized by God's gracious hospitality. Norén explains this approach to pastors:

> When you conduct a funeral or otherwise lead Christian worship, one thing you are doing is embodying and proclaiming God's gracious initiative toward us. It is a kind of hospitality to people in sorrow, reminiscent of the Risen Christ's invitation to his followers to "Come and have breakfast" by the Sea of Galilee. Jesus did not force-feed the disciples, and neither should we as we lead worship. We should invite participation, but we should not coerce people or shame them if, for whatever reason, they do not feel ready to take part.[4]

Simply opening the church doors in the aftermath of crisis proclaims in a clear and comforting way the gospel of the God who is always there.

Worship serves as a form of pastoral care in times of crisis in several other ways, Norén says. Providing people with information—as much as is possible and appropriate—is a way of caring for them. Providing a safe place for people to lament a loss—a place where they can express their raw emotions to God—also is a way of caring for them. And in that safe place, yet another pastoral-care strategy is to maintain the familiar. Norén explains, "People in crisis are in a state where boundaries and routines have been disrupted." Providing the normal rhythms of the liturgy as it is usually practiced in their congregation can be a soothing balm for hurting people.

This pastoral care happens over time as well, as the urgency of the crisis begins to dissipate. Worship planners must realize that the impact of the crisis will last far beyond the crisis itself and the first few Sunday services. Jill Hudson writes that worship planning in the year following a traumatic event requires "careful monitoring of the congregation's progress toward healing. Leaders and planners should remember that people will be in different places in their separate journeys toward wholeness." But "gradually, as life seems to settle down, overt mention of the trauma may be replaced with more subtle, thematic references. Assessing this shift is an art and may best be determined in consultation with others."[5]

Worship planning groups must be in contact with other leaders in the congregation to determine the pace at which the congregation is healing, and therefore the way that the process can best be encouraged and acknowledged in worship. Hudson reminds us that "life does go on, and part of releasing the traumatic past to God's care is letting go of how trauma defines the congregation. Remembering is always important, but the way we remember and the intensity of focus on the remembrance should alter as time goes on."[6] For worship planners and pastors, keeping in step with the pace of the congregation's healing will be important, knowing that the pace will differ widely for the church members and for the worship planners themselves.

Initially, some church members may struggle to bring themselves to worship during a difficult time. They may be challenged so severely with questions about God and God's providence that they have no desire or ability to worship. Church leaders must take care to tend to these people with sensitive pastoral care through notes, calls, or visits, rather than judging their absence as lack of commitment or lack of faith. Their struggles may actually be indicative of strong faith and tenacious wrestling with God.

Also, leaders should be aware of their own struggles and reactions to the crisis, and how those feelings will affect their leadership and those they lead. They should confide their own feelings about the crisis to a colleague or mentor, both to grow in self-understanding, and to express their own sadness or frustration in a safe context that will not affect the morale of the congregation. Pastors and worship leaders also need both information and comfort in times of crisis.

Lament: Being Sad and Mad in Worship

An essential way to enable worship to function as pastoral care in a time of crisis is to allow people to be sad and angry, and to express these emotions in worship as lament. As they are experiencing feelings like rage or fear, lament is an action that rises out of those emotions and functions as an element of worship. The psalms of Scripture are filled with lament and sometimes juxtaposed with praise, another expression of emotion that serves as a component of the liturgy. The Christian church has seen lament as a legitimate element of worship throughout its history, though it has not always been practiced regularly, especially in more recent Protestant traditions. While lament is too seldom included as an element of worship in many congregations, crisis situations especially call for it. Gathering up the feelings of anger, betrayal, and fear that accompany a crisis, lament provides a way to express them to God—not as doubt, but as an act of faith.

J. Frank Henderson, editor of the *National Bulletin on Liturgy* of the Canadian Conference of Catholic Bishops, writes that

> we Christians know, even in times of violence and oppression, that God does not turn away from us. Nor does God turn away from any person who suffers or from any other part of creation that experiences disaster. So when we lament violence or disaster,

we do not "grieve as those without hope" (1 Thess. 4:13): The
life, suffering, death and resurrection of Jesus reveals to us God's
steadfast love. The Spirit of God abides with us.[7]

Worship planners are often pressured to make worship joyful
and uplifting. Daniel Migliore and Kathleen Billman, professors at
Princeton Theological Seminary and Lutheran School of Theology
at Chicago, respectively, note that "instead of providing space for
protest and grief, what churches often offer are worship services
that are 'unrelentingly positive in tone.'"[8] Worship in North America today seems to lean more toward praise than lament, although
both are expressed in biblical worship and certainly in the Psalms,
the "songbook" of Israel's worship. A time of crisis may actually bring balance to a congregation's worship. As Roman Crews
of Columbia College puts it, "The tension between the sense of
God's absence and God's presence, between 'the not yet' and 'the
already' of salvation, between lament and praise, characterizes
faithful worship."[9]

According to Carl Bosma and Ron Nydam, professors of Old
Testament and pastoral care, respectively, at Calvin Theological
Seminary, the prevalence of "praise and worship" services does
not fully honor either the biblical expressions of worship or the
ways in which people need to worship God. There is a time to
lament, a time to be sad; and often such times follow a crisis. Authentic worship requires us to acknowledge the struggles of life in
the presence of God and ask for help to get through the difficult
times. Worship can be a way to "teach people how to be sad and
mad" when difficulties come their way.[10]

According to Bosma and Nydam, worshipers need words and
music that will carry them into their sadness so that they can bring
their suffering to God. They also need a community in which to
do this. The body of believers can give them the courage to face
suffering in whatever form it is experienced, because it is in the
midst of sadness that we realize how deeply we valued whoever or
whatever was lost. It is in sadness that we meet God, and in the
experience of our tears that we come "face to face" with God as
the "healer and restorer of hope" (Psalm 42).

The biblical psalms can be a good model for expressing anger, fear, and bewilderment in times of crisis, according to John D. Witvliet. "When faced with an utter loss of words and an oversupply of volatile emotions, we best rely not on our own stuttering speech, but on the reliable and profoundly relevant laments of the Hebrew Scriptures."[11] He suggests that the basic form of the lament psalm be contextualized to a particular tragedy and used to give structure to the entire worship service, as follows:

- Begin with an invocation, a startling confession that even in times of crisis, we approach a personal and accessible God.
- Address this personal God through the picturesque gallery of images used in direct address in the psalms, such as a rock, fortress, hiding place, or bird with encompassing wings.
- Continue with bold lament, bringing our most intense theological questions right into the sanctuary, understanding through the psalms that doubt can be expressed as an act of faith.
- Lift up specific petitions to heal us, free us, save us.
- Conclude the prayer with expressions of hope, confidence, and trust, however muted they might be by the present situation, because lament is eschatological prayer: it always looks to the future.[12]

Of course, we also can pray the psalms themselves to express our lament. Witvliet suggests that we "choose Psalm 69 for a crisis of shame, 51 for a crisis of guilt, 38 or 41 for medical crises, 88 for times of utter despair, 71 for the afflictions of old age, and 143 for occasions of oppression or victimization."[13] When we use these strong biblical words to express our lament, we should read them with power and passion, but not too quickly. Lament takes time. It elicits emotions that should not be easily swept away. Especially when the pain is acute, worshipers need time to face their anguish before God and to experience the comfort God brings to the community. That is why Witvliet recommends that worship planners consider expanding lament to encompass an entire service, taking a full hour to pray through a given psalm of lament, such as Psalm 13, using silence, quiet hymns, and brief spoken meditations to unpack the meaning of each section of the psalm.

Two extremes should be avoided when incorporating lament into the worship service. The first is the tendency to "leave worshipers behind in lament, hastening too quickly to return to normalcy, to songs and prayers of well-being." The second is "to linger in lament, praying week after week concerning a given crisis with a sense of despair that fails to sense the magnetic pull of Christ-centered hope."[14] As mentioned above, worship planners must be sensitive to the emotional state of the congregation and the progress they make over time, helping them to express lament, but also to move on in hope. Witvliet adds that the goal should be to "shepherd worshipers over time through disorientation to reorientation, through lament to praise." This need could be addressed through a series of services that focus on the Psalms, perhaps beginning with Psalm 13 and moving to Psalm 30 and then to 146, encompassing disorientation and reorientation, lament and praise. The goal of such services is "not to solve the problem of evil, but rather to lead worshipers more deeply into these biblical prayers."[15]

Using lament in worship provides a way to speak boldly to God about our pain, knowing that it is real, but not the last word in the biblical scheme of things. It gives us a structure for doing so, following the psalms, and it also lends greater integrity to the praise we offer, after we have expressed our lament. It provides a way for individuals caught up in isolated and lonely struggles with tragedy or injustice to find a voice in a community of worshipers, and it gives suffering worshipers biblical landmarks to anchor personal prayer and worship. "It gives us a place to put a bookmark in our Bibles. It gives us texts to recall at family reunions and anniversary commemorations. This is a tangible gift that thoughtful liturgy can provide in times of crisis,"[16] says Witvliet.

Other good resources for helping a congregation express lament in a time of crisis are new translations of the psalms, including the well-known paraphrase *The Message,* by Eugene Peterson, which offers this translation of Psalm 13:

Long enough, GOD—
    you've ignored me long enough.
I've looked at the back of your head
    long enough. Long enough
I've carried this ton of trouble,
    lived with a stomach full of pain.
Long enough my arrogant enemies
    have looked down their noses at me.

Take a good look at me, GOD, my God:
    I want to look life in the eye,
So no enemy can get the best of me
    or laugh when I fall on my face.

I've thrown myself headlong into your arms—
    I'm celebrating your rescue.
I'm singing at the top of my lungs,
    I'm so full of answered prayers.[17]

Another fine volume is *Voicing God's Psalms* by philosopher and author Calvin Seerveld, which includes a CD recording of the author reading his own psalms.[18] Listening to the audio could allow worshipers to reflect on the words more attentively than if they were reading them aloud in unison—a practice that can distract worshipers from the very words they are reading. Providing a printed copy or projecting the words on a screen as they listen may help them to hear the psalm even better.

Seerveld's translation of Psalm 13 is reproduced here in two versions, the second designed to be sung to GENEVAN 13, the tune for this psalm in the Genevan Psalter, a compilation of musical settings for the entire Psalter gathered by 16th-century Reformed Christians in Geneva, Switzerland. Many of these tunes continue to be sung throughout the world.

1   How long, LORD God, how long will you keep on forgetting me!
     Forever?
    How long will you hide your face from me?

2   How long must I always be second-guessing such things
       deep inside myself,
    and have worrisome pain in my gut all day long?
    How long will my enemy have me in its triumphant power?

3   Take a good look, O LORD, my God, please hear me with an
       answer!
    Keep my eyes bright with life lest death itself put me to sleep,
4   and my enemies roll in the aisles when they see me about to
       break down—

5   But I still sense I am safe in your covenantal love.
    My deepest heart rejoices in your always coming through to
       the rescue.
6   I will sing out to the LORD!
    Yes, the LORD has always helped me grow more sure of
       God's enduring love.

© Calvin Seerveld, *Voicing God's Psalms,* 2005 Wm. B. Eerdmans Publishing Company, Grand Rapids, Michigan. Reprinted
by permission of the publisher; all rights reserved.

Psalm 13 (versification)
How long, O LORD, will you ignore—
how long face me like a closed door?
How long must I brood on what went wrong,
suffer with pain, worry all day long,
blocked by the enemy's cruel war?

Take a close look, LORD, answer prayer!
Keep my eyes bright, safe in your care
lest I succumb to hateful death's hour,
caught in the grip of evil's power
which laughs while I wrestle despair.

But I sense I am safe with you.
Your covenant love remains true.
My heart is happy in your favor;

I celebrate the LORD my savior:
God always has brought me rescue!

Seerveld writes other poignant "voicings" of the psalms of Scripture, as well as a powerful "Congregational Lament" that includes verses for various particular crises and concludes with these words:

Why, Lord, must any child of yours be hurt?
Does all our pain and sorrow somehow please you?
You are a God so jealous for our praises—
Hear this lament as prayer that fills the earth.
We plead: repair the brokenness we share.
Chastise no more lest it destroy your creatures.
Hear this lament as intercessory prayer,
and speak your powerful word to make us hopeful.

Seerveld wisely points out that "the *comfort* the psalms give is not what makes you 'comfortable.' It is the comfort of knowing that you are safe and not alone as you walk through troubled waters. Genuine comfort is not the end of misery or the resolution of problems, but is having somebody you love hold you close while you are hurting."[19] In worship we experience the love of God holding us close in our pain.

Worship Planning after a Crisis

While the suddenness and pain of a crisis often interrupts family, school, and work schedules, it usually does not disrupt worship itself. Worship goes on, but pastors and worship planners need to acknowledge the crisis in some way and answer the question of the people, which is usually: "Is there any word from the Lord in this situation?" Norén says the church must "announce the prophet's answer—'There is'—through preaching and other parts of the liturgy."[20] How that is accomplished will make all the difference in whether worship really does become a form of pastoral care to people. It may involve giving up some already-laid plans and substituting new plans.

Worship planners and pastors will want to ask some questions like these when working on the Sunday-after-the-crisis service, whether it's a national emergency, natural disaster, tragedy in the community, or trauma in the life of the congregation or its members:

- How close is the crisis to our congregation?
- Does the text with which we have already been working for this service have words to address the crisis?
- What other parts of worship may address the crisis, such as prayers, songs, readings, offerings?
- What will be the duration of the crisis; that is, is it an unfolding situation that may be addressed through worship at other times? or elsewhere?[21]

Pastors and worship planners need to consider the elements of the service through new filters because of the crisis. They need to realize that because of the crisis or calamity, the "acoustics" of the situation have changed and the gospel will be heard differently. That's why the message of Psalm 46 was so poignant for Americans in the weeks following 9/11. "God is our refuge and strength, an ever-present help in trouble" was heard through ears that had been opened in a new way by the terrifying attacks on the United States.

The normal themes of the church year are also affected by these new acoustics; they "sound" different in a turbulent time. Congregations going through a crisis may find certain seasons in the church year more difficult to observe because their circumstances either intensify or contradict the meaning of the season. For instance, the longing and waiting of Advent may seem more urgent in a time of crisis. Church members may need a gentle leader to help them understand why they have difficulty singing Christmas carols in the aftermath of a crisis—or why they may want to sing *only* carols and avoid the feelings evoked by Advent hymns. With careful guidance, they may discover in Advent a new appreciation for the longing reflected in Scripture.

On the other hand, a time of crisis may bring deeper meaning to a particular time of year. For instance, in a Lenten season that occurs during or soon after a crisis, the contemplation of Christ's suffering may be particularly comforting to parishioners in pain and grief. Wise worship planners tune their ears to the new acoustics brought by the crisis, and make adjustments accordingly.

Often in difficult situations the impulse of leaders is to pretend that everything is fine and therefore not to "mess up" the worship service—especially if the crisis has to do with an internal problem like a firing or the sudden departure of a pastor or staff person. Some may assume, or hope, that ignoring the problem will be better for the people. However, if the matter is public knowledge, then avoiding mention of it may be counterproductive. The people will already be somewhat disturbed, so ignoring the obvious may only heighten their stress. A better way to lower the congregation's anxiety would be to acknowledge the difficulty publicly, both honestly and prudently, and to make it a matter of prayer. One church-shopping couple visited a congregation on the day the suspension of its pastor was announced. They kept coming to see how the church would respond and observed the honest and open way it dealt with the crisis. They are still members of that congregation, 15 years later.

Worship planners and leaders will need to anticipate the reaction of their own congregation to the crisis and what the needs of the people will be, and that will require communication with the leadership body of the congregation. They need to ask:

- Do parishioners need information? Comfort? Stability? An action plan?

- Will they feel angry? Afraid? Shocked? Sad? Bewildered?
- Will this difficulty be short-lived? Long-term? Or will it cause permanent damage?

All of these needs and emotions may arise and can be acknowledged by careful service planners through the words they choose and the readings they offer. Sensitivity to timing is also important. Wise worship planners will be sure to give the congregation some breathing room as well—some "time off" from the crisis. Like counselors, they need to remember that the therapeutic hour is only 50 minutes, and that everyone needs a break from dealing with difficult issues.

Themes for Worship in Times of Crisis

Worship planners will want to discern carefully the biblical themes that will be most helpful in the context of a particular crisis. Jill Hudson argues that even those churches that don't usually follow the lectionary may want to in difficult times. She notes that in a crisis the prevailing question often is "Why did this happen?" and then, also, "Why did God let this happen?" In the face of such questions, pastors and worship planners may want to look to the lectionary for guidance, because it follows the ongoing story of God's faithfulness to God's people. Focusing on that story may be "the most consistent way of demonstrating that God does not break promises."[22] Furthermore, the congregation is likely to find itself connecting with that story in new ways in this situation.

For congregations that don't follow the lectionary and decide to address the crisis more directly through special themes, here are a few suggestions:

- God's providential care for all creation and creatures (Ps. 55:22, Matt. 10:29; Acts 14:15–17, 17:24–28; Rom. 8:38–39).
- God's promise always to be with us (Isa. 43:1–3, Matt. 28:20).
- God's promise of forgiveness and reconciliation (Eph. 2, 1 John 1).

- God's call for justice and peace (Amos 5, Micah 6).

Other overarching biblical themes can also be fitting in times of crisis, such as the ongoing narrative of redemptive history, the promise of forgiveness through the cross, the eschatological hope in the second coming, and the restoration of the new heavens and the new earth. In worship we can move the focus beyond ourselves to the bigger family of God and God's plan for the world, which is far beyond our understanding. We can trust in God's providence—that indeed all things work together for good for those who love God—even when the situation we face doesn't seem good at all. As Professor John Cooper of Calvin Theological Seminary explains:

"All things" does not necessarily mean "each and every thing." More likely it means "the totality of things." Understanding it this way implies that God may allow some instances of evil and suffering that do not lead to greater good. But his whole plan, ordained from before the foundation of the world, does work together for the good of those who are called according to his purpose (Rom. 8:28). That plan includes bad things that God does directly turn to our good. It includes perplexing things whose purpose takes a while to figure out. It includes awful things that are much worse than any good that comes from them. But all of these things work together for the ultimate good according to God's plan. The Gospel is that whether or not bad things lead to good things, God is always with us, loving and sustaining us even through the greatest pain and darkest despair. "Nothing... will be able to separate us from the love of God that is in Christ Jesus our Lord" (Rom. 8:39 [NIV]).[23]

Helping the congregation to remember God's love, and to look ahead and trust in God's ultimate purposes for the kingdom of Christ, can bring hope and comfort in the wake of a crisis. Knowing that the world and the church are in God's hands assures us that we will not be in distress forever. Communicating these important themes of assurance in each element of the worship service is essential in times of crisis. The following liturgical resources are provided as models for worship planners and may serve them well as starting points when little time is available.

Liturgical Resources

Opening of Worship

The opening of worship sets the tone for the service through the call to worship, the opening prayers or opening sentences, and God's greeting and mutual greetings. In all worship services, the first words a leader says are important, but they are even more vitally important at funerals and crisis-related services than on normal Sundays. According to Norén, "Your tone of voice and body language, as well as the words you speak, set the tone of the service and help (or hinder) the congregation in worshiping God."[24] Even with a minimum of preparation time imposed by the impending events of the crisis, worship leaders should plan their opening words with great care and much prayer.

Opening Sentences

No matter what the crisis is, opening sentences and calls to worship that emphasize God's nearness, caring, and strength will be fitting, such as the following texts:

- Psalm 28:6–7a
- Psalm 34:18
- Psalm 46:1
- Psalm 55:22a
- Psalm 95:6–7
- Psalm 124:8
- Psalm 145:18–19
- Habakkuk 2:20
- Matthew 11:28–29
- 2 Corinthians 1:3–4

A creed or confessional faith statement may also be an appropriate opening to worship—an affirmation of belief in God in the face of crisis. One good example is the first question and answer of the Heidelberg Catechism:

Q. What is your only comfort in life and in death?

A. That I am not my own,
but belong—
body and soul,
in life and in death—
to my faithful Savior Jesus Christ.

He has fully paid for all my sins with his precious blood,
and has set me free from the tyranny of the devil.
He also watches over me in such a way
that not a hair can fall from my head
without the will of my Father in heaven:
in fact, all things must work together for my salvation.

Because I belong to him,
Christ, by his Holy Spirit,
assures me of eternal life
and makes me wholeheartedly willing and ready
from now on to live for him.[25]

Such a statement, read responsively by the leaders and the congregation, may give them an opportunity to speak words that are hard to believe, and yet that build confidence as they are spoken. We speak the words of the creeds both to state the things that we believe and *in order to* believe them.

Another fine example comes from the Belgic Confession, written by 16th-century martyr Guido de Brés in the face of severe persecution in what was then the southern part of the Netherlands, now Belgium. His statement of faith, which became one of the doctrinal standards of the Reformed churches, offers comfort in crisis in the words of Article 13 on "The Doctrine of God's Providence." Two excerpts follow:

We believe that this good God,
after he created all things,
did not abandon them to chance or fortune
but leads and governs them according to his holy will,

in such a way that nothing happens in this world
without his orderly arrangement.

· · · · · · · ·

This doctrine gives us unspeakable comfort
since it teaches us that nothing can happen to us by chance
but only by the arrangement of our gracious heavenly Father.
He watches over us with fatherly care,
keeping all creatures under his control,
so that not one of the hairs on our heads
(for they are all numbered)
nor even a little bird can fall to the ground
without the will of our Father.
In this thought we rest,
knowing that he holds in check
the devils and all our enemies,
who cannot hurt us without his permission and will.[26]

The truly memorable memorial service of a denominational leader stricken 10 months earlier by a brain tumor began with a recording of this powerful article—spoken in his own voice—and reassured family and church members of the providence of God.

Greeting of God

When the pastor or worship leader brings the greeting of God, a crisis may call for something different from the typical Pauline greeting of "Grace and peace to you from God the Father and the Lord Jesus Christ." If a congregation is accustomed to a fixed liturgy in which the words of the greeting are always the same, however, then the disruption of replacing it may outweigh the benefits of tailoring the reading to the crisis situation. But for those congregations that do use greetings of God from different parts of Scripture, finding one that is especially fitting to the crisis situation may bring new insight and comfort. For example, after a natural disaster, the words of Isaiah 43 may be especially fitting:

Do not fear, for I have redeemed you;
I have called you by name, you are mine.
When you pass through the waters,

I will be with you;
and through the rivers,
they shall not overwhelm you;
when you walk through the fire
you shall not be burned;
and the flame shall not consume you.
For I am the LORD your God,
the Holy One of Israel, your Savior.

—Isaiah 43:1b–3

Or these verses from Isaiah 54:

"For a brief moment I abandoned you,
but with great compassion I will gather you.
In overflowing wrath for a moment
I hid my face from you,
but with everlasting love
I will have compassion on you,"
says the LORD, your Redeemer.

—Isaiah 54:7–8

Opening Prayer

Likewise, the opening prayer is crucial to setting the tone for the
worship service. Worship leaders will want to communicate with a
calm tone that places trust in God, even when it is appropriate to
express fear and frustration. Often, words of Scripture offer that
tone. Here is one example from Lamentations, printed for responsive reading:

Let us call to mind the reason for our hope:
Because of the LORD's great love we are not consumed,
for his compassions never fail.
They are new every morning;
great is your faithfulness.
I say to myself, "The LORD is my portion;
therefore I will wait for him."
The LORD is good to those whose hope is in him,
to the one who seeks him;

it is good to wait quietly
for the salvation of the LORD.

—From Lam. 3:21–26 (NIV)[27]

Or, a prayer from the Iona Community:

We come to worship God in our need,
bringing with us the needs of the world.
We come to God, who comes to us in Jesus,
and who knows by experience what human life is like.
We come with our faith and with our doubts,
we come with our hopes and with our fears.
We come as we are because it is God who invites us to come,
and God has promised never to turn us away.

> Excerpt by Ruth Burgess from *The Pattern of Our Days: Worship in the Celtic Tradition from the Iona Community,* edited by Kathy Galloway, 33, alt. Copyright © 1996 by the authors, Paulist Press, Inc., New York/Mahwah, N.J. Used with permission of Paulist Press. www.paulistpress.com

In traditions that begin worship with a Prayer of the Day that captures the themes of the appointed lessons, leaders will want to determine whether that prayer is most fitting, especially on the first Sunday after the crisis. If the prayer of the day doesn't introduce a theme that would be awkward or unhelpful, it could be used as is. If the appointed prayer leads in a direction the worship leader does not plan to go, he or she could modify the prayer or write a new one, following the pattern typical of these prayers. Or the worship leader might choose lessons and prayers appointed for another Sunday or special rite, such as that used for the burial of the dead or for healing or confession.

Confession and Assurance

Most Christian traditions include an element of confession in worship, but it can come at various points—from the very beginning as preparation for worship to just before the Eucharist as preparation for receiving the sacrament. In a time of crisis, the confession and assurance section of the liturgy will take on a different tone no matter where it is placed in the liturgy. Some congregations may not be accustomed to including it at all, but may discover its appropriateness in a time of crisis and continue to practice it in the weeks and even years following the difficult time.

If the crisis is due to intentional evil such as war or rioting or a terrorist attack, a corporate confession that appeals to the Prince of Peace may be appropriate. An example from *The Worship Sourcebook:*

O Prince of peace,
from peace that is no peace,
from the grip of all that is evil,
from a violent righteousness,
deliver us.
From paralysis of will,
from lies and misnaming,
from terror of truth,
deliver us.
From hardness of heart,
from trading in slaughter,
from the worship of death,
deliver us.
By the folly of your gospel,
by your choosing our flesh,
by your nakedness and pain,
heal us.
By your weeping over the city,
by your refusal of the sword,
by your facing of horror,
heal us.
By your bursting from the tomb,
by your coming in judgment,
by your longing for peace,
heal us.
Grant us peace. Amen.

Peace litany (20th c.), source unknown, in *The Worship Sourcebook,* 101.

But if the crisis is caused by a failure of leadership or a public sin in which the congregation is wronged, then congregants may need to confess their frustration and betrayal, and their difficulty in forgiving even as they need to be forgiven. A confessional prayer follows, naming many of the inadequate reactions people have to crisis:

Merciful God,
for the things we have done that we regret,
forgive us;
for the things we have failed to do that we regret,
forgive us;
for all the times we have acted without love,
forgive us;
for all the times we have reacted without thought,
forgive us;
for all the times we have withdrawn care,
forgive us;
for all the times we have failed to forgive,
forgive us.
For hurtful words said and helpful words unsaid,
for unfinished tasks
and unfulfilled hopes,
God of all time,
forgive us and help us
to lay down our burden of regret. Amen.

Likewise, the assurance of pardon will become very important in such a difficult time. If disaster or accident strikes—unpredictable evil—then assurance that God is in control is needed. The words of the psalms may offer exactly that assurance:

> The LORD is faithful in all his words,
> and gracious in all his deeds.
> The LORD upholds all who are falling,
> and raises up all who are bowed down.
>
> —Psalm 145:13b–14

> The LORD builds up Jerusalem;
> he gathers the outcasts of Israel.
> He heals the brokenhearted,
> and binds up their wounds.
> Great is our Lord, and abundant in power;
> his understanding is beyond measure.
>
> —Psalm 147:2–3, 5

Or other passages may serve as fitting for the assurance of pardon, such as this one from Romans 8:

> Who will separate us from the love of Christ?
> Will hardship, or distress, or persecution, or famine,
> or nakedness, or peril, or sword?
> No, in all these things we are more than conquerors
> through him who loved us.
> For I am convinced that neither death, nor life,
> nor angels, nor rulers,
> nor things present, nor things to come,
> nor powers, nor height, nor depth,
> nor anything else in all creation,
> will be able to separate us
> from the love of God in Christ Jesus our Lord.
>
> —Romans 8:35, 37–39

Proclamation

Because people dealing with difficult situations need a word from the Lord, the preaching of the Word in the worship service takes on great significance. The preacher offers a message from God in the midst of the crisis—a message that brings stability in chaos and comfort in loss. The fact that God is always with us and will continue to rule the world in spite of this dire situation is the underlying message of all preaching in times of crisis.

Preaching professor and pastor Craig Satterlee suggests a possible structure for preaching through congregational transitions that is also appropriate for the suddenness of a crisis. Following Walter Brueggeman's lead, he proposes four movements with the following four verbs: *lament, assure, promise,* and *invite:*

> *Lament*—Name the loss in vivid images and address the loss to God, who is implicated in it. Dare to give voice to the pain, loss, grief, shame, indignation, bewilderment, and rage that the community is feeling.

> *Assure*—Assert that God is present in our circumstances, bringing newness out of seeming defeat. Anticipate what God is about to do.

> *Promise*—Paint a picture of God's promised future that will more fully embody God's intent for the whole world. Be concrete and specific. Ground the promise in God, not in circumstance or in human efforts.

> *Invite*—Invite the hearers to abandon their despair and live the promise. Give examples rather than absolutes, possibilities rather than certitudes.[28]

These four elements do not need to be present in every sermon but can provide a pattern for preaching over time.

In addition to these themes and the themes listed earlier in this chapter, consider the following texts for preaching:

- Psalm 25, a prayer for guidance and deliverance that acknowledges the need for confession and assurance.
- Psalm 46, a psalm that recognizes God as the people's defender.
- Psalm 90, a text that acknowledges God's eternity and human frailty.

- Psalm 102, a prayer for help from the eternal King.
- Psalm 130, a cry to the Lord from one waiting for redemption.
- Jeremiah 31:31–34, an assurance of God's covenant promises.
- Ezekiel 11:19–20, a promise that God will restore his people.
- Matthew 6:9–15, an account of the Lord's Prayer.
- Matthew 11:28–30, a call to bring burdens to the Lord, whose yoke is easy.
- Matthew 22:34–40, the summary of the law and call to love neighbors.
- John 15:12–17, Christ's command to love one another.
- Romans 6:1–14, Paul's instruction to die to sin and rise with Christ.
- Colossians 3:1–17, the call to break with the past and press on toward the goal of life in Christ.
- Peter 5:6–11, the call to endure suffering and enjoy Christ's restoration.
- 1 John 1:1–2:2, the promise of forgiveness through the atoning work of Christ.

Many more texts can be found that will be appropriate in times of crisis, and some may fit a particular situation better than those listed here. Preachers will find that they also hear the text in new ways in the context of a crisis. Passages may come to mind as the preacher reflects on the crisis, or he or she may consult a minister's manual such as Norén's or a book like Satterlee's. Another helpful approach would be to ask others close to the situation, "What words from the Bible are you clinging to as you come to grips with this traumatic event?"

Prayers

Prayers are very important in times of crisis because they put words to people's feelings and struggles, and give them an avenue for expressing those emotions to God. Those who lead prayer in worship have the challenge of speaking to God on behalf of people who are feeling many different things. Listening to the people as much as possible will help leaders to speak for them, as well as imagining the various reactions that could be provoked by the crisis. Furthermore, as Professor Ron Byars of Union Theological Seminary puts it, worship leaders are called to pray for those who *can't* pray, those who *don't* pray, and those who *won't* pray.[29] Leaders need to put themselves in others' "shoes"—and hearts and minds—as they think through and plan their prayers for worship. Byars writes in *A More Profound Alleluia: Theology and Worship in Harmony:*

> Karl Barth's well-known suggestion that one should preach with the Bible in one hand and the newspaper in the other applies with at least equal force to the church's prayers. The sermon may or may not address some pressing issue in society, but the Prayers of the People will always hold up before God whatever brokenness in the world has come to our attention.[30]

In *Worship as Pastoral Care,* William Willimon addresses the need for humility in prayer, even in critical times, and asks:

> [Do] our prayers show a sense of trust, a basic belief in a larger, benevolent source of help; or do they smack of bargaining, pleading, and cajoling a despotic and capricious God into acts of goodness toward us? Do our petitions in prayer convey a sense that God owes us specific benefits, prompt solutions to problems, and magical aid; or do they refer and defer to a transcendent power that has its own unfathomable purpose that although at times may be inscrutable to us, is a good purpose toward which all creation moves?[31]

In prayer the eschatological hope of the church triumphs over the crisis. As Byars writes, "When the church prays, it not only lifts up the immediate needs of the world but does so in anticipation of God's new creation, the reign of God (the kingdom of God)."[32]

Using the prayers of Scripture, especially prayers of lament, is especially appropriate during a difficult time when words are hard to find. This practice will also help to connect the people with the biblical narrative in new ways and will bring balance to worship that so often tilts more toward praise. Kathleen Billman and Daniel Migliore argue for creating such balance by increasing the use of lament. They ask, "How can praise be free and joyful if the realities of broken human life are not named and lamented?" and "How can intercession be strong if our language does not reflect knowledge of the real sufferings of those for whom we pray?"[33]

Those who lead in prayer need to acknowledge the anguish without losing confidence in God's providence. And they should be sure to pray for the whole church, including those who may have been hurt by the crisis, those who must lead the church through the difficult time, and those who are absent and unable to deal with the situation. They should look for or write prayers that are both honest and caring. Two examples follow from *Celebrate God's Presence: A Book of Services for The United Church of Canada.*

God of compassion,
you watch the ways of all of us,
and weave out of terrible happenings
wonders of goodness and grace.
Surround those who have been shaken by tragedy
with a sense of your presence and love;
hold them in faith and strength.
Though they are lost in grief and shock,
may they find you and be comforted;
through Jesus Christ, who died but lives again with you. Amen.

> *Book of Common Worship,* 836, as found in *Celebrate God's Presence: A Book of Services for The United Church of Canada,* 564. Used by permission.

Caring God,
we acknowledge before you our fears;
we acknowledge before you our anxieties;
we acknowledge before you our doubts.
Help us to recognize in the depths of our being
that we are not alone,
but that you are truly present in this painful hour.
We pray that you might ease our burdens
by the assurance of your companionship,

by the knowledge of your abiding love,
and by the hope we share in Jesus Christ,
in whose name we pray. Amen.

The following prayer was printed in the bulletins that were never used at Rayne Memorial United Methodist Church in New Orleans on the fateful Sunday of evacuation as Hurricane Katrina approached in August 2005. It became the starting place for pastors who gathered for mutual support in the months following the devastating loss of their homes and churches.[34]

O God, most loving Comforter,
I pray that you will always turn what is evil into good,
and what is good into what is better.
Turn my mourning into joy,
my wandering feet into the right path,
my ignorance into knowledge of your truth,
my lukewarmness into zeal,
my fear into love,
all my material goods into a spiritual gift,
all my earthly desires,
all that is transient into what lasts forever,
everything human into what is divine,
everything created and finite into that sovereign and immeasurable good
which you yourself are,
O my God and Savior. Amen.

      —Thomas à Kempis, 15th century

Silence

Henderson notes that "communal silence is an important yet often overlooked part of liturgy. It is not the unavoidable 'dead time' that occurs in the theatre between scene changes. Nor is it even the hushed anticipation of a concert audience awaiting the next movement. Instead, it is deliberate quiet, held in common, so that the assembly can ponder together what it has just proclaimed and heard."[35] Times of silence can be especially meaningful in pondering a crisis, when led with sensitivity and in a way that allows people to be comfortable rather than confused. "The presider must resist the temptation to fill the silence with his or her own speech. If no one chooses to offer prayers, reflections or responses aloud, after a respectable period of silence the liturgy continues."[36]

Sometimes it is most helpful to offer times of silence with no expectation that anyone speak aloud. The purpose of such silence is to be open to whatever God might "say" in directing the thoughts of the worshipers, or to contemplate the crisis situation without anyone's attempting to put words to worshipers' thoughts and feelings. Or, it could simply be a time to rest in the presence and the love of God.

Songs

Liturgical choices of readings and songs can do much to acknowledge and heal a difficult situation. At the very least, worship planners need to be aware of the power of music in an emotional time. Whether familiar or new, a hymn chosen for such a service may become forever associated with the crisis in some people's minds. And that association can be part of the healing process. For instance, when "Come, You Disconsolate" was chosen as the opening hymn of the service held the morning after the tragic death of the pastor's daughter, the final line of the first verse became an oft-repeated phrase in the congregation: "Earth has no sorrows that heaven cannot heal."[37]

Reactions to music used in funeral services are similar; the songs sung are linked to the event, and even to the person's passing, in the minds of many attending. For this reason, certain familiar hymns may open the floodgates of emotion; but worship leaders who expect this reaction and are prepared for it can help people understand that tears are all right, because they express the grief and pain that all share in this time of sorrow. In fact, familiar hymns may bring comfort in an uncertain time. Although this may not be the time to learn a lot of new songs, a particularly

well-worded song of healing may be appropriate and helpful, such
as "We Cannot Measure How You Heal" by John Bell of the Iona
Community in Scotland.

> We cannot measure how you heal
> or answer every sufferer's prayer,
> yet we believe your grace responds
> where faith and doubt unite to care.
> Your hands, though bloodied on the cross,
> survive to hold and heal and warn,
> to carry all through death to life
> and cradle children yet unborn.
>
> The pain that will not go away,
> the guilt that clings from things long past,
> the fear of what the future holds,
> are present as if meant to last.
> But present too is love which tends
> the hurt we never hoped to find,
> the private agonies inside,
> the memories that haunt the mind.
>
> So some have come who need your help
> and some have come to make amends,
> as hands which shaped and saved the world
> are present in the touch of friends.
> Lord, let your Spirit meet us here
> to mend the body, mind and soul,
> to disentangle peace from pain
> and make your broken people whole.

Another resource from the Iona Community is the volume
When Grief Is Raw: Songs for Times of Sorrow and Bereavement,

which employs the full emotional range present in the Psalms. As John Bell and Graham Maule note in the introduction, the songs in it were written to "enable God's people to speak honestly to their Maker when grief is raw, just as other songs enable their praise to be represented when joy is deep."[38] Other songs appropriate in times of crisis can be found in the following hymnals:

Sing! A New Creation[39]
62	Psalm 130: In Deep Despair I Cry to You
69	We Cannot Measure How You Heal
130	I Want Jesus to Walk with Me
180	You Are My Hiding Place
183	Psalm 46: God, Our Help and Constant Refuge
185	On Eagle's Wings
188	Don'na Tokidemo/Anytime and Anywhere
189	Through It All
200	When the Storms of Life Are Raging
205	Healer of Our Every Ill

Psalter Hymnal[40]
446	If You But Trust in God to Guide You
500	How Firm a Foundation
538	Come, You Disconsolate
556	Great Is Thy Faithfulness

With One Voice[41]
735	God! When Human Bonds Are Broken
739	In All Our Grief

Sing the Faith[42]
2177	Wounded World that Cries for Healing
2180	Why Stand So Far Away, My God?

Gather Comprehensive[43]
381	Dust and Ashes
586	O Lord, Hear My Prayer
592	Mayenziwe/Your Will Be Done
603	How Can I Keep from Singing

614   O God, Our Help in Ages Past
644   Within Our Darkest Night

Glory & Praise[44]
342   Turn to Me
473   Show Us Your Mercy
474   Remember Your Love
478   Precious Lord, Take My Hand
597   Do Not Fear to Hope
605   Though the Mountains May Fall

Hymnal: A Worship Book[45]
343   My Hope Is Built on Nothing Less
355   Savior, Like a Shepherd Lead Us
589   My Shepherd Will Supply My Need
637   When Grief Is Raw

The United Methodist Hymnal[46]
130   God Will Take Care of You
517   By Gracious Powers

The African American Heritage Hymnal[47]
141   Cast Your Cares
160   The Lord Is My Light
395   I Love the Lord, He Heard My Cry

Sacraments

In most congregations, the administration of the sacraments will proceed with the usual frequency regardless of a crisis, but in some traditions there is more flexibility about when sacraments are offered. In such churches, a time of crisis might cause leaders to question whether it is appropriate to celebrate the sacraments. But in actuality, the sacraments bring assurance to people, especially in difficult times. When the sacrament of baptism is administered after a crisis, the congregation will be comforted and encouraged by this community-affirming event. When a new member of the church family is baptized, the congregation reaffirms both God's ongoing care for all the members and the continuing mission and growth of the church, in spite of crises.

Furthermore, as Columbia College religion professor Roman Crews writes, baptism signifies that we are "free from sin and death and opens the way to eternal life. Baptism is nothing less than God's triumph over evil."[48] In times of crisis that result from evil in the world, baptism is a testament to God's faithfulness in the face of evil. Baptism redeems us from the chaotic waters in which we die to sin and rise in Christ. The baptismal liturgy renounces the evil that often feels very near in times of crisis.

Likewise, the practice of celebrating the Lord's Supper can bring healing to the gathered congregation as the people focus on their union with Christ. Professor Crews asserts that

> communion is a crisis—a turning point—for the entire creation. The sacrament intends nothing short of God's complete transformation of life: 'Christ has died; Christ is risen; Christ will come again.' The communion liturgy is strange, shocking speech. With these words the congregation proclaims a world-changing prophecy: God's new creation is coming. In communion, as in baptism, we see it beginning to appear.[49]

When the sacraments are administered in times of crisis, it is wise to use prayers and readings that note the circumstance and the importance of the sacraments as signs and seals of God's promises to the church, despite the troubles it faces. Or perhaps a few simple words of introduction would suffice, such as, "Today we celebrate the baptism of another child of God, even as we are acutely aware of the fragility of our earthly lives"; or "This sacrament reminds us of God's faithful promises to us, no matter what circumstances we face"; or, "Throughout history the church has faithfully celebrated the sacraments instituted by Christ, and we do also today, in spite of the dire circumstances we face."

Closing of Worship

The closing of worship during a time of crisis is just as important as the opening of worship. Leaders should be conscious that the tone they set will last throughout the week among the people, so their parting words should be chosen with care. This tone is reflected in the sending portion of the service through words of dedication or exhortation and challenges to the people to be faithful, together with an assurance that God's strength will support them in this endeavor. Texts that both challenge and comfort are appropriate here, such as Micah 6:8, Matthew 22:36–40, Matthew 28:19–20, and Colossians 3:17.

Closing Prayer

In this time of prayer, worship leaders will want to express gratitude for the gathering and ask God's blessing on those who have attended. Some models for the closing prayer follow:

> O Creator and Mighty God,
> you have promised strength for the weak,
> rest for the laborers, light for the way,
> grace for the trials, help from above,
> unfailing sympathy, undying love.
> O Creator and Mighty God,
> help us to continue in your promise. Amen.

> Pakistan, source unknown, based on a poem by Annie Johnson Flint, in *The Worship Sourcebook*, 358.

> Tender and compassionate God,
> you long to gather us in your arms as a hen gathers her chicks.
> Draw us to yourself in love,
> surround us with your grace,
> and keep us in the shelter of your wings
> so that in our time of testing we may not fall away. Amen.

> *Hymnal: A Worship Book*, 746. Copyright © Brethren Press, Faith and Life Press, Mennonite Publishing House, 1992. Used by permission.

Blessing

Receiving the blessing of God is especially important in a crisis for the reassurance that God has not abandoned his people but continues to bless them as they face tragedy. The Aaronic blessing can be powerful here because of its conclusion in the granting of peace:

> The LORD bless you and keep you;
> the LORD make his face to shine upon you,
> and be gracious to you;
> the LORD lift up his countenance upon you,
> and give you peace.
>
> —Numbers 6:24–26

Another blessing based on Philippians 4:7 also calls attention to the peace of God:

> The peace of God,
> which passes all understanding,
> keep your hearts and minds
> in the knowledge and love of God,
> and of God's Son, Jesus Christ, our Lord;
> and the blessing of God Almighty,
> the Father, the Son, and the Holy Spirit,
> remain with you always.[50]

Other appropriate parting blessings include:

> In your journeys to and fro
> God direct you;
> in your happiness and pleasure
> God bless you;
> in care, anxiety, or trouble
> God sustain you;
> in peril and in danger
> God protect you.
> The grace of God be with you all, now and always.

Timothy Olufosoye, Nigeria, in *Partners in Prayer,* Forward
Movement Publications, as found in *The Worship Sourcebook,*
364.

May the grace of God,
deeper than our imagination;
the strength of Christ,
stronger than our need;
and the communion of the Holy Spirit,
richer than our togetherness,
guide and sustain us today
and in all our tomorrows.

Roger D. Knight, in *Book of Worship, United Church of Christ,*
552, alt. Copyright © Roger D. Knight. Used by permission.

Planning Worship
Practices for the Rest of the Week

Worship planners may want to think beyond the Sunday services
as they provide opportunities for people to deal with the crisis in
other areas of congregational life that flow naturally out of worship. Planners could provide resources for personal devotions, or
for devotions in all groups and committees, that provide consistency with the worship liturgies and comfort for those who struggle
with the crisis. These resources may also help members move into
a deeper understanding of the issue the congregation faces. The
same passage of Scripture could be read in worship and also before
prayer at all church meetings, giving a sense of unity through the
time of crisis.

Other activities could be planned that would supplement worship in the process of healing—discussions and meals, and opportunities to be together to talk about "the issue," as well as times
for fellowship specifically planned not to deal with the main crisis.
Like the worship services, these activities should be planned with
sensitivity to the people's response to the crisis. Discerning leaders
take the congregation's temperature often and note symptoms of

discomfort, so that they can administer appropriate remedies for healing at the right dosage.

The children and young people of the congregation may need special consideration in a time of crisis. If special services are planned—for lament, or confession, or healing—leaders should make sure the young people understand what is happening and why. Explaining these things to children often gives clarity to the adults who overhear as well. Thinking of the children may help leaders decide how much information is appropriate in public worship. It will also encourage them to be pastoral and caring. If the congregation is not accustomed to a children's time or children's message in the service, this explanation and preparation can happen in another setting, such as Sunday school or children's worship.

Hudson gives suggestions for helping young people in time of crisis.

- Tell them what happened in words they can understand. Give correct information, but not necessarily all the details. If you don't know, say so, say you'll find out, and then do it.
- Listen carefully to what they say—encourage them to talk about their thoughts and feelings about what happened. Don't put down their responses.
- Make allowances for grumpiness, unusual eating, or difficult sleep.
- Accept the fact that children will want to play about the event—how they accept emotionally difficult information...they may pretend to be dead or act violently.
- Never say "Everything will be OK." Everything isn't OK for them right now. Be honest about safety, take action if necessary.[51]

While this advice applies generally to dealing with children facing a crisis, it will guide worship planners as well as they go about their work, attempting to keep all ages in mind as they plan worship services. These reminders are also applicable for most congregational transitions, the topic of the next chapter.

Chapter Five

Worship in Times of Transition

The practice of worship does not cease, even when crisis hits, as observed in chapter 4. That is also true during congregational transitions. Worship goes on but is always affected by such transitions, whether the congregation is adjusting to a new pastor, a new building, or a new vision for ministry. Congregational worship is also affected by transitions that involve losses—of leaders, facilities, key members, groups of members, or longstanding patterns of ministry. In a sense, congregations are always in transition, because things never stay exactly the same. Even when it seems as though nothing is changing or that nothing has changed in a very long time, the congregation itself is in transition, perhaps decline. If a congregation is a living organism, as explained in chapter 2, it follows that change is necessary. Organisms that do not change and grow are not living organisms—they're dead!

Types of Transitions

In this chapter we will explore some typical transitions that congregations undergo, as well as ways that worship planners and worship leaders can best perform their roles during these transitional times. We will also consider suggestions for the liturgy during various transitional times.

Certainly each transition requires different responses—different modes of planning as well as different emphases in the elements of worship. However, these varied situations all bring stress to the congregation and therefore require thoughtful responses from leaders. These unique circumstances bring opportunities for creativity, but also call for calm and sure leadership, since transitions can be anxious times for many.

Transition, as defined in chapter 2, is a changing situation that can be noticed and named—and of which most people in the congregation are aware. When asked how their church is doing, they will say something like, "We are going through _____," and will fill in the blank with their situation. They may even be able to articulate the progress of the congregation through the transition—"we are just starting to let go of the old ways," or "we are trying to figure out what to do next," or, "we are finally getting our act together again after a long stretch of uncertainty."

Worship will be affected in various ways, depending on the congregation's progress through the transition. If it is just beginning the "ending" phase, the parishioners may need to lament and grieve the losses involved. If they are in the middle of the transition, a steady look at God's promises in Scripture may be required. Or if they are just coming out of the transition and beginning something new, it may be time to celebrate.

Worship during a transitional time should offer both stability and flexibility. When the pace of change is intense, worship that is constant, and for the most part stable and predictable, will comfort some who find change difficult. The familiarity of the worship service, no matter what form or style a congregation typically observes, will give a sense of stability and connection to the past that grounds the congregation in changing times. At the same time, worship needs to flex with those changing times, to establish forward momentum that will avoid stagnation. Creativity in worship can encourage and sustain that momentum. The transition may produce new ideas for worship and even involve new people in worship because of their roles in the transition.

Because transitional times produce anxiety, a congregation needs a deep reservoir of congregational maturity to manage the transition well. Congregations that have strong roots and understand who they are and what they stand for will be able to bend more easily in the transition and perhaps even sprout a few new branches despite the winds of change. So especially in the midst of transition, careful attention should be paid to building up the congregation into a growing, maturing body of Christ. One good way to build up the body is through education that adds to or deepens the reservoir. Congregations that learn how transitions affect the body will be more stable as they move through the transition.

The variety of transitional winds that blow around and through congregations will result in a variety of effects on worship. Such transitions fall into four general categories—transitions in leadership, space, membership, and vision. We will look closely at these four categories, and at the worship changes that have become common in North American congregations in the 21st century—changes that may not result from any of the categories named above, but from cultural and societal pressures to change worship itself.

Leadership Transitions

Leadership transitions include such changes as the arrival of a new pastor or another staff member, as well as the departure of a leader for a new call, for retirement, or because of suspension or even removal from the ministry. It is quite possible for an anxious or difficult time to result from a positive transition or for people to have positive feelings about a troublesome transition. The presence of new leaders, no matter how well received, will create stress in the congregational system. Likewise, when leaders depart, the congregation may respond with regret or relief, but either way, the turbulence of a transition is bound to follow. Sometimes vacancies are quickly filled by a new person assigned by a denominational office; in other cases transitions involve a lengthy process of strategic planning and searching for and calling a new leader. Church consultants Carolyn Weese and J. Russell Crabtree note that during leadership transitions, congregations with a more fixed liturgical tradition, such as those of the Roman Catholic Church, have some advantages. In such congregations, the liturgy "is shaped by history, not by the innovation of the pastor," and "the worship experience at Parish A is nearly identical to that at Parish B regardless of the pastoral leadership" so that the transition in leadership has less impact on the worship of the congregation.[1] Although these congregations are not free to choose their new leader, they know that in most cases the liturgy will not change with the leader's arrival.

However, since the publication of the *Constitution on the Sacred Liturgy* of the Second Vatican Council (1962 to 1965), the Roman Catholic Church has made enormous changes in its liturgy, and Catholic congregations can be found to vary greatly in the practice of worship. Therefore, the similarity from parish to parish and its advantages can no longer be assumed. Joyce Zimmerman, director of the Institute for Liturgical Ministry in Dayton, Ohio, and founding editor of *Liturgical Ministry* magazine, notes that while Catholics have done the work of adapting the liturgy, they are just beginning the real work of liturgical renewal. Some congregations are just beginning to implement the changes of the Vatican Council, while others are still hoping to return to a pre-Vatican II liturgy.[2] So even in the so-called fixed-liturgy traditions, we live in a period of significant change.

In other church traditions, the liturgy is very much shaped by the pastor or worship leaders, so leadership changes and the inherent preferences and style of the leader will have a distinct impact on the worship of the congregation. But no matter what the liturgical tradition of a congregation, a change of pastors will have some impact because each person leads in a particular way. Congregants can become so accustomed to their pastor's voice and style of leading that any other leader will take some getting used to. In congregations where a pastoral vacancy usually results in a string of guest preachers, worship planners would be wise to select and train liturgists from within the congregation to provide some consistency of tone and voice in worship. This practice will also help prevent the congregation from becoming fatigued by a parade of preachers and styles.

Congregations going through leadership transitions should ask the following questions:

- Are we likely to be without a regular worship leader for a long time? If so, how will we adjust in the interim?
- Would it be wise for us to retain an interim pastor for a time?
- How should we select and train lay leaders to take on new roles in the liturgy during the transition?

- Should we take some time to evaluate our ministries and our values before we take steps to replace our leader?
- How can we prepare for a new leader?
- What can we do to help a new leader understand us and be able to figure out what is or isn't fitting for us, given our congregational history?

Whether the leadership transition is planned or unexpected, the congregation needs time to adjust to the change. Prevailing wisdom argues for the use of a supply pastor—someone who can continue the basic pastoral tasks, such as preaching, teaching, and pastoral care. Better yet, an "intentional interim pastor" can also use the opportunity to help the congregation reflect on its ministry and plan next steps for the future.

Alban Institute founder Loren Mead recommends that churches call a full- or part-time interim pastor:

> The leadership of a congregation often finds itself overloaded with responsibility during the period between installed pastors. The management of the search process is a significant call for leadership energy, and the board can find itself overwhelmed by trying also to locate regular preaching and worship leadership, handle the regular and crisis pastoral care, and continue all the community building pastors provide in congregations. Having a professional on call to cover those bases can relieve leadership for the tasks of the transition.[3]

Mead points to three situations in which a trained interim pastor can be valuable. The first is following a long pastorate, about 12 years or more. An interim pastor allows the congregation to get used to new leadership—even the different pace at which another pastor leads the liturgy—so that the adjustment to the next pastor will be easier. The second is the situation after "the previous pastorate ended in unhappy conflict and polarization."[4] If events related to the pastor's departure left the congregation in factions, an interim pastor can help parishioners work through the conflict and clean up the mess somewhat before the next pastor arrives. Otherwise the next pastor will be the victim of the inherited conflict. The third situation occurs when the congregation is large and has multiple staff members—in which case the interim pastor takes the leadership role, avoiding conflicts over who's in charge when the senior pastor leaves. While there, the interim pastor not only can lead the congregation through the transition, but he or she can also ensure that the church is running well with various people fulfilling their responsibilities. The interim can also intervene with the former pastor to ensure that boundaries are set and respected.

Lutheran pastor and preaching professor Craig Satterlee offers three biblical stories and images for preaching during pastoral leadership transitions that interim pastors will want to consider. They assure listeners of God's faithfulness through the transition they face. In Philippians 1:3–6 Paul thanks God for the readers and expresses "confidence that God will continue to do good works through them." In Joshua 24:1–27 the review of the history of the people of God and the covenant they have with him "helps the people to focus on the task at hand and the decisions they need to make." John 14:18–27 records Jesus's promise not to leave his disciples as orphans, nor let them be "overwhelmed by too much change." All three texts have the potential both to comfort and to assure the congregation of God's care in and through the transition.[5]

Good interim pastors will understand the importance of acknowledging the ending and beginning of a leadership transition. Preacher and author Anthony B. Robinson gives the following advice to congregations:

> When a pastorate ends, ritualize the ending with a liturgy that acknowledges the conclusion of the covenant between pastor and congregation. "You are no longer our pastor." "You are no longer the congregation I serve as pastor." Name it. Solemnize it. Ritualize it. Include a pastor's family members: they have been included in and affected by the ministry and relationship. And offer it all to God with prayers of gratitude and prayers for forgiveness.[6]

In *Saying Goodbye: A Time of Growth for Congregations and Pastors*, Edward A. White offers some ideas for liturgical resources and sermon texts for the time following a pastor's departure.[7] Here are his suggestions for scriptural texts:

- Genesis 31:44–46, 48–49, 50b; "the Lord watch between you and me when we are absent one from another."
- Genesis 12:1–9; Abraham's departure from Haran and God's promise to bless him.
- Deuteronomy 18:15–18; God will raise up a prophet like Moses.
- Deuteronomy 32:1–9; the farewell of Moses.
- Joshua 24:1, 14–25; Joshua's farewell to his people.
- Ecclesiastes 3:1–7, 7:8, 10, 13–14; a time for everything; better the end than the beginning.
- Matthew 9:35–38; "The harvest is plentiful, but the laborers are few."
- Luke 12:35–38; the faithful servant.
- John 10:14–18; the ministry of the good shepherd.
- John 21:15–19; "Feed my sheep."
- Acts 16:9–10; Paul's call to Macedonia.
- Acts 20:17–22, 25–28, 32, 36–38b; Paul's apologia for his ministry at Ephesus.
- 1 Corinthians 3:4–11; Paul planted, Apollos watered, God gave growth.
- Philippians 4:1–10, 23; "Rejoice in the Lord always."
- 1 Thessalonians 5:12–25; Paul encourages the ministry among the Thessalonians.
- 2 Thessalonians 2:13–3:5; Paul gives thanks for the success of the gospel.[8]

White recommends that congregations acknowledge the conclusion of the pastoral relationship in worship. He proposes the following litany:

Pastor: On the ___ day of _____, (year), I began ministry in this congregation. I have, with God's help and to the best of my abilities exercised this trust.

After prayer and careful consideration, it now seems to me that I should leave this charge, and I publicly state that my tenure as pastor of this church ends this day.

Bishop/executive/elder: Do you, the people of _____, recognize and accept the conclusion of this pastoral relationship?

People: We do.

Prayer, spoken together by the pastor and the people:

O God, you have bound us together for a time as pastor and people to work for the advancement of your kingdom in this place. We give you thanks for the ministry which we have shared in these years now past.

Silence

We thank you for your patience with us despite our blindness and slowness of heart. We thank you for your forgiveness and mercy in the face of our many failures.

Silence

Especially we thank you for your never failing presence with us through these years, and for the deeper knowledge of you and of each other which we have attained.

Silence

We thank you for those who have been joined to this part of Christ's family through baptism. We thank you for opening our hearts and minds again and again to your Word, and for feeding us abundantly with the Sacrament of the Body and Blood of your Son.

Silence

Now, we pray, be with those who leave and with us who stay; and grant that all of us, by drawing nearer to you, may always be close to each other in the communion of saints. All this we ask for the sake of Jesus Christ, your Son, our Lord. Amen.

Edward A. White, *Saying Goodbye: A Time of Growth for Congregations and Pastors,* 72. Copyright © 1990 the Alban Institute. Used by permission.

Some service books recommend that a statement of purpose be used, such as the following:

Our church, like any community, changes.
Babies are born.
Children grow up.
Loved ones and friends grow old.
People move into our community and church.
Others leave us, moving on to new places,
new experiences, and new opportunities.

Let us not forget that the ministry in this place
is Christ's ministry, entrusted to us as part of his Body.
Our ministry belongs to Jesus and is ongoing.

When a minister comes into our church,
we covenant with one another;
we promise to walk together as God's People,
deepening our commitment to Jesus Christ
and growing closer to God.
God's covenant with us never changes,
but our covenants with one another do change.
We gather now to mark the ending of the covenant between N.,
the N. United Church(es)/Pastoral Charge,
and *N. Presbytery.*

> *Book of Worship, United Church of Christ,* 696, alt. Adapted
> with permission to include work by Beverly C. S. Brazier and Bev
> Irwin. Copyright © 1986, 2002, United Church of Christ, Lo-
> cal Church Ministries, Worship and Education Ministry Team,
> Cleveland, Ohio. All rights reserved.

This liturgy points out the benefit of ritual in leadership transitions. Of course, much more can and should be said when a pastor departs from a congregation, but this liturgy offers a basic pattern and an official acknowledgement of the conclusion of the relationship. Rituals that include visual symbols may be helpful as well. One congregation commissioned a potter to create communion vessels in honor of their pastor's "first communion" in their midst as a newly ordained minister and presented that communion set to her as a parting gift when she left for another position.

Leadership transitions involving other staff members or associate pastors should also be acknowledged liturgically. Even if the person departing did not usually function as a worship leader, a public ritual to honor the transition is important, both to honor his or her past role in the congregation and to declare publicly the conclusion of that role.

Space Transitions

Transitions that involve space can have major implications for worship—especially if the congregation must worship in a temporary space for a time, or adjust to a brand-new space. Space transitions may involve renovation of an aging facility or repairs to church facilities after a fire or natural disaster, relocation to a more fitting building, or the construction of a new church building. In each of these situations, the reality of the change may make the congregation more aware of its surroundings. Some of those changes will lead to great appreciation for facilities—especially in the case of natural disaster. Others will lead to more critical evaluation as the issue of inadequate facilities is addressed. Especially when moving into a new space, some congregants may be quick to express their likes and dislikes, and compare those to "the way it used to be." Others will find freedom and refreshing flexibility in the process of renovating or moving.

In fact, these situations are wonderful times for examining space as a theological issue. Congregations should ask themselves questions like these:

- What do we believe about the church, and what does that mean for the space in which we worship?
- If we believe the church is a community, what does that mean for how we sit together in worship?
- How can we design space to make room for visual arts that will enrich our worship?

- What is the visual focal point of our worship space, and what does that communicate about what we believe? Is the pulpit central, or the table and the font?
- How can we use banners and projected images to enhance our worship?

It is possible for congregations to see worship-space transitions not simply as building programs, but as theological adventures into a fresh understanding of the congregation and its relationship to God. Chapter 3 recognized some important principles of worship—that it should be dialogic, trinitarian, covenantal, and contextual. How do these concepts influence choices in worship space and visual arts? The congregation will learn much in any transitional situation. Wouldn't it be great if the result of a space transition was not, "We learned that we don't want to deal with another bricks-and-mortar project for a long time!" but rather, "We discovered a lot about what worship means in the process of designing a space to hold and nurture it."

One seminary renovated its worship space and discovered that the process itself was formative for members of that educational community as they worked to design a space that was fitting to the values and theological traditions of the school. One administrator noted gratefully that it "improved and strengthened our community. The sustained conversation, the careful listening to one another, the commitment to embrace differences rather than reduce them to 'win-lose' decisions, and the learning that resulted—all these efforts and attitudes animated not only the chapel renovation committee but also the seminary community."[9]

In dealing with worship-space transitions, it is important to involve worship planners and leaders as well as musicians and artists in the planning. Often the planning tasks are left to the building and grounds or facilities and finance committees. But to address broader questions about worship and the impact of space, the technical and facility experts should be joined by those who can help the group reflect theologically and artistically about worship space. Educators should also be included or consulted to suggest ways to consider the needs of children, and pastoral caregivers can give good advice for making the space accessible to those with disabilities.

Even if the space transition faced by the congregation does not directly involve the worship space—for example, if an educational or administrative wing is added to the church facility, planners will want to acknowledge the change in the context of worship and to celebrate its progress and the benefits it brings to the congregation.

Chapter 3 highlighted the story of a congregation that incorporated windows from its former structure into a new church facility. Congregations may also want to preserve furniture or other items of significance, such as the font and table, the pulpit and pulpit Bible, the communion vessels and baptismal bowl, or particular visual art installations, such as banners or paraments that are identified with the congregation's history. In fact, making a procession of such items from one space to another in a mobile or progressive worship service can be a powerful symbol of the people of God moving into a new place. Because of the meaningful associations attached to visual objects, when there are items that cannot be transferred to the new space, worship services that acknowledge and remember what is being left behind are appropriate and necessary.

Membership Transitions

The third transition category, changes in the congregation's membership size, average attendance, or demographic makeup, might include an influx of young families and new babies, the aging of the congregation, sudden growth due to the construction of a nearby housing project or retirement community, the merger or consolidation of one congregation with another, or a decline caused by changing demographics in a community coupled with the inability of the congregation to adjust to the new neighbors around them. These sorts of transitions will affect more than the number of people in worship; they will also shape the variety of gifts to be found among those available to lead worship and to be involved in various roles. They may even change the content of worship, in response to the changing makeup of the congregation. Such transitions could involve a sense of loss as gifted members leave the congregation, or an excitement about fresh ideas as new people and gifts are discovered and employed in worship. Sometimes transitions in membership lead to even more momentous events such as beginning a congregation by planting a daughter church, giving new life to an older congregation in the rebirth of a church, or simply ending a congregation's active ministry. Such transitions should be celebrated or honored in worship as well.

In "Merger as a New Beginning," Alban Institute consultant and author Terry Foland writes that in a merger, different practices and traditions need to come together. No matter how much the merging congregations are alike, there will be differences—in the frequency with which they celebrate communion, perhaps, or their traditions for holiday services. Such things should not be decided on a "whose way wins" basis, but after a careful analysis of the vision of the new congregation and the practice that will be most fitting for it. "At times, congregations have to compromise or negotiate to find the appropriate wedding of the two sets of traditions and practices. At other times, they need to discontinue what each congregation has done and create something new."[10] Congregations that have merged for healthy, forward-looking, hopeful reasons should be able to blend old ways and new dreams into a new way.

When congregations merge, the location for worship is an important issue. Prevailing wisdom says that a new facility would be better than either of the congregations' previous church buildings, if they really are to make a fresh start. Former facilities have many memories attached—they may seem like sacred space to parishioners. If they must choose one space or another, finding a way to include certain meaningful artifacts in the new facility is helpful. Services of closure could be held at each location, with movement toward a joint service of celebration and dedication that establishes the new congregation.[11] As mentioned above, the procession of artifacts from the former locations to the new home can be an effective way to ritualize the move of the congregation, not unlike Old Testament processions to worship.

Other membership transitions may be less conspicuous in worship because they don't warrant entire services to acknowledge the change. But even in those situations—when a larger-than-usual number of people come or go—it would be appropriate to deal with the subject in prayer. Such prayers can celebrate growth and lament decline with a healthy and honest intercession about the losses involved in both cases, and the effects on the congregation as well.

Sometimes congregations in decline due to changing demographics know they need to refocus their efforts on the community around them. However, what they often don't realize is that this decision will require them to change. According to Missouri pastor Robert T. Roberts, congregations naively turn to their communities to find "replacements for the lost members and leaders of the past. When few 'genuine factory replacements'" are found, they try to "fashion substitute spare parts into something as near the originals as possible." Few of them comprehend "that if the future was in the neighborhood, it was the congregation that would need to change."[12] This new focus will undoubtedly lead to changes in worship as well, because as the congregation changes, what is most fitting in its worship will also change. If the median age of the congregation changes markedly over time, worship planners will want to adjust accordingly, either by including more elements that appeal to younger people, or those that are remembered fondly by older members. Changes in the ethnic diversity of a congregation may offer opportunities to praise God through songs of other cultures and languages. Changes in the theological bent of a congregation may affect a congregation's comfort level with liturgical innovations. Members who have not been accustomed to such changes in their previous congregations may struggle to adjust in their new surroundings.

Transitions in Vision

The fourth category of transition includes changes in the vision or direction of a congregation, which often will entail changes in the style or form of worship. Such transitions may occur as a result of the three types of transitions mentioned above. A change in leadership, such as the arrival or departure of a pastor or staff member, may bring a time of congregational strategic planning, or at least a time of reevaluation of the congregation's mission and ministry. A facility transition may open up new possibilities for ministry that prompt the congregation to revisit its purpose and goals for ministry in its setting and context. A major change in membership will in effect create a new congregation, and will also require an adjustment in the congregation's plan for ministry. All of these transitions may lead to a new direction in the mission or philosophy of the congregation, or a new emphasis in ministry or programming.

Even if the change isn't directly about worship, such changes do have a major impact on worship. Because worship is an expression of the community in a specific time and place, changes in that context or in the congregation's goals will influence worship as well. For instance, when a congregation decides to be more outreach-oriented or more accessible to people of cultures and ethnicities not presently found in the congregation, this move will have implications for worship. Should the congregation adapt to the preferences of the people they hope to attract (if they actually know what those preferences are and aren't simply making assumptions)? Or should they try new things until they hit on something that seems to work? Or should they try whatever worked well in some megachurch and is touted in books and conferences?

Most often transitions of this type will involve changing an inward-focused congregation to an outward-reaching one. To propose a vision to focus only on church members is simply untenable, because it's not biblical. A congregation may become more inward-focused and exclusive over time, if it is inattentive to the matter, but that is not likely to happen as a result of a "visioning process." Most congregations that have been established for any length of time struggle to stay outreach-oriented. And in a society where fewer people find church attendance to be an important aspect of life, churches have to persuade people to come. Whether the change toward more vigorously reaching out evolves from a desire to follow God's Word and commands more closely, or from a sense of panic over declining numbers, the motivation will probably determine its effectiveness.

It is conceivable that a congregation—whether a newly organized church or an established church in a rapidly changing neighborhood—could become so involved in outreach that it would neglect to care for its members and regular attenders. In that case, the vision for outreach needs to be combined with a vision for care and education of all who are connected with the church—new contacts as well as those who have been around a while. Extending hospitality to all worshipers—visitors, members, and regular attenders—is important, and being hospitable includes helpfully explaining the patterns of worship as well as providing invitations to further learning and fellowship opportunities. In fact, all changes in worship should be implemented while placing a high priority on hospitable ways of helping people understand the change and the rationale behind it.

In *Beyond the Worship Wars: Building Vital and Faithful Worship,* Thomas G. Long notes that when congregations go through worship reform or worship renewal, some congregational conflict is inevitable. Pastors and church leaders should expect some resistance to changes in worship. "Congregations know when they are being stretched and challenged to worship more effectively and when they are being bullied into submission by leaders with a chip on the shoulder. Even so, the healthiest of worship reforms encouraged by the gentlest and wisest of pastors will always be accompanied by some measure of conflict."[13] Long declares that pastoral leadership is key to worship renewal and that to change worship, significant lay involvement is necessary. So to effect worship renewal in a congregation, pastors and lay leaders should have a good understanding of the dynamics of a congregational system, as explained in chapter 2, and an understanding of conflict and its effects, which will be explored further in the next chapter.

Recent Worship Transitions in North America and Beyond

The four types of transitions described in this chapter do not account for all the changes that congregations face today. Recent worship changes in North America are more generally following the trend toward the use of praise bands and presentational technology—what some people call "contemporary" worship. That description is a misnomer, however, since what was considered contemporary a decade ago and is still practiced in many churches is now regarded as out of date by today's young people. Nancy

Beach, programming director at Willow Creek Community Church in South Barrington, Illinois, notes that at age 30, the congregation is adjusting to this reality. "I see God laughing at those of us who started Willow because we were a reaction, and now in the age I am now, I am in meetings with young 20-somethings telling us that they don't like our music and our communication is irrelevant to them. I sit there and I try to be open and everything about the emerging culture and the postmodern influence. I've read a lot and I'm in dialogue with them, and a lot of them are my friends, but the joke's on us. It's a cycle." She says that congregations need to "find that blend of the rich heritage of our past, whether it's our recent past or hundreds of years ago, with what is new and what is fresh and what will communicate most effectively to the next generation."[14]

In some congregations, the young people are connecting with very old things—the historic liturgies and worship practices of the early church. Congregations adopting so-called contemporary worship practices to retrieve the young people who are leaving established churches en masse should investigate the new trends among the young. What they will quickly discover is that worship trends are not necessarily age-specific. In fact, it could be that since middle-aged baby boomers who grew up listening to rock-and-roll bands are the most likely to enjoy the contemporary praise-and-worship style, that mode of worship may not last beyond their generation. But for much of North America, "praise and worship" is still the primary model being adopted by many congregations, and too often transition in worship is equated with installing a screen and using projected lyrics and music for singing. These are technical matters that should not substitute for thoughtful theological reflection on the purpose of the church and the expression of worship in a specific congregation.

United Church of Christ pastor and workshop leader Michael Bausch notes that these transitions may not be as simple as some worship committees and pastors assume.

While new technologies may make it more convenient to use electronic media in worship, congregational practice or tradition may not welcome them into the sanctuary. A pastor or worship committee in touch with a congregation and knowledgeable about the realities of parish ministry knows that bringing such technology into the worship setting is a change that will concern some people.

As long as this change fits the core values of a congregation and flows out of a congregation's historical sense of purpose and mission, the change will be less jarring. The changes that people perceive to be peripheral to the mission and purpose of their church are the changes they will most resist. Technology that is seen as just another expensive furnishing in a church, or as a source of theological friction, is technology that is disconnected from the heart and soul of a church. Unless multimedia technologies are linked to the core values of a congregation and church's sense of mission and purpose, they will be seen as an undesired change.[15]

Congregational leaders would be wise to heed Bausch's caution and to be sure that they are implementing changes for thoughtful, fitting reasons rather than because of popular trends, or change for change's sake. Change does not need to be a negative experience, though most churches experience the fallout from change negatively because they have not learned to anticipate the anxiety that will arise in the congregational system. United Methodist Bishop William Willimon takes a different approach, noting that "one of the positive pastoral effects of change and innovation in worship is that it may invite or promote a greater sense of openness among the congregation. They may discover new and helpful ways of expressing and experiencing their faith. Persons' reactions to liturgical innovation can give a discerning pastor clues to their particular stance of faith."[16] Worship renewal, then, does not need to be contentious, but it can be an opportunity for growth and learning for both the worship leaders and the people in the chairs and pews.

Fittingness and Discernment

Quentin Schultze, professor of communication arts and sciences at Calvin College, offers good advice for dealing with a transition in worship style, especially when it involves introducing new technology—the change many congregations are currently facing, and a change that can be related to or result from any of the four transition categories described above. In his book *High-Tech Worship? Using Presentational Technologies Wisely,* Schultze argues for avoiding a one-size-fits-all approach, or a "that church does it this way and is growing like crazy" approach. Rather, he argues for "fittingness"—choosing technology that is fitting for good worship, and fitting for a particular congregational context. Furthermore, according to Schultze, "we ought to be creative and flexible in our worship planning but without discarding the valuable practices instituted by earlier generations of worshipers. Fittingness has theological and historical as well as contemporary and practical components."[17] He proposes the following six ways to move forward when a congregation considers adding technology to its worship:

1. Learn about liturgy so that technological skill is adapted to liturgical wisdom.
2. Borrow from low-tech as well as high-tech worship.
3. Progress slowly with new technologies to allow for more reflection and adjustment in this learning process.
4. Consider the quality of fellowship that technology should support, not divert.
5. Adapt the old to the new and the new to the old.
6. Seek sincere and beautiful worship that is a sweet fragrance to God.[18]

In making changes that will require contemplating the meaning and purpose of worship, we need to remember that worship is not meant to be entertainment for us or for those whom we invite to church. Worship is first of all for God. As Presbyterian pastor and author Tod Bolsinger puts it:

Our worship practices must always be judged by how well they reflect God's direction and example. The primary questions are not about relevance to the world, or inspiration for people, *but faithfulness and submission to God.* This begins in the necessary and honest affirmation that we *gather to worship God at God's gracious invitation and that the gathering merits us nothing.*

Even in our gathering we are responding to the "command performance" of a sovereign Lord who honors us by inviting us into
his presence.[19]

Bolsinger urges remembering that "our 'performance' is not an
improvisational soliloquy, but submission to a divine scriptwriter,
director, and leader. If nothing else, this approach should cause
us to reflect carefully on our attempts at creativity in worship,
lest we invent new forms of worship that God does not inspire or
inhabit."[20]

Likewise, in the move toward cultural adaptation in North
American worship, worship planners and leaders ought to be discerning of the spirits of the age, and especially of the Spirit of
Christ. Calvin Theological Seminary President Cornelius Plantinga, Jr., and Notre Dame doctoral student Sue Rozeboom make this
point in *Discerning the Spirits: A Guide to Thinking about Christian Worship Today*. Noting that cultural adaptation of worship is
not only inevitable and even desirable, but also risky and messy,
they encourage their readers to seek the wisdom of the Word of
God and especially the Word made flesh, whose life on earth was
characterized constantly by cultural adaptation. These authors encourage "the fitting adaptation of worship to culture. What we
want is to make worship the object of adaptation, with culture
as its context, rather than making culture the object of adaptation, with worship as its context. Worship should be culturally
connected not for the sake of culture but for the sake of worship.
First things first." Such discernment ought to be done communally,
since "discernment is a gift of the Spirit given not to individuals
but to a community," one that extends around the globe and back
2,000 years into history.[21] Discernment, then, is the key for worship planners and leaders whose task is to making fitting choices
for their congregations.

Appreciative Inquiry

To help with this discernment process, a new approach called
"appreciative inquiry" can be very useful. Developed in the early

1980s by David Cooperrider of Case Western Reserve University, it has been applied to congregational process by others, such as Fuller Theological Seminary's Mark Lau Branson. Branson's thesis in *Memories, Hopes, and Conversations: Appreciative Inquiry and Congregational Change* "is that an organization, such as a church, can be recreated by its conversation. And if that new creation is to feature the most life-giving forces and forms possible, then the conversations must be shaped by appreciative questions."[22] Both the analysis of the congregation and the positive reinforcement— appreciation—for what the members have done well and what they are particularly gifted in will provide motivation for positive change. It is a process based on hope for the future in God's plan, rather than on desperate attempts at survival, which lack confidence in God's power and promises.

Appreciative inquiry (AI) avoids the problem-solving approach that fools congregations into thinking that the problem has been "fixed"; it promotes a process of reflection that leads to the learning needed when a congregation is faced with an adaptive challenge. Most transitions that congregations face are not simply problems to be solved with what Harvard's leadership specialist Ronald Heifetz calls "technical solutions."[23] Rather, congregational transitions usually present challenges to churches and their members that require reflection and learning on the part of the congregation. This is called an adaptive challenge: the congregation must adapt to what God is calling it to be—it must bridge the gap between what it is and what it ought to be. Changing circumstances in transitional times will make that gap more apparent than ever to congregations, but appreciative inquiry will help them to sort out the best and most fitting ways to bridge the gap. So, rather than making changes in worship style out of an attempt to stem the flow of members out of the congregation, or to attract an influx of visitors, such changes will come in response to questions about what this congregation is good at and gifted in, and how it can best express its worship of God at this time and place in its history.

The biblical framework for appreciative inquiry is the theme of gratitude. According to Branson, "congregations need encouragement and guidance to frame their lives in gratitude. Biblical resources for this formative agenda abound."[24] Imagine the effect that planning a series of worship services on the theme of gratitude would have in a time of congregational transition. It may seem easier to be grateful for positive transitions in congregational life—new facilities, new leadership, new members, new vision for ministry. But how would a theme of gratitude in worship be expressed in the aftermath of a church fire, or the sudden suspension of a pastor, or the departure of a faction of members involved in a serious conflict or opposed to a new direction for ministry? Discerning some reasons for gratitude in the face of these difficulties will give the congregation hope, because the reasons will connect with God's faithfulness in the past and promises for the future.

Branson writes that "without this posture of gratefulness, we lose our way. While there are times when other orienting positions become dominant—anger, confusion, despair, blindness—our responsiveness to God, our vulnerability to grace, requires foundational gratefulness. And, as the parable of the lepers teaches us, silent thankfulness is insufficient. We become saved/whole as we voice our praise in the company of believers."[25] So, as Branson emphasizes, congregations need to heed the words of Philippians 4:8: "Finally, beloved, whatever is true, whatever is honorable, whatever is just, whatever is pure, whatever is pleasing, whatever is commendable, if there is any excellence and if there is anything worthy of praise, think about these things."

Describing the case study of a congregation involved in a difficult transition, Branson first notes that "during worship the mood was subdued, perhaps even wounded. There was significantly more energy in sidewalk conversations than in either worship or in education classes." After two years of AI with this congregation, Branson reports that the congregation is "more empowered, imaginations are more engaged, and new initiatives are being welcomed. The tone, the mood, of the church is one of expectancy, knowing that we have hard work to do while also confident that we are in the midst of generative trajectories."[26]

The following assumptions of appreciative inquiry demonstrate the positive power of this approach:

1. In every organization, some things work well.
2. What we focus on becomes our reality.
3. Asking questions influences the group.
4. People have more confidence in the journey to the future when they carry forward parts of the past.
5. If we carry parts of the past into the future, they should be what is best about the past.
6. It is important to value differences.
7. The language we use creates our reality.
8. Organizations are heliotropic [leaning toward their source of energy].
9. Outcomes should be useful.
10. All steps are collaborative.[27]

When appreciative inquiry is applied to worship, questions are asked to help congregations appreciate what they are doing well and live into what they want to be. Possible questions: "What are the most valuable aspects of our congregation's worship? In worship experiences at our church, what do you believe has been most significant, most helpful in making worship alive and meaningful? When worship is at its best, how does it shape us? How has worship helped connect us with God? Describe those times when we are most engaged in and shaped by worship."[28]

Susan M. Weber of the Indianapolis Center for Congregations describes appreciative inquiry as "the study and exploration of what gives life to human systems when they function at their best. It assumes that extended conversations about strengths, successes, values, hopes, and dreams are themselves transformational and can make a lasting contribution to building up an organization."[29]

She notes that Cooperrider developed appreciative inquiry on the basis of a belief in collective human capacity and a desire to challenge conventional patterns of change that fragment and isolate individuals and organizations. True, in many congregations, difficult times of transition lead to fragmentation and isolation. Appreciative inquiry offers another way. "Clearly, Appreciative Inquiry is very different from traditional problem solving

or planning methods. Rather than focusing on gaps or defi-
cits, AI leverages strengths and qualities that give life to an
organization."[30]

Weber lists these examples of using appreciative inquiry:

- Imagine beginning a pastoral team meeting by asking team
  members to describe the *best* thing that has happened to
  them since the last meeting.
- What would happen if all members of a congregation were
  invited to tell about a time when they saw the congregation *flourish* rather than a story about deep conflict or
  division?
- What if a covenant group of pastors began each gathering
  by telling a story about a time when they experienced the
  presence of God in their ministry?

Weber argues for the use of stories in an appreciative inquiry
approach. She writes, "Over the centuries generations have passed
on stories of hope and inspiration drawn from the depth of human
experience. Scripture is filled with stories and parables of the mystery and love of God, which in turn forms and deepens our faith.
Stories become part of our human and institutional memories and
serve to teach, inspire and give us strength to move ahead."[31] The
stories generated through the use of appreciative inquiry will motivate congregations to live into the future, giving them hope and inspiration as they discern their way through a transition that seems
more like an opportune time than a difficult time.

Practices for Transition

Stories are a key way for a congregation to connect beliefs and
practices—to work out the learning that comes from addressing an
adaptive challenge. As the congregation makes progress through
a transition, it will find encouragement from connecting the biblical story with its congregational story, and even with its members'
individual stories. In *From Nomads to Pilgrims: Stories from Practicing Congregations,* researchers for the Project on Congregations

of Intentional Practice Diana Butler Bass and Joseph Stewart-Sicking gather a collection of stories from pastors and congregations that have gone through transitions and have emerged from them as vital communities, rather than suffering the fragmentation that so often happens when churches deal with change. According to Bass, "certain common themes were threaded throughout their accounts of congregational change. In every case, leaders practiced discernment by paying attention to cultural change, listening to the voices of the congregation, and relating the biblical story and God's call to the gathered community."[32]

They discovered that "intentional engagement with Christian tradition as embodied in faith practices fostered a renewed sense of identity and mission in congregations." The ultimate goal of these congregations was not church growth in numerical terms, but growth in the area of "Christian communal life, that of the organic body of Christ journeying toward shalom."[33] To accomplish this aim, these churches "worked hard at developing certain disciplines and making them the core of their life together. [They] saw an engagement with tradition not as the tyranny of the dead but as a living body of wisdom."[34] They recognized that honoring tradition is especially helpful as a practice for times of transition.

More congregations are now realizing the value of tradition, and the folly of casting it all aside, as so many North American churches have done in the past few years. Pastor and author Eugene Peterson encourages pastors and church leaders to be faithful to tradition. Speaking to students and faculty at Calvin Theological Seminary in January 2006, he pointed out, "Tradition is not what's old but what continues to live. There are no dead traditions." He went on to explain that living only in the present results in "a very thin life." But being faithful to tradition "doesn't mean repeating the past. It means continuing the livingness of the past. For a tradition to stay alive it has to stay alive in the present— the local. The roots might be dirty and invisible, but they're alive."[35]

The living, vital congregations that Bass and Stewart-Sicking studied found that reaching postmodern people meant "serving as spiritual bridges from the nomadic life to a life of faithful discipleship." They found that three practices were key to this process: "Discernment helped the congregation see the stranger; hospitality welcomed the stranger; and worship provided strangers a connection to the community and to God. Working together, these three practices not only opened the way to congregational renewal, but they initiated the movement of the individual from being a spiritual tourist to being a Christian pilgrim."[36] While the specific practices differed greatly from congregation to congregation, they were alike in "inverting a potentially destructive cultural pattern into a faith-filled way of life. By providing intentional congregations based on Christian practice, they offered a path for nomads to become pilgrims." All congregations going through transitional times could learn from these groups and the importance of these three practices as well, because all congregations, to one extent or another, face the same postmodern cultural patterns of "individualism, aimlessness, consumption, fragmentation, and forgetfulness—the conditions of American life that foster nomadic spirituality."[37]

One way to envision how worship can help congregations remember who they are and explore where they are and where they should be going is to think of it as "balcony space." Many churches have balconies, which are not just overflow areas; they provide occupants with an overview of the event proceeding below. From their vantage point, balcony dwellers can see the bigger picture of how everything fits together. Heifetz and Linsky compare this perspective to leaders' imaginative move to the balcony—mentally putting themselves above the mundane or conflictual matters of daily church and ministry life to think about broader concerns.[38] It's what they do when they rise above the mechanics of a worship service—whether the sound system worked and the musicians were in the right places and the readers entered at the right times—and evaluate whether it really did function as worship for God. When they rise above the specifics and the comments about preference ("I liked this; I didn't like that"), they are getting up into the balcony. Getting some mental distance from the situation, they are freer to discern and evaluate.

But not only do worship planners and leaders need to get into the balcony when reflecting on worship; the practice of worship actually helps the entire congregation do that very thing. In worship, congregations are reminded of the great promises of God in the sweep of redemptive history and see that their difficult transition is not so bad in comparison, and that it is a way to grow in dependence on God. Transitions can also be part of God's ongoing creation of the world, God's plan to reconcile and restore all creation. In this sense, transitions are more than something to endure. The refinement that comes through difficulty—whether of sudden onset or in a longer, drawn-out process—actually strengthens the congregation in the long run. In worship the members can focus on these larger themes and remember the purpose for which they go through the ups and downs of transition in congregational life.

So if worship provides balcony space for congregations going through transitions, how can congregations and worship planners use it as a vantage point from which they can see the bigger picture of who they are in Christ? In worship they step back from the details of their own individual stories and their congregational story, and consider the much greater scope of God's story. In considering the biblical story, they may understand their own history better. By reflecting on the parts of the biblical story that resonate with them best now, or fit with another point in their history, they may find enlightenment for the present. Furthermore, following the trajectory of redemptive history in the biblical story will also guide their congregational planning into the future.

Although a more valuable exercise would be for a worship planning team to come up with biblical stories and texts that fit their current situation, here are a few suggestions that may help start the process of reflection.

Leadership changes:

- Exodus 13–40; Israel's wanderings in the wilderness.
- Exodus 18; the assistance of elders to help Moses judge cases.
- Deuteronomy 34–Joshua 1; from Moses to Joshua.
- 2 Kings 2; from Elijah to Elisha.

- Acts 6; the assistance of helpers to meet the needs of widows on behalf of the disciples.
- Deuteronomy 34; Moses's parting words, or Acts 20; Paul's parting words.

Space changes:

- Ezra/Nehemiah for rebuilding.
- Israel's wanderings in the wilderness for relocations.
- The tabernacle, made for mobility and temporary spaces.

Changes in membership and vision:

- Jeremiah 29 and trust in God's plans.
- Jeremiah 34 and the change from old to new covenant.
- Acts 15 and the council of Jerusalem on the inclusion of Gentiles.
- The vision of Cornelius in Acts 10.
- The call to transformation in 2 Corinthians 3.

Some other important biblical themes for transitional times include affirming one another as the body of Christ, and considering again such questions as What is the church? Who are we as the body of Christ together? A facilitator or interim pastor could help the congregation find itself in the biblical narrative—find a biblical story that fits with its current situation. Then, that passage might be used as a reading in worship—even juxtaposed with a testimony, a remembering, of the church's history. Congregations that follow the lectionary may look for other ways, such as through Scripture songs and prayers or in the prayers of the people, to bring out these themes.

Liturgical Resources

While the vast variety of transitions and congregational situations makes it impossible to compile any complete list of resources, a few are noted here as examples that can be used in transitional times, or that may spur the imaginations of worship planners as they search for fitting resources for their own congregations.

Responsive Readings

The following reading is appropriate for the opening of worship in a time of transition, noting the passing of time and honoring the God of all time.

> God of the past, who has created and nurtured us,
> **we are here to thank you.**
> God of the future, who is always ahead of us,
> **we are here to thank you.**
> God of the present, who is here in the midst of us,
> **we are here to thank you.**
> God of life, who is beyond us and within us,
> **we rejoice in your glorious love.**

> Excerpt by Ruth Burgess from *The Pattern of Our Days: Worship in the Celtic Tradition from the Iona Community,* edited by Kathy Galloway, 92, alt. Copyright © 1996 by the authors, Paulist Press, Inc., New York/Mahwah, N.J. Used with permission of Paulist Press. www.paulistpress.com

Another opening prayer uses these simple words:

> Holy God, be with us in our worship.
> As we open to Christ's Spirit guiding each of us,
> help us to cherish our memories,
> and to move forward with your grace. Amen.

> Bev Irwin, in *Celebrate God's Presence: A Book of Services for The United Church of Canada,* 697. Used by permission.

The following reading focuses on the God of the covenant and the faithfulness of our God.

God, who has called you into fellowship
with his Son, Jesus Christ, our Lord, is faithful.
**He is a faithful Lord, keeping his covenant of love
to a thousand generations of those who love him
and keep his commands.**
His faithfulness reaches to the skies
and continues throughout all generations on into eternity.
**We therefore praise the faithfulness
of our Lord Jesus Christ in this assembly, saying,
"Great is your faithfulness!
We will exalt and praise your name,
for in perfect faithfulness you have done marvelous things.
Great is your faithfulness to us, O Lord, our God."**

> Paul E. Engle, *Baker's Worship Handbook,* 84. Copyright © 1998 Baker Books, a division of Baker Publishing Group. Used by permission.

Prayers of Confession

Following is a prayer of confession acknowledging that we don't always worship God well. A time of transition could be a good time to name this issue.

Lord, you have called us to worship you.
We gladly gather!
As we praise you, though,
our own inadequacy reminds us
of how we have broken our relationship with you.
Because we have sinned against you,
even our worship fails to be what it could.
We often treat it as a show.
We simply go through motions,
failing to recognize that you want to engage us deeply.
Renew us, we pray, according to your steadfast love.
Remind us of your covenant faithfulness
and have mercy on us in the name of Jesus Christ. Amen.

> John D. Witvliet, "Worship—Taking a Closer Look," *Reformed Worship* 56 (June 2000): 32, alt.

Prayers

Worship leaders should set an example of praying with confidence and yet acknowledging the ambiguity of the situation. It may help to offer prayers that narrate the community's history. Following the pattern of a historical psalm, such as Psalm 105 or 106, members can retell the story of God's working in and through their particular congregation. The reminder of God's faithfulness will provide encouragement to go forward, trusting in God's promises.

It is a good idea to involve the governing board of the church in leading the prayers of the people. Board members are most likely to know the mood or state of the congregation, and should be able to pray in an appropriate tone. Their visible leadership will also increase the congregation's confidence in them and calm some anxieties about the transition.

This prayer is a helpful example for transitional times:

Holy God, your love for all is everlasting.
Help each of us to trust in the future which rests in your care.
The time we were together in your name provided
laughter and tears, hopes and disappointments.
Guide us as we hold on to these cherished memories
and move forward in new directions.
Keep us one in your love forever,
through Jesus Christ. Amen.

> *Book of Worship, United Church of Christ,* 703. Adapted with permission. Copyright © 1986, 2002, United Church of Christ, Local Church Ministries, Worship and Education Ministry Team, Cleveland, Ohio. All rights reserved.

Or, for the ending of a congregation or for moving out of a building:

The time has come for us to go now from this house,
and to journey in faith in new and unfamiliar ways.
We do so with sadness but also in hope.
We do what so many faithful people have done before,
walking with trust and confidence in you,

knowing you do not abandon us,
but lead us always with your Light.

> "The time has come for us to go now from this house," 13T013-707, from *Celebrate God's Presence,* United Church Publishing House, 2000. Reprinted with permission.

The following prayer is from a service for the dissolution of a pastoral call, but could be appropriate in other transitional situations as well:

Loving God, Alpha and Omega,
you are both beginning and end.
Our endings and our beginnings
are rooted in your love.
Whether near or far,
we are held close by your love,
and kept safe from any lasting loss.
Let our time together end with your blessing.
Touch all memories with your grace and peace.
Help us to live with courage and gladness
in the future you present us.
In every time and place,
may we offer you our highest and our best,
through Jesus Christ our Lord.
Alleluia! Amen.

> *Book of Occasional Services: A Liturgical Resource Supplementing the Book of Common Worship,* 1993, 246–247. Used by permission.

This prayer from a congregational anniversary service could also fit in many transitions:

Receive our gratitude, Holy God,
for the years through which you have led us,
and open us to the future you promise.
In the years that lie ahead,
grant us your encouragement in the work of ministry,
your consolation in our defeats,

and your challenge to our complacency.
Give us such trust in your abiding Holy Spirit,
that we may find joy and peace in our common life,
strength and courage to live in the world for your reign,
and hope in the gospel of Jesus Christ our Lord. Amen.

Book of Occasional Services, 251. Used by permission.

A prayer for the uniting of congregations:

God of grace,
in Jesus Christ you have broken down our divisions,
accomplished our unity,
and given us in love to one another.
In humility, we confess our reluctance
to welcome your gifts,
to let go of our differences
and accept each other.
In every way, we are creatures of earth,
fearful of change,
even as we yearn for the new things
you are doing among us.
Forgive us, Gracious God,
and free us to embrace each other in your love.

We acknowledge that we are also your children,
who hope in your promise
and trust in your love.
In confidence, we confess our hope
that your love can transform us,
that the gifts you give us are for our good,
that the bonds you forge among us
will free us for strong and joyful service.
In all things, Loving God, grant us your grace,
that we may live fully into the gift of our baptism,
and welcome the new life you bring to birth in us,
in Christ Jesus our Lord. Amen.

Book of Occasional Services, 254–255. Used by permission.

Songs

The following songs may be helpful in times of transition. They call for God's leading in changing times, and for trusting God by letting go of things that seem secure.

This Is a Day of New Beginnings
This is a day of new beginnings,
time to remember and move on,
time to believe what love is bringing,
laying to rest the pain that's gone.

For by the life and death of Jesus,
Love's mighty Spirit, now as then,
can make for us a world of difference,
as faith and hope are born again.

Then let us, with the Spirit's daring,
step from the past and leave behind
our disappointment, guilt, and grieving,
seeking new paths, and sure to find.

Christ is alive, and goes before us
to show and share what love can do.
This is a day of new beginnings;
our God is making all things new.

*In faith we'll gather round the table
to show and share what love can do.
This is a day of new beginnings;
our God is making all things new.

Alternate text for Holy Communion

Words: Brian Wren
© 1987 Hope Publishing Company, Carol Stream, IL 60188. All rights reserved. Used by permission.

Gracious Spirit

Gracious Spirit, heed our pleading; fashion us all anew.
It's your leading that we're needing; help us to follow you.
Refrain: Come, come, come, Holy Spirit, come.
Come to teach us; come to nourish those who believe in Christ.
Bless the faithful; may they flourish, strengthened by grace unpriced.
(Refrain)
Guide our thinking and our speaking done in your holy name.
Motivate all in their seeking, freeing from guilt and shame.
(Refrain)
Not mere knowledge, but discernment, nor rootless liberty;
turn disquiet to contentment, doubt into certainty.
(Refrain)
Keep us fervent in our witness; unswayed by earth's allure.
Ever grant us zealous fitness, which you alone assure.
(Refrain)

> Wilson Nigwagila, Tanzania; tr. Howard S. Olson.
> Text copyright © Lutheran Theological College, Makumira,
> Tanzania, admin. Augsburg Fortress. Used by permission.

Faith Begins by Letting Go

Faith begins by letting go, giving up what had seemed sure,
taking risks and pressing on, though the way feels less secure:
pilgrimage both right and odd, trusting all our life to God.

Faith endures by holding on, keeping mem'ry's roots alive
so that hope may bear its fruit; promise-fed, our souls will thrive,
not through merit we possess but by God's great faithfulness.

Faith matures by reaching out, stretching minds, enlarging hearts,
sharing struggles, living prayer, binding up the broken parts;
till we find the commonplace ripe with witness to God's grace.

> Words: Carl P. Daw, Jr.
> © 1996 Hope Publishing Company, Carol Stream, IL 60188. All
> rights reserved. Used by permission.

Jesus, Lead the Way
Jesus, lead the way
through our life's long day.
When at times the way is cheerless,
help us follow, calm and fearless;
guide us by your hand
to the promised land.

Jesus be our light,
in the midst of night.
Let not faithless fear o'ertake us,
let not faith and hope forsake us;
may we feel you near
as we worship here.

When in deepest grief,
strengthen our belief.
When temptations come alluring,
make us patient and enduring;
Lord we seek your grace
in this holy place.

Jesus, still lead on
'til our rest be won:
if you lead us through rough places,
grant us your redeeming graces.
When our course is o'er,
open heaven's door.

> Nicholas L. von Zinzendorf, tr. Jane Borthwick, in *Gather Comprehensive* 632, alt.

Sacraments

The vows that a congregation makes in baptism will remind the people not only of what is really important in the church, but also of what it is that holds them together. A baptismal service should remind all of their baptisms and the meaning of being part of God's family. Such reminders can be especially assuring to the congregation in transition. Pastors and worship leaders could transition into the baptism service with words such as,

> Even though our congregation is going through the uncertainties that come with a transition [or a change in leadership, space, membership, or vision], we know this for certain: God loves us and extends that love to us in this sacrament of baptism. As we baptize *[name]*, may we recall the many baptisms we have witnessed and the promises God made to all of us as adopted children in the family of God.

The celebration of the Lord's Supper can also be an occasion of remembrance and reassurance, and a time for parishioners to reaffirm their love for Christ and one another as they gather together around the table. The sacrament provides an opportunity to think ahead to the banquet that awaits them, where the painful effects of earthly transitions will be absent. A communion service can also offer opportunities for parishioners to express both their faith in Christ and the concerns they face. In *Worship as Pastoral Care,* Willimon relates a practice of John Carr, professor of church ministries at Emory University, who led an early communion service every Sunday morning at his former parish. That service

> began providing a place for parishioners to signal personal needs. When John would see a person, couple, or family at that early morning service for the first time, his pastoral sensitivity would tell him that their presence might signify some special need they had or some crisis they were going through. He therefore made a point to allow himself sufficient time to talk with people after the service, to allow them the opportunity to make contact with their pastor if they wished to do so. Time and again, the service became an opportunity for parishioners to alert their pastor to their needs (whether the parishioners consciously or unconsciously knew this was what they were doing), to seek pastoral care through their actions in public worship.[39]

While not every church and pastor will be able to add a communion service, each can watch for pastoral care opportunities when the sacrament is celebrated.

Planning Together

A church's governing leaders often miss opportunities by not connecting with the worship planners during transitional times, and worship planners don't always see the value of connecting with the leaders. But working together will not only signal cooperation and stability in a difficult time; it will also result in worship services that are more fitting, given the other issues going on in the congregation. Communication between church leaders and worship planners is crucial during these times. In fact, forming a worship planning team that is organically connected with the congregation's governing body during the transitional time could be crucial for the health of the congregation and its worship life. Worship planners can make more appropriate choices if they are aware of the current congregational dynamics.

Transition is also a good time to implement a practice of evaluating worship. Though the presenting issue is to test whether worship services are addressing the transition well, worship planners and church leaders should think beyond the transition to whether the services truly bring the congregation's best worship to God. This challenging time could even be a learning opportunity for worship planners to explore a theology of worship, when the interest in such topics is high. Involving the elders or the governing body in worship planning is especially appropriate when a system of regular evaluation is put into place. A process developed for evaluating worship during a difficult time can also be transferred to easier times. In fact, church leaders that spend time regularly evaluating and discussing worship will find themselves better able to address difficult times and crises when they do come up. The groundwork will be laid for better worship planning in the long run.[40]

When congregational leaders are dealing with a major transition, such as replacing a pastor or planning a new facility, they should give the congregation as much information as possible. Regular updates, even if they don't contain a lot of new information, will help the congregation feel informed and confident in the leaders. Especially when there is an interruption in staff, congregations should be assured that careful plans are being made. Printing a schedule of upcoming worship themes and guest preachers can be helpful in this regard. It is also a good idea to make sure to give guest preachers a sense of what the congregation has gone through and how church members have handled it, to let them know which themes have been treated in worship, and help them avoid themes that either don't fit well, or may have been emphasized too frequently.

Worship planners should keep records of worship themes, texts, and songs used, so that balanced choices can be made. If the transition involves introducing new songs or ethnically diverse elements of worship, it will be important to pace the changes carefully with enough repetition to encourage learning, but not so much that tedium results. If the transition calls for addressing a particular theme, from "refinement by fire" to "welcoming the stranger," wise planners will both highlight the theme and discern when it is time to move on. They should avoid hitting the same themes each week and "wearing the people out" with them. For example, if they've been focusing on forgiveness for a long time, they should take a break from that theme, remembering the need to balance the values of stability and flexibility in transitional times.

A Word for Pastors and Leaders

"One of the hardest things about being a pastor is the transitions. My heart never moves as fast as the schedule of events,"[41] writes Craig Barnes. Many pastors may find this comment to be true and will need to face their own reactions to the transition even as they lead the congregation through it. This matter will be addressed further in chapter 7, but some advice from Barnes about transitional times may be helpful here.

Barnes writes in *Leadership* of the Hebrews' transitional journey through the desert to the Promised Land, noting that they brought "the rabble" with them. According to Barnes, "These were not true believers in this journey or in the God who called them to it. The rabble's toleration for discomfort was low and their capacity for complaint was high."[42] Most churches going through transition will find those in their midst who act like "the rabble." Furthermore, as Barnes points out, even though "the rabble" tend to threaten to leave if they don't get their way, and leaders are often tempted to simply take them up on the offer, they usually don't leave.

Instead of continuing to be frustrated with them, Barnes finds a "holy purpose for the rabble" in that they force the pastor into "the awkward position of standing between the people and the God they cannot see. The grace of that awkwardness is that it forces the pastor to pray, looking for the One who is present but not apparent." As pastors lead congregations though transitions, they must remember the role to which God has called them.

> When you're in leadership it is tempting to think your job is to get the people to the Promised Land. But that's actually God's job. Your job is to bear their burdens while they're in the wilderness. We prefer just the opposite. Let God love the people and we'll just move them along. But pastors are called to serve as wilderness guides, wandering through the ordinary with their people, loving them enough to point to the manna that keeps them spiritually alive even when it is unappreciated.[43]

All congregational leaders should take such a pastoral approach to the people and the ministry of the congregation in transitional times, and apply it not just to "the rabble," but to all those connected with the church. As they lead their congregations through the next transition, they should remember to make space for the congregation to appreciate its heritage and gifts and to dream its way into a fitting future. Leading such a process will not only point to the theme of gratitude that is so important for a healthy transition; it will also produce gratitude in the congregation, an attitude and practice that will serve it well during the transition and long afterward. Congregations that can stay focused on God's gifts to them and the Spirit's guidance while navigating a transition may be able to circumvent the most turbulent rapids of congregational conflict, the topic of the next chapter.

Chapter Six

Worship in Times of Conflict

"An old farmer once said, 'Go slow. Churches are a lot like horses. They don't like to be startled or surprised. It causes deviant behavior.'" Larry Osborne, author and pastor of North Coast Church in Vista, California, remembered this saying when a conflict developed with a couple in his new congregation—mainly because he had dropped the closing hymn in the worship service! He didn't realize that so small a change would have such an impact, but he learned from the experience to slow down when introducing changes. From then on, he tested the waters with new ideas like "moving across town, adding a new staff member, or changing the church logo" to see how people would react, and he did it in informal, smaller groups in social contexts. As he explains, "Larger groups tend to silence introverts and inhibit candor, while formal settings or full-blown presentations cause most people to assume I'm asking for their approval rather than their opinion."[1] Osborne learned that testing the waters helps prevent conflict because it provides information about whether, and to what extent, the leader's dissatisfaction with the status quo is shared by others, which changes not to make, which aspects of the change will cause the most resistance, and the source of that resistance.

Osborne has a healthy attitude toward those who resist change and try to instigate conflict. Instead of labeling them as "adversaries," he calls them "advisers," and considers them "a necessary link in the process of transforming a good idea into a great idea. Their resistance is useful," he writes. "Like pain in the body, it lets me know something is out of adjustment." From their reactions he learns "where change is most likely to go wrong," and "what hidden psychological barriers must be overcome" for people to accept

the change. He also recommends that leaders avoid first presenting
new ideas in formal public gatherings of the whole church, because "initial responses are often negative" and "public responses
are usually permanent."[2] People have to get used to new ideas
before they are comfortable taking public stands on them, and
they like to know who else is supporting the new idea before they
weigh in with their opinion. Osborne found this method successful
for making conflict-free changes, whether altering worship style in
the morning worship service or replacing the evening service with
home Bible studies.

Osborne supplies good advice for pastors and church leaders
in congregations that are going through change. While not every
change will lead to a major conflict, some level of conflict will
always be present, and often a segment of the congregation will
experience the conflict rather acutely. Leading a conflicted congregation in worship is especially difficult, because some parishioners carry intense feelings about the conflict with them to worship
services. Even if those strong feelings don't boil over in visible or
audible ways, astute worship leaders can sense them simmering
just below the surface.

Congregations and Conflict

Most congregations are uncomfortable with conflict. They want
it resolved; they don't enjoy discord between fellow church members. More than that, they worry that conflict could be a sign of
disobedience to God. They know the call of Scripture to "love one
another" and to "bear one another's burdens." They may realize
that being in conflict is part of the brokenness of this world, but
since they know it's not the way God's people should act toward
one another, they feel guilty. Congregations and their leaders need
to be reminded that conflict is normal. As observed in chapter 3,
change and growth are themselves signs of a healthy organism, but
change will usually produce some conflict, which can be a good
thing and is not necessarily to be avoided, according to Alban Institute consultant Gil Rendle. He defines conflict, tongue in cheek,
as "two or more ideas in the same place at the same time."[3] That

broad definition would require labeling almost every church meeting as a conflict.

Conflict should be thought of both as a normal part of congregational life, and as something that needs to be worked through and resolved if congregations are to fulfill their calling to be the body of Christ. Life in Christ means participating in genuine confession, forgiveness, and reconciliation, and thereby emulating Jesus Christ more and more. The task of the church is to include more people in the family of God, and together to become more unified in being Christlike. Working through conflict is one part of fulfilling that task.

The unity of the church is an important gift of God, and it is good to remember at the outset of this chapter that it *is* a gift. Even though church members are called to the task of becoming one in Christ, they have already received the gift of unity from the Holy Spirit. The disunity the church experiences is evidence that the Spirit's gift has not been fully embraced in the life of the church because of its sinful, broken condition. Congregations that work toward greater unity by resolving conflict in their midst are working to become who and what they already are in Christ. This unity of the church, which is both a gift and a task, is expressed well in two articles of the *Contemporary Testimony* of the Christian Reformed Church in North America, "Our World Belongs to God," as follows:

> The church is a gathering of forgiven sinners,
> called to be holy, dedicated to service.
> Saved by the patient grace of God, we deal patiently with
>   others.
> Knowing our own weaknesses and failures,
> we bring good news to all sinners
> with understanding of their condition, and with hope in God.
> We grieve that the church, which shares one Spirit, one faith,
>   one hope,
> and spans all time, place, race, and language,
> has become a broken communion in a broken world.
> When we struggle for the purity of the church
> and for the righteousness God demands,

we pray for saintly courage.
When our pride or blindness blocks
the unity of God's household, we seek forgiveness.
We marvel that the Lord gathers the broken pieces
to do his work, and that he blesses us still
with joy, new members, and surprising evidences of unity.
We commit ourselves to seeking and expressing
the oneness of all who follow Jesus.[4]

The concept of becoming who and what the congregation already is can be seen also in baptism. In that sacrament, believers are washed clean of their sin and clothed with new life in Christ; but they still live out their days striving to embrace that life in reality. So, too, the body of Christ is *one* in faith, hope and love, and also *is becoming one* in that reality. Until unity in Christ is fully experienced in the restoration of all creation, conflict will be evident in congregations and is both to be expected and to be overcome.

In this chapter we will consider the effects of conflict on the congregation and its leaders and discuss ways that worship can help a congregation through the healing process. As in previous chapters, specific ideas for thoughtful, fitting worship in such situations will be suggested, with special attention given to the elements of confession, forgiveness, and reconciliation.

The Effects of Conflict: Rules and Rituals

Learning about conflict and how it typically affects churches will be helpful for all those involved in such situations. Retired Alban consultant Speed Leas, an expert in dealing with congregational conflicts, provides much information about the subject as well as strategies for dealing with it. Congregational leaders will find it helpful to read and discuss together his resource *Moving Your Church through Conflict*.[5] At the same time, they need to know their particular congregation and observe carefully how it responds to conflict. Leas says that different congregations have different tacit rules for conflict—certain understandings or ways of doing things that are never really talked about. Such rules include:

- Ignore conflict. Pretend it's not there, talk about everything but the conflict, and let it fester.
- Don't allow any yelling. Use lots of euphemisms, and basically avoid genuine conversation about the issue. Keep your voices down.
- Placate angry ones. Let the most dysfunctional people in the system control it. The rest of the congregation will be fearful because of the conflict between a few or because of the ones vocalizing it.
- Triangulate. Don't talk to the person you disagree with. Talk to a third party, and exaggerate the problem.[6]

Obviously these are not the kinds of rules you want to find in your congregation. If you do find them present, you have more to work on than the presenting issue of a particular conflict. A review of congregational systems and the effects of conflict will be helpful, as will practical resources such as those found in the Indianapolis Center for Congregations and the Alban Institute's online Congregational Resource Guide.[7]

Leas also points out that the rituals of a congregation—and especially the rituals of worship practices—can function as "anxiety binders" because they truss or tie up people's anxious feelings in conflictual situations. Negative examples of anxiety binders include turning to alcohol or abusing other substances to numb anxious feelings, or overfunctioning to block out anxious feelings— for example, by focusing on excessive busyness. Positive rituals for binding anxiety in the church take the form of prayer and worship, more appropriately bringing concerns and anxious feelings to God, as Peter recommends: "Cast all your anxiety on him, because he cares for you" (1 Pet. 5:7). People who are tense because of conflict can find peace and reassurance in worship, which points them back to the God who is in control of all things and reminds them that "all things work together for good for those who love God" (Rom. 8:28).

While the entire liturgy is a ritual that can bring comfort in anxious times, prayer is especially helpful as a way of both expressing the worries raised by a conflict and calming the fears of those affected by the conflict. So the prayers of regular worship services or of special services held in light of the conflict should focus on the faithfulness of God and the call of the church to be one. These prayers should be offered out of a genuine desire to bring comfort, not as a strategy to "guilt" people into submission. Prayer should never be used as a weapon or as a way to scold or deliberately embarrass anyone. The point of intercession is to ask for help, confidently petitioning God to act. A beautiful by-product of prayer is that congregations can experience comfort even before the prayer finishes.

Ritual can also be used to signal to the rest of the system that a part of the system has changed. The ritual binds the anxiety produced by the change. For instance, a wedding functions in that way, as does a funeral, when the rituals and activities signal a change in a family and provide a way to internalize that change. In worship the worries and fears of the people can be gathered up and held in a service of prayer, or some kind of guided meditation that will guard people's minds and hearts in a trying time.[8] This approach can be especially effective as congregations go through an intervention process to address the conflict and work toward resolution. Naming difficult issues, like lancing boils, can be painful but necessary for the health of the organism. Soothing the pain with the balm of a prayer or a service of confession and reconciliation can bring healing to those who are hurting.

Some of the hurt comes when words and motives of conflict are revealed. It takes a mature congregation to expose such secrets and still make room for those who disagree on the issues to remain present. Worship can be this safe space, especially because the focus is on the presence of God, who knows all of our motives and nonetheless forgives and loves us. As Calvin College English professor Debra Rienstra writes in *So Much More: An Invitation to Christian Spirituality,* "Worship services reveal a church's most important secrets. Not because you find out the latest news about people during prayer-request time but because worship structures and styles reveal what a congregation really believes church is all about—whatever they might say."[9] Worship should be a safe place for expressing both the pain and the frustration of a conflict. In worship the family of God is gathered together, and its members can express their concerns openly and honestly, without attacking or accusing others. If they are reluctant to bring their concerns before God and the community, then they are probably not truly looking to resolve the conflict.

Richard Blackburn, director of the Lombard Mennonite Peace Center, teaches church leaders how to deal with conflicts in the church, cautioning that if they don't, unresolved conflicts from the past may come up again. Blackburn understands that sometimes those conflicts have more to do with the parishioners' past or present struggles than with the conflict at hand. He explains how church members tend to project their own issues onto the pastor in a church conflict with this telling phrase: "The clergy collar is the screen upon which parishioners show home movies."[10] Discerning leaders need always to be alert to the possibility of these "home movies" being projected on them, while showing sensitive pastoral care to those individuals who are transferring their concerns.

Rather than being divided by conflict, according to Blackburn, congregations can be bound together and strengthened by conflict if the following conditions are present:

1. Issues and people are separated. Members are properly hard on issues and soft on people. (They disagree agreeably.)
2. Conflict is viewed as an opportunity.
3. Disagreement means engagement and involvement.
4. Leaders welcome open disagreement.
5. In the stress of conflict, many voices are heard (members are energized), and direct dialogue increases.
6. Individuals interact thoughtfully with the views of others. Individuals offer their own responses only after making an obvious effort to understand others.
7. Discussion focuses on the process.
8. Timing is steady. People foresee issues, plan procedures, examine options (allow plenty of time here), and then prepare proposals for a final decision.
9. [People have] a willingness to move calmly through the inevitable periods of uncertainty as all options are considered.
10. Each individual is consciously aware of his or her own past hurts or unresolved conflicts and takes responsibility not to project these in the current situation.[11]

This list could be a significant educational tool for any church board or worship planning committee. While many of these statements could also apply to other areas of congregational life besides worship, a deep understanding of these realities is essential to planning worship that is fitting in tone and language, and that both acknowledges the existence of conflict and intends to help the congregation move through the difficult time.

Language and Conflict

The matter of language—how people speak to one another conversationally in a time of conflict and the words they use in public worship—is an important consideration. Are words being used as weapons or propaganda, or are they being used to calm and stabilize? Are leaders choosing their words carefully, speaking the truth but doing it in a grace-filled way? Thomas G. Long argues that "language is one of the ways we maintain Christian community."[12] The words used by individuals in a community shape and form them, so leaders and members need to be especially aware of this effect in difficult times, when words are noticed and offhand comments are not easily forgotten.

In his book *Testimony: Talking Ourselves into Being Christian,* Long points out that "sometimes the wisdom about how to speak as Christians is born of apparent failure."[13] He illustrates this point by referring to Dietrich Bonhoeffer's time leading a small seminary in Finkenwald, Germany, where "he proposed a remarkable rule for how the Christians living together in that community, faculty and students alike, ought to talk. As an expression of the gospel, no person in the community, he said, should talk about another Christian in secret, even when the intent is to help and to do good. When Christians speak about each other, Bonhoeffer maintained, they ought to do so truthfully, out in the open, and in the hearing of the person being talked about." Long notes that "if Bonhoeffer's rule were observed among Christians today, there would be no gossip, no secret whispering about others, no strategy meetings on how to handle 'difficult' people," and he concludes that "much of our daily conversation would be silenced."

Long goes on with the story:

> Hard as they tried, residents of Bonhoeffer's seminary community were not able to abide by the rule either. But by trying, failing, and trying again, the members of that community gained deep insights about the constructive and destructive power of words and were renewed in their commitment to honor other people in everyday speaking. Bonhoeffer's biographer, Eberhard Bethge, observed that by attempting to live by this rule and resolving to try again when they failed, the students and faculty at Finkenwald learned almost as much as they did from sermons and Bible studies.[14]

Congregations in conflict may not want to try to enforce such a rule, but they could learn from this story the value of avoiding secretive talk that often leads to unhealthy patterns of conflict.

The careless or ungracious use of words is not the only potential language hazard in a situation of congregational conflict. Sometimes the broader issue is not just how to talk about the conflict, but whether to talk about it at all. However, in most instances, naming the struggle rather than ignoring it is important for the health of the congregation—for lowering the congregation's level of anxiety, and for ultimately bringing reconciliation. Worship planners and leaders will be tempted to avoid the subject at the heart of the conflict but must carefully consider how best to help the congregation. It may take courage to face and name the reality, but if members realize that openness is encouraged and problems shared are matters for prayer, not gossip, then they as individuals and the congregation as a whole will grow spiritually and more closely follow the New Testament injunctions against gossiping (Rom. 1:29, 2 Cor. 12:20, 1 Tim. 3:11, 5:13).

Tension in Worship

Worship planners need to remind themselves that during a time of conflict, it is hard for some people to worship. Some will find confession and assurance awkward because of underlying conflict.

Others may experience the tension especially during the administration of the Lord's Supper, which offers time for reflection and penitence, as well as the communal sharing of a meal. They may prefer to avoid convictions that arise from reflecting on their sin even as they are receiving the signs of God's grace, or to avoid gathering around the table with members of the church family with whom they should be reconciled. Becoming aware of and talking about these realities will help worship planners to be sensitive to them and plan ways to address them, perhaps by acknowledging the difficulty verbally and calling people to repentance, while still inviting them to take part in the sacrament. The administration of the sacrament should also be led with sensitivity to these issues.

Congregations that have been experiencing conflict in another area of their ministries may find tensions over worship issues heightened as well. Parishioners who are upset about the conflict may focus their frustration on worship issues instead of on the actual cause of the conflict. For example, a person who normally wouldn't complain about songs she doesn't like may be prompted to speak out against them, out of heightened anxiety related to the conflict. Instead of reacting quickly to every complaint, leaders should absorb some of the complaints and anxieties and respond in a calm, measured way to indicate that careful planning of worship will continue. The complaints are good data or evidence to help leaders assess the anxiety level of the congregation.

Leading Worship in Times of Conflict

By the time a conflict is named in a congregation, many people will have taken sides, and worship leaders will face parishioners who either are upset with one another, with some person or organization in the community, or with the leaders of the church itself. Pastors and worship leaders need to be aware that anything they say or do may be interpreted as evidence that they are taking one side or the other in the conflict. People will wonder: What did he mean by that comment? Was it a subtle message to us for opposing his viewpoint? Or was he trying to communicate support for those on the other side? Why did she choose that text? Is she trying to get us on her side and persuade us to change our minds? The challenge for leaders will be to lead worship well, despite the conflict, the leader's position in the conflict, and any personal feelings about it.

One principle of good leadership to be explored in chapter 7 is to keep the "opposition" close—to stay connected with those who disagree with you so that you can stay in relationship with them, both to listen genuinely to them and to influence them. The purpose of staying connected is to keep the lines of communication open and to avoid the polarizing of factions that can paralyze a congregation's ministry. Staying close to those who differ is especially important in congregations because the church is the body of Christ. Congregations really don't have the option of cutting off an arm or a leg, but must make every effort to keep the body whole. Of course, a time may come when parts of the body choose to separate and join another congregation, but this outcome should not be the goal of any congregation. The desire of the body of Christ is to be unified and to grow more like Christ, not just individually but as a community.

Since worship is the main corporate activity of the church, it is the occasion when the body gathers, and when missing parts of the body will be noticed or feuding parts of the body will show up next to each other. So worship becomes a natural way to keep the opposing sides of a conflict in relationship with one another. Those who drift away should be sought out and brought back. Those who are hurt or angry over the conflict should receive empathy and listening ears. But there are several hazards in bringing factions together. Doing so could escalate the tension, breed resentment by ignoring the needs and concerns of some sides of the disagreement, or encourage hypocrisy by not acknowledging the brokenness of the church.

Carefully planned and thoughtfully led worship will be required to avoid these hazards. The main way to avoid escalating tensions between factions is to focus on the worship of God and not on the disagreement. After all, as observed in chapter 3, worship is first and foremost about God, not about the worshipers. Their purpose in worship is to bring glory to God first, and only subsequently to present their requests and concerns to God. So, while they bring their needs with them to worship and filter their experience of worship through those concerns, they also must acknowledge that the worship they bring to God should not be tainted by their squabbles.

At the same time, worshipers cannot pretend that everything is fine when it isn't. Doing so would imply that it is not all right to express lament and hurt in the congregation. Part of becoming one in Christ is naming failings and learning from them so that the congregation can become a healthier body. Church leaders and church members need to know which parts of our body are hurting, and why. They need to remain open and care enough to listen genuinely to one another and desire the unity to which they are called. Hiding the struggle will breed hypocrisy and allow it to fester; uncovering the wound and cleaning it out will be painful for a time, but will eventually bring soothing and healing through caring and sensitive leadership.

Often conflict doesn't just affect worship: it's *about* worship! Conflicts can develop in churches over styles of worship and especially over choices of music, both songs and instrumentation. Recent conflicts over worship have often focused on the use of electronic technology (computers, projectors, and screens) with praise bands versus singing from hymnals with organ accompaniment. Congregations may benefit from remembering that years ago the organ itself was viewed as a secular technology invading the worship of the church, and the invention of the printing press was one factor that led to a great protest in the church called the Reformation.

More important, congregations need to recognize that the underlying and more significant issue is related to the style and content of the songs and hymns themselves. When congregations take the time to consider the deeper meaning and purpose of worship, as described in chapter 3, and only after that discussion make appropriate and fitting musical, visual, and technical choices for their congregation, they end up with better decisions and less polarization. Finding things they can agree on is helpful—especially when those things are of God. Remembering what they together believe will help them deal with the disagreements that are less important when put in perspective.

Leaders Who Understand Conflict

Congregational leaders especially need to remember that conflict can be a sign of health. How does it make for healthier churches? *Leadership* journal editor Marshall Shelley lists three reasons given by church consultant Eddy Hall. First, conflict shows that a congregation is not succumbing to "lowest common denominator decisions." It is not seeking the path of least resistance or becoming paralyzed by inaction, but deciding to address the issues. Second, conflict is a way of deepening relationships by dealing with differences and forging the trust that comes from working through conflict in a constructive way. And third, conflict avoids the temptation to become complacent—"it forces people to look deeply at what their priorities and commitments are." Hall says that "one of the most important responsibilities of leaders is to create the right kind of tension." Shelley adds that "this happens when you make people aware of the gap between the way things are and the way God wants them to be. Conflict does that almost automatically."[15]

In the foreword to Diana Butler Bass's *The Practicing Congregation: Imagining a New Old Church,* Loren Mead refers to Speed Leas's teaching on church conflict:

> He always told me that the most important thing in working in a hot fight is to recognize that everybody wants to simplify the issues so you have clear reasons for killing each other (spiritually, of course, in *most* church conflicts). He said that the most important thing one can do is to "complexify things." What he meant, I think, is that only when you begin to see new dimensions of what is going on are you able to get beyond dead ends. When you see all ten sides of the issue you'd mistakenly thought had only two, only then can you begin working out of the polarization.[16]

Leaders would do well to help their congregations see that there are more than two sides to any issue, and that a healthy discussion to reveal all the angles will at first seem to "complexify" the issue, but eventually will bring greater clarity.

In *The Practicing Congregation,* Bass goes on to say that during a time of conflict, "whatever the situation, however different this church is from others, one thing almost always remains the same—people want someone to blame for their troubles.... Whoever—or whatever—churchgoers blame for congregational turmoil, typically the troublemaker can be found within the building." The congregation may blame the pastor, a worship leader, a musician, or some other high-profile person in the congregation, so people in these roles should be prepared for accusations and resist the temptation to overreact to them. Bass continues:

> The same goes for denominational conflict—people blame internal factors for their struggles with change. Fault for denominational stress is placed on women's ordination, liberals or conservatives (depending upon the church) "taking over the seminaries," the new hymnal or liturgies, the rise of contemporary worship, or the election of a controversial leader. People tend to blame something *inside the denominational structures* for the tensions, pressures, and stresses associated with change in American churches.[17]

What they often do not see is that there may be no one to blame—the conflict is due to factors outside the denomination or congregation. Bass says that sometimes conflict is "the result of institutions reacting and responding to larger cultural changes—trends, ideas, and practices *outside the church building.* People bring their fears about large-scale social change with them to church. These cultural anxieties are often a hidden source of congregational conflict. Congregants overfocus on what is at hand and forget the stress and anxiety of global cultural changes that are affecting nearly every human being on the planet at this juncture of history."[18] Understanding these realities will help leaders to function more effectively in a time of conflict.

Conflict and Change

One parishioner who was upset about changes in the order of the liturgy was confronted by his pastor as to the cause of his resistance. The older gentleman said, "Everything's changed in my life: my kids moved away, we never used to go out for lunch on Sunday and now we do . . . and everything else seems to be changing in my life. But by cracky, I'm not going to put up with change in church!" This man wasn't trying to start a conflict; he was trying to preserve some stability in his life.

Bass tells of a church conflict that was addressed by the pastor from the pulpit as a "Tevye tension"—referring to the main character in *Fiddler on the Roof* who struggled with change and tradition. He compared Tevye in that story to the congregation, which like many churches was having a fight "between hanging onto the past and moving toward the future 'by adapting, changing, and growing.'" Bass concludes that the pastor was wrong in that interpretation. "The conflict was not between tradition and change. *The conflict was between rival versions of tradition.*" So they really were "arguing over *what tradition* formed the center of congregational identity."[19] Other congregations may be helped if they realize that the conflict may not be so much about which changes to adopt, as about which tradition to appropriate and encourage in their context.

Congregations are constantly interpreting their past and translating it into the present and future—making choices, setting priorities. It's not a matter of choosing between tradition and change, but of choosing how the tradition will be transmitted to the current generation. Bass argues that many congregations are actually in a process of "retraditioning"—a reaction to a time several decades ago when they "muted their traditional identity in favor of generic versions of Christian belief and worship to better serve a 'post-denominational age.'"[20]

Some churches are finding that clarity about their identity and tradition is helpful in gaining commitment from new members. But that requires knowing the church's history and appropriating it for the present—the process Bass identifies as "retraditioning." In congregations with competing core values, the retraditioning process can lead to conflict. For instance, sometimes a segment of a congregation is very interested in worship and in using a variety of the gifts of the people. And the people are, indeed, quite gifted. But another segment in the congregation has different gifts and is more interested in neighborhood outreach and assistance programs, which focus on people who do not attend worship. The congregation needs to decide how to hold these competing values in place without ending up in a conflict with one another.

When the Conflict Concerns Worship

Sometimes the conflict isn't about whether worship is the most important value of the congregation, but about which kind of worship takes precedence. Thinking about conflict as the result of differing values breaks down the typical "traditional vs. contemporary" debate, especially when it comes to worship style. Various worship styles are practiced today, and in a sense they are all contemporary, even though that word has become attached to certain styles and types of songs and patterns of worship. By definition, any worship that happens *today* is contemporary, whether it uses brand-new music or appropriates music from years past.

Recent authors have been much more interested in the diversity of worship experience than in promoting a particular worship style. Debra Rienstra tells of her journey with a group of college and seminary students in Great Britain, and of the insights they gained into the worship style discussion from the people they met along their way. She writes of three musicians and theologians from three very different traditions:

> Matt Redman, a singer-songwriter-worship leader active in Britain's contemporary worship movement, talked with us about balancing the old and new in worship. His view of the matter was that having only brand-new music and words in worship would not be compassionate; it would not respect how people are nourished by what they have learned to love over many years. On the other hand, using only old forms would not be prophetic: it would not challenge us to see the world in new ways.
>
> . . . .
>
> Alison Adam, a founder of a Scottish worship renewal group called the Wild Goose Resource Group, explained that worship ought to both "bless and disturb" us. All through our discussions about worship, we talked about these kinds of balances: between form and freedom, old and new, comforting and challenging.

. . . .

[Anglican Bishop of Durham] N. T. Wright explained to my group that when we worship, "we are dipping into the stream of the church's worship in all times and places." If the worship of God is a stream we dip into, it is always the same stream but also always shifting and moving, with different qualities of light playing on its surface.[21]

The key is to realize that worship should not be about this *or* that, but about this *and* that. It ought to be old *and* new, comforting *and* challenging, compassionate *and* prophetic. Worship should be planned and led in a way that acknowledges the variety of styles that are blessed by God.

As one church struggled with the typical worship-style controversy, the sides became polarized along generational lines. To facilitate communication between the sides of the conflict, a discussion group of older people and teenagers was gathered and divided into pairs with one older person and one teen in each pair. The task of each pair was to explain to each other what they preferred in worship—what songs, especially—and why. After hearing each other out, they were to repeat back to each other what they had heard. So the teenagers had to say to their elders what the elders preferred in worship and why, and the elders had to do likewise for the teenagers. Through the conversations and the listening and echoing back, and in learning why the "other side" had its preferences, the two groups came to better understand and appreciate each other. As a result, they also became more tolerant in worship when songs of the other generation were used, not just because they knew who liked it, but because in light of their growing relationships, they too began to appreciate the others' choices and learned to worship more fully through them. The point is that individuals and congregations need to appreciate one another and be willing to talk together to understand each other's preferences and to appreciate the deeper issues of what worship and fellowship are all about.

Confession

Part of the process of learning to appreciate one another's preferences and being able to worship along with them is to mend fences—to

confess and forgive any offense that may have been given in the
buildup of the conflict. Rienstra points out that worship is also the
place to get that right:

> Worship has taught me how to say "I'm sorry." It's taught me the
> posture of getting down on my knees: we don't do that literally
> in my particular worship tradition, unfortunately, but we do it in
> spirit. In worship we should be able to face the truth of our fail-
> ures, both as individuals and as congregations, denominations,
> nations, racial groups and so on. We ought to learn to recognize
> what we have done wrong, to speak the "I'm sorry" and taste
> the forgiveness that enables us to move on. In doing this we be-
> gin to trace a kind of penitential parabola—down and up, dying
> and rising, that fundamental rhythm of the Christian life. "I'm
> sorry" can also be about compassion. We can learn to say "I'm
> sorry" as a lament emerging from our own suffering and to kneel
> down in solidarity with the suffering of others.[22]

That "solidarity" is what can become stronger in a congregation that has endured and survived a conflict. When members of
God's family care enough about each other and about God to work
through a conflict rather than let it fester or fade, that congregation
is already on the way to health and strength. In worship they remember that even as God is willing to forgive them their trespasses,
so they must also be willing to forgive the trespasses of those who
sin against them. Only then will they begin to feel "one" again.

So when it comes to the liturgy, it is crucial for the matter of
confession to be addressed carefully. Worship planners will wonder, "When do we address it? How? Is it possible to do it wrong
and cause more trouble? What is appropriate? What isn't? What
Scripture passages are instructive and helpful?" The answers to
these questions depend on the context of the church and the unique
situation it is facing.

The main thing for worship planners to remember is that confession in worship must be honest, not forced. They don't want
to create hypocrites by requiring people to say words that they
don't feel or believe. Even as pastors and worship leaders offer
prayers of confession, they can acknowledge that perhaps not all

parishioners will be able to fully embrace that confession. It may be helpful to point out to the worshipers that they usually pray in words that express *what they believe,* but sometimes they say words in prayer *in order to believe them.* Just as in a time of crisis they may confess that "God is our refuge and strength, a very present help in trouble," even when that help seems far away, still, they say it again in order to believe it—to reinforce their belief during a time when it is being shaken. In a time of conflict they may offer a prayer of confession *in order to* believe it—both confessing their sin and receiving God's pardon as a way of reinforcing their belief in a forgiving God.

If leaders are concerned that the congregation's confession be authentic and not hypocritical, they may find comfort in knowing that they aren't the first to wonder about this question. Cornelius Plantinga, Jr., writes that "in part, the Reformation grew right out of that very question." Martin Luther began to worry about the possibility that he might be a hypocrite, wondering, "How do I know that my confession of sin is sincere? How do I know my heart is really contrite? . . . What if I'm deceiving myself?" Plantinga concludes that, as Luther learned, believers need to trust in the grace of God. "There are lots of reasons why we need the grace of God. One of them is that we don't even know how sincere we are. We don't know how divided or deceived we are. We don't know each other's hearts, and we don't even know the maze in our own hearts." But "what makes God's grace so amazing is that it comes not just for the proud and the envious and the angry, but also for us hypocrites."[23]

So even in conflicted congregations, confession is appropriate for all, no matter whether they see their need for it. And even as people are given space to offer confession in their own way and at their own pace, by the use of times of silence or voluntary prayers, leaders must challenge them to be open and to seek reconciliation with one another, even as God offers forgiveness and reconciliation to them. Tom Long puts it this way:

> Confession of sin in worship takes place within the context of a merciful relationship with God. . . . Confession of sin happens not in fear but in trust, and its purpose is not punishment

but self-awareness, deep and honest relationship, and healing forgiveness. For every word of confession in worship, there is an assurance of pardon. For every honest admission of warfare against God, neighbor and self, there is the announcement that "the peace of the Lord Jesus Christ be with you."[24]

The peace that comes from Christ is extended beyond worship into the lives of the congregation. Confession expressed to God in worship should lead to confession to one another as well and, one hopes, to mitigating the effects of the conflict.

Forgiveness and Reconciliation

Once leaders have initiated the process of confession in the congregation, they must also recognize that while forgiveness is granted in worship in the words of absolution or assurance of pardon, the process is not necessarily over for those individuals and groups in conflict. Congregations tend to forgive too soon, and then, thinking they have dealt with the issue, lose the openness to continue to learn through the process. In worship they can learn that confession and forgiveness are needed all the time—and every Sunday—all part of a long process of becoming more loving of one another and of Christ.

Forgiveness takes time and should not be rushed. Former Fuller Theological Seminary professor Lewis Smedes has helped many to understand the dangers of superficial, too-fast forgiveness: "We will not take healing action against unfair pain until we own the pain we want to heal. It is not enough to feel pain. We need to appropriate the pain we feel: Be conscious of it, take it on, and take it as our own. . . . I worry about fast forgivers. They tend to forgive quickly in order to avoid their pain."[25] They may find that they didn't really forgive in their hurry to feel better about things. Then they can be sure that the old issues will surface again—as if asking to be dealt with.

Sometimes congregations will also forgive too quickly to avoid the pain of the conflict—whether the object of their forgiveness is a pastor who fell into misconduct, a member who caused great dissension among them or defrauded them in some way, or factions that have caused hurt through gossip and backbiting. Either they cannot forgive the hurts they have had to endure, or they cannot admit to their part in the problem, and have deceived themselves into thinking they or their leaders are innocent. Worship planners and pastors can design services and prayers that will gently nudge all toward the realization that no one is without fault and that all need to take responsibility for the pain they feel and the pain they have caused. Only then can they move toward forgiveness and reconciliation.

Steven Chase, professor of Christian spirituality at Western Theological Seminary, points out:

> Forgiveness and reconciliation are crucial to the maintenance of relationship. Forgiveness and reconciliation do not simply cover or push aside the pain, loss, and grief we inflict on others or ourselves. In fact, the opposite is the case. To forgive is to shine a light on our participation in and personal responsibility for brokenness and hurt. It means that we confess our participation, whether alone or with others, ask for pardon, and work toward reconciliation. Relationship sustained through forgiveness and reconciliation in prayer is thus a four-step process: (1) finding those places in our life where we have participated in breaking rather than mending relationship, (2) acknowledging and confessing our participation, (3) actively seeking and asking for forgiveness and (4) working toward true reconciliation.[26]

These four steps provide a fitting approach toward healing a congregational conflict, whether they occur in an intervention of some sort, or as a frame for worship. Pastors and worship leaders could guide a congregation through these steps in prayer in one service, or in a series of services. They could choose a series of psalms or other Scripture texts that highlight these four themes, and allow times of silence in between the readings, or they could plan entire services based on those texts. The context of worship and the transforming power of prayer will remind parishioners that forgiveness and reconciliation for each person and for the whole community are possible because of God's commands and promises in Scripture. As Chase reminds us:

> The pattern of transformation in prayer is often a loop between personal, transforming experience and living out that experience in community. But transformation can also move in the opposite direction. Common prayer, liturgy, and witness can transform personal lives. Both directions within this pattern are essential for living out the Christian call to service and transformative living. Individuals express their experiences of transformation by writing a memoir, preaching a sermon, or engaging in acts of kindness, compassion, or hospitality. Communities express their experience of transformation often by communal action or communal witness. Thus, it is important to highlight the role of liturgical or common prayer in transformation.[27]

Congregational leaders need also to be realistic about the time moving toward true reconciliation will take. It will not happen overnight, and may take many weeks or months; in some cases, it may not come at all. It is one thing to forgive—individuals or groups on different sides of a conflict can do that alone. But reconciliation requires the other sides to acknowledge and receive that apology. All parties need to participate genuinely if reconciliation is to happen.

In *Moving Your Church through Conflict,* Speed Leas tells how his mother used to force him to make up with his brother after an argument. He did as he was told but did not experience genuine reconciliation. Reflecting on that experience, he writes:

> In human terms reconciliation is not something we can make, something we can do, something we can create, like a milkshake, if we only have the right ingredients. We can do all in our power to create an environment in which the possibilities of reconciliation are increased, but human beings don't know how to "force" or mandate it. . . . Thus, our "work" in conflict management cannot be the creating of reconciliation. That is God's work. Our aim, rather, is to help one another to be faithful, to seek to create environments in which the possibilities of reconciliation are

increased. We are to invite others into new relationships and to invite ourselves into those new relationships—not to force them. Forced, renewed relationships are not a gift. Forced, they are our will imposed on others (including God); invited and accepted, renewed relationships take on the character of grace.[28]

That grace is the best focus of worship in times of conflict.

A special focus on confession, reconciliation, and healing might be scheduled for a separate service, so that people can choose whether to participate. The timing of such a service or any special focus on these issues should be carefully planned. It probably wouldn't work immediately after an extremely contentious congregational meeting, for instance. It should be held after the congregation has had an opportunity to learn about their situation and to take steps toward resolving it.

One example of such a service comes from Blackburn's *Mediation Skills Training Institute* and is included here as a model.

Service of Healing and Reconciliation

Call to Worship

Leader:	Bless the Lord, O my soul; and all that is within me, bless God's holy name!
People:	**Bless the Lord, O my soul, and forget not all God's benefits,**
Leader:	Who forgives all your iniquity, who heals all your diseases,
People:	**Who redeems your life from the grave, who crowns you with steadfast love and mercy,**
Leader:	Who satisfies you with good as long as you live,
People:	**So that your youth is renewed like the eagle's.**

Invocation

Hymn: "The Church's One Foundation"

Scripture Reading: Luke 15:1–2, 11–32

Meditation: "The Ministry of Reconciliation: Reflections on Rembrandt's *Return of the Prodigal Son*"

Statements of Gratitude and Affirmation

Prayer of Thanksgiving

All: **We thank you, O Lord,**
for all the ways you have blessed us here
at Second Faithful Church.
You have given us gifted leaders;
You have blessed us with a community of faith;
You have endowed our lives with goodness;
You have given us the Holy Scriptures.
But most of all,
you have given us the gift of your Son Jesus Christ
and the healing power of your Holy Spirit.
For all these blessings and more,
we praise and thank you.
Through Jesus Christ we pray, Amen.

Statements of Regret and Confession

Prayer of Confession

Leader: If we claim that we have no sin,
we deceive ourselves, and the truth is not in us.

People: **But if we confess our sins,**
God who is faithful and just
will forgive our sins
and cleanse us from all unrighteousness.

Leader: In silence, let us confess our sins against God
and our neighbor.

Moments of Silence

People: **Merciful God, Father of our Lord Jesus Christ;**
maker of all things; judge of all persons:
we acknowledge the many sins and failures

that we have committed
by thought, word, and action
against each other and against you.
We earnestly repent.
We are deeply sorry for our damaging words
and our destructive behaviors.
In your mercy forgive what we have been,
help us to amend what we are,
and direct what we shall be,
so that we may delight in your will
and walk in your ways, giving you the glory. Amen.

Leader: Hear the good news!
           The saying is sure and worthy of full acceptance,
           that Christ Jesus came into the world to save sinners.
           He himself bore our sins in his body on the cross,
           that we might be dead to sin
           and be alive to all that is good.
           In the name of Jesus Christ,
           embrace God's forgiveness and peace.

Holy Communion

Hymn: "Blest Be the Tie That Binds"

Closing Prayer

Benediction

Richard Blackburn, *Mediation Skills Training Institute*, F-23–24. Copyright © Lombard Mennonite Peace Center, 2004. Used by permission. www.LMPeaceCenter.org.

Liturgical Resources

While each congregational context is different and each conflict situation will have its own idiosyncrasies, some suggestions follow that may help worship planners to design services that are fitting for times of conflict. As they plan, they should consider how worship could either precede or follow some congregational conversations that address the conflictual situation. The services could lay the groundwork for those events, or provide a ritual for gathering up the feelings and thoughts expressed in such conversations.

Some denominations have service books that contain liturgies for various occasional services—including liturgies of services for individual and corporate confession. Some of these services would work well exactly as they are published; others may need some modification for the particular situation. Other helps can be found in journals and on Web sites, or in resources such as *The Worship Sourcebook,* which offers a variety of ideas for every part of the liturgy, and does so in a way that will fit in many traditions.

In planning services for congregations that have experienced conflict, it will be good to remember the need to focus on grace. As Willimon notes, "Many worship services are heavy on the penitence and humility and light on grace and affirmation."[29] While both emphases are important in times of conflict, the balance should be tipped toward an awareness of God's grace. The goal will be to name the conflict without trying to resolve it, and to look for the direction the congregation can move in Christ.

Gathering or Opening Prayers

> God of Peace, we come to you
> recognizing that the people whom you love
> have not always been faithful to you.
> In the wilderness,
> in foreign cities,
> in Jerusalem, and the Promised Land:
> it has always been difficult for your people
> to live in peace with one another
> Yet, your will for us is the peace that passes all understanding,
> the peace that only you can give.
> Be with us now.
> Help us hear your voice,
> and feel your peace in our time and place. Amen.

Betty Lynn Schwab, in *Celebrate God's Presence: A Book of Services for The United Church of Canada,* 672. Used by permission.

The Prayer of St. Francis of Assisi
Lord, make us instruments of thy peace.
Where there is hatred, let us sow love;
where there is injury, pardon;
where there is doubt, faith;
where there is despair, hope;
where there is darkness, light;
where there is sadness, joy;
for thy mercy and for thy truth's sake.
Amen.

Prayers of Confession

Because confession is so important in a time of conflict, a number
of sample prayers of confession are included here.

Dear friends, let us love one another,
because love comes from God.
Whoever loves is a child of God and knows God.
Jesus Christ, life of the world and of all creation,
forgive our separation and grant us peace and unity.
The peace that Christ gives is to guide us in the decisions we make,
for it is to this peace that God has called us together into one body.
Jesus Christ, life of the world and of all creation,
forgive our separation and grant us peace and unity.
With his own body he broke down the walls of separation.
By his death on the cross Christ destroyed our divisions.
Jesus Christ, life of the world and of all creation,
forgive our separation and grant us peace and unity.

> Based on Ephesians 2:14–22; 4:3–6; Colossians 3:15; 1 John 4:7,
> World Council of Churches Assembly Worship Committee, in
> *Jesus Christ—the Life of the World: A Worship Book for the*
> *Sixth Assembly of the World Council of Churches,* 64, alt. ©
> 1983, World Council of Churches.

O God, your will is that
all your children should be one in Christ.
We pray for the unity of your church.

Pardon all our pride and our lack of faith,
of understanding and of charity,
which are the causes of our divisions.
Deliver us from our narrow-mindedness,
from our bitterness, from our prejudices.
Save us from considering as normal
that which is a scandal to the world
and an offense to your love.
Teach us to recognize the gifts of grace
among all who call upon you
and confess faith in Jesus Christ, our Lord. Amen.

> French Reformed Church liturgy, in *The Complete Book of
> Christian Prayer,* 440, alt. © 2000 The Continuum International
> Publishing Group. Reprinted with the permission of the pub-
> lisher, The Continuum International Publishing Group.

Loving God,
in your compassion forgive our sins,
both known and unknown, things done and left undone,
[*especially those we name silently now...*].
Forgive us.
Uphold us by your Spirit that we may truly live in your presence,
walking closer with you
and in deeper harmony with one another. Amen.

> Adapted from page 168 of *The Book of Alternative Services,*
> copyright © 1985 by the General Synod of the Anglican Church
> of Canada; published by ABC Publishing (Anglican Book Cen-
> tre); used with permission.

Followed by:

Declaration of Hope
Do you believe that God is willing to forgive our sins?
We do.
Do you resolve to forgive those who have offended and hurt
you?
We do.

Do you resolve to seek the forgiveness of those you have hurt or
    offended?
We do.
Do you resolve to keep yourself open to the Holy Spirit, so that
    you may resist what is wrong and do what is good?
We do.

Book of Worship, United Church of Christ, 676. Adapted with
permission. Copyright © 1986, 2002, United Church of Christ,
Local Church Ministries, Worship and Education Ministry Team,
Cleveland, Ohio. All rights reserved.

A Prayer of Confession for Those Who Have
Reached Agreement after a Serious Conflict
Almighty God, Father of our Lord, Jesus Christ;
maker of all things, judge of all persons:
we acknowledge our many sins and the wickedness which we
    have committed
by thought, word and actions against each other and against you.
We earnestly repent.
We are deeply sorry for our damaging words and our destruc-
    tive behaviors;
the very memory of them causes us much grief.
Have mercy on us, have mercy on us, most merciful Father.
For thy Son, our Lord Jesus Christ's sake, forgive us all that is
    past;
and grant that we may ever hereafter serve thee in newness of
    life and unity,
to the honor and glory of thy name;
through Jesus Christ our Lord. Amen.

Norman Shawchuck, *How to Manage Conflict in the Church:
Conflict Interventions and Resources,* 44. Copyright © 1983,
Spiritual Growth Resources. Used by permission. Call 800-359-
7363 for further information.

O gracious and gentle and condescending God,
God of peace, Father of mercy, God of all comfort:
we confess before you the evil of our hearts;

we acknowledge that we are too inclined
toward anger, jealousy, and revenge,
to ambition and pride,
which often give rise to discord and bitter feelings
between others and us.
Too often have we thus both offended and grieved you,
O long-suffering Father.
Forgive us this sin and permit us to partake of the blessing
you have promised the peacemakers,
who shall be called the children of God.
Through Jesus Christ, our Lord. *Amen.*

> Johann Arndt, in *The Complete Book of Christian Prayer*, 246,
> alt. © 2000 The Continuum International Publishing Group.
> Reprinted with the permission of the publisher, the Continuum
> International Publishing Group.

Gracious God,
you have called us to be a new community in Christ,
and yet we remain divided.
Forgive us our fear, anxiety, prejudice, and misunderstandings.
Strengthen our common bonds and deepen our resolve
to promote the unity of your church. Amen.

> Janet Crawford, in *Celebrating Community: Prayers and Songs
> of Unity*, 24.

Forgive us the sins of disunity, O Lord:
pride and jealousy and narrow-mindedness.
Forgive us the sins of false unity:
lack of imagination, apathy, and indifference.
Make us one in genuine love and mutual trust.
Make us many in gifts and talents and vision. Amen.

> Simon H. Baynes, in *Prayer for Today's Church*, ed. Dick Wil-
> liams, 88, alt. Copyright © 1972, R. H. L. Williams. Used by
> permission of Falcon Press c/o Christian Pastoral Aid Society.

Assurances of Pardon

You are a chosen race, a royal priesthood, a holy nation, God's own people, in order that you may proclaim the mighty acts of him who called you out of darkness into his marvelous light. Once you were not a people, but now you are God's people; once you had not received mercy, but now you have received mercy. People of God, all of us together have received God's mercy in Christ.

In Christ we are forgiven, redeemed,
and made to be a community united in faith.
Thanks be to God.[30]

           —Based on 1 Peter 2:9–10

The LORD works vindication
and justice for all who are oppressed.
He made known his ways to Moses,
his acts to the people of Israel.
The LORD is merciful and gracious,
slow to anger and abounding in steadfast love.
He will not always accuse,
nor will he keep his anger forever.
He does not deal with us according to our sins,
nor repay us according to our iniquities.
For as the heavens are high above the earth,
so great is his steadfast love toward those who fear him;
as far as the east is from the west,
so far he removes our transgressions from us.
As a father has compassion for his children,
so the LORD has compassion for those who fear him.
For he knows how we were made;
he remembers that we are dust.
As for mortals, their days are like grass;
they flourish like a flower of the field;
for the wind passes over it, and it is gone,
and its place knows it no more.

But the steadfast love of the LORD is from everlasting
to everlasting
on those who fear him,
and his righteousness to children's children,
to those who keep his covenant
and remember to do his commandments.

—Psalm 103:6–18[31]

In some traditions the passing of the peace follows the assurance of pardon. In conflicted congregations this practice reinforces the fact that the peace of Christ is available to all and extended to all through one another. So the ritual of repeating "The peace of Christ be with you," and hearing the reply, "And also with you," is a good way of remembering the source of true peace even as parishioners attempt to reach out to one another with that peace.

Creeds

Many Christian traditions have creeds and confessional statements of what they believe. Reciting a creed or confession will remind the worshipers of what they have in common, and will point them to the God whose tent is big enough for all of them to live together. Some denominations have updated confessional statements, such as the *Contemporary Testimony* of the Christian Reformed Church mentioned above. These declarations of belief can be used effectively as unison readings in times of conflict.

Baptism

When a congregation has gone through a conflict, or as it is moving out of a conflict, leaders may want to hold a "Remembrance of Baptism Service," such as the one found in *Sing! A New Creation*, as a way of recalling their dying and rising in Christ, as well as the affirmation of membership in the body of Christ.[32] A baptismal remembrance service could be introduced with the following prayer:

Brothers and sisters in Christ,
we worship today in the context of a very significant event
in the life of our congregation:
[*explanation, as appropriate, of circumstances*].
At this important time, we need to claim again God's promises
        to us.
We need to recommit ourselves to service in Christ.
We need to place our only hope and trust in God
and pray for the work of God's Spirit in our midst.
Baptism is a sign of God's faithful covenant promises,
under which we live as a congregation each day.
Let us remember now our baptism and be thankful.

> *The Worship Sourcebook,* 289–290. Used by permission.

The words of Scripture could also serve as a prayer to remember
the unity that is evident in baptism:

There is one body and one Spirit,
just as you were called to the one hope of your calling,
one Lord, one faith, one baptism,
one God and Father of all,
who is above all and through all and in all.
                                        —Ephesians 4:4–6

Scripture Themes and Texts

A number of biblical themes and passages are appropriate for use
in times of conflict. Perhaps the most often suggested are from the
gospel of Matthew. The fifth chapter includes the passages about
turning the other cheek and loving your enemies, and the 18th
chapter speaks of going to those who sin against you and, if they
won't listen, taking the issue to the church. Interestingly, it is in
the context of Matthew's discussion of conflict between believers
and questions about how many times they should forgive one another that this well-known verse occurs: "For where two or three
are gathered in my name, I am there among them" (Matt. 18:20).

Christ's promise is that he will be present with his people, even when they are in conflict.

Mennonite pastor and professor Arthur Paul Boers gives the following list of texts for times of congregational conflict in his book *Never Call Them Jerks: Healthy Responses to Difficult Behavior:*

- Accept conflict: Romans 14:1–8, 10–12, 17–19, 15:1–7.
- Affirm hope: Ephesians 4:15–16.
- Commit to prayer: James 5:16.
- Go to the other: Matthew 5:23–24, 18:15–20.
- Restore another in the spirit of humility: Galatians 6:1–5.
- Be quick to listen: James 1:19, Proverbs 18:3.
- Be slow to judge: Romans 2:14, Galatians 5:22–26.
- Be willing to negotiate: Acts 15, Philippians 2:1–11.
- Be steadfast in love: Colossians 3:12–15.
- Be open to mediation: Philippians 4:1–3.
- Trust the community: Acts 15.
- Be the Body of Christ: 1 Corinthians 6:1–6.[33]

Norman Shawchuck points out in *How to Manage Conflict in the Church* that conflict has always been a part of the Christian church, as is apparent in passages like Galatians 2, 1 Corinthians 1, Philippians 3, and Acts 15.[34] Congregations may find themselves in these stories and be able to evaluate their own condition by studying Paul's letters to these churches and the way the council of Jerusalem dealt with conflict in Acts 15. In addition to looking at texts where biblical figures deal with conflict, such as Moses and the prophets and Jesus himself, other texts worship planners may consider are:

- Matthew 22:34–40: The summary of the law of love.
- John 15:12–17: Love one another as I have loved you.
- 1 Corinthians 1:10: Paul's appeal to the Corinthians in Christ's name to agree, to eliminate divisions, and to be of one purpose.
- 2 Corinthians 5:17–20: The ministry of reconciliation.

- Ephesians 4:1–6: Bearing with one another in love, one body and one Spirit, one Lord, one faith, one baptism, one God and Father of all.
- Philippians 2:1–11: Be of the same mind, having the same love; follow Christ's example of emptying himself.
- Colossians 3:12–15: As God's chosen ones, holy and beloved . . . forgive each other; just as the Lord has forgiven you, so you also must forgive.
- Romans 5: While we were yet enemies, God reconciled us.
- Colossians 1: God reconciled all things making peace through the blood of the cross.

Celebrate God's Presence offers several Scripture suggestions under the heading "To Reconcile and Make New":

- Psalm 25: Teach me your ways, O Lord.
- Psalm 90: Have compassion on your servants.
- Isaiah 1:15–18: Make yourselves clean.
- Jeremiah 31:31–34: I will put my law within them.
- Matthew 6:14–15: Forgive and be forgiven.
- Matthew 11:28–30: Come to me all who labor.
- Matthew 22:34–40: Which is the great commandment?
- Romans 6:1–14: Walk in newness of life.
- Colossians 3:1–17: Old life and new.
- 1 John 1:1–2, 5–2:2: When we confess, God is faithful.[35]

Prayers of the People

The model for prayer in times of conflict is our Lord's own prayer in Matthew 6, where he instructs his disciples to pray with these words: "Forgive us our debts, as we also have forgiven our debtors" (Matt. 6:12). Other prayer models follow:

We pray, O Lord, for the church,
which is one in the greatness of your love,
but divided by the littleness of our own.
May we be less occupied with the things that divide us,

and more with those we hold in common
and the love that enfolds us all. **Amen.**

> United Society for the Propagation of the Gospel, *Network*
> (Winter 1978), 14, alt.

Lord, make our hearts places of peace
and our minds harbors of tranquility.
Sow in our souls true love for you and for one another,
and root deeply within us friendship and unity
and concord with reverence.
So may we give peace to each other sincerely
and receive it beautifully. **In Christ, Amen.**

> Native American, in *A Wee Worship Book,* 38, alt. Copyright ©
> 1999, Wild Goose Resource Group, Iona Community, Scotland.
> GIA Publications, Inc., exclusive North American agent, 7404 S.
> Mason Ave., Chicago, IL 60638. www.giamusic.com, 800-442-
> 1358. All rights reserved. Used by permission.

God,
good beyond all that is good,
fair beyond all that is fair,
in you is calmness, peace, and concord.
Heal the dissensions that divide us from one another,
and bring us back to a unity of love
bearing some likeness to your divine nature.
Through the embrace of love
and the bonds of godly affection,
make us one in the Spirit by your peace,
which makes all things peaceful.
We ask this through the grace, mercy, and tenderness
of your Son, Jesus Christ, our Lord. **Amen.**

> Dionysius of Alexandria, in *The Worship Sourcebook,* 737–738.

That we may manifest the unity of the Spirit in the bond of peace
and together confess that there is only one body and one spirit,

one Lord, one faith, one baptism,
let us pray to the Lord:
Lord, have mercy upon us.
That we may soon achieve visible communion in the body of
    Christ
by breaking the bread and blessing the cup around the same
    table,
let us pray to the Lord:
Lord, have mercy upon us.
That having been reconciled to God through Christ
we may be united in one ministry of reconciliation,
let us pray to the Lord:
Lord, have mercy upon us. Amen.

> Based on 2 Corinthians 5:18–19; Ephesians 4:4–6. Eucharistic
> Liturgy of Lima (Geneva, Switzerland: Faith and Order Com-
> mission of the World Council of Churches, 1982).

O God, from you come all good desires and deeds.
We thank you for your loving forgiveness of us,
and for your presence embracing us even when we are unaware.
Give to us, we pray, that peace which only you can give;
help our hearts yearn to forgive others
and to seek their forgiveness of us;
help our hearts yearn to follow all your ways;
and grant that we may live in true peace with you.
In Jesus' name we pray. Amen.

> *Book of Worship, United Church of Christ,* 677. Copyright ©
> 1986, 2002, United Church of Christ, Local Church Ministries,
> Worship and Education Ministry Team, Cleveland, Ohio. All
> rights reserved.

The following prayer in litany form comes from *Soul Pearls:
Worship Resources for the Black Church:*

Leader: As we walk through the valley of the shadow of grief,
    pain, and death, anoint us with your blessedness, that we

might confess, in preparation for seeking and embracing forgiveness.

People: **When we harm others, or when others harm us, help us acknowledge the wrongdoing and forgive ourselves and others for our and their mistakes.**

Leader: Help us not judge others unfairly, so that we will not be judged unjustly by you or by others. Let us live the life of joy and contentment, open to forgiving those who do us harm.

People: **Help us practice the habits of hospitality and kindness. Melt the hatred in our hearts, so that we many know the peace that comes with the sacrament and testament of forgiving others.**

Leader: O God of our salvation, deliver us, and forgive us our sins, trespasses, and debts for the sake of righteousness and for your glory, from everlasting to everlasting.

People: **In the mystery of forgiveness, let us be your light, your vessel, that others may desire to be in relationship with you, coming to know that indefinable, gentle peace.**

> Cheryl A. Kirk-Duggan, *Soul Pearls: Worship Resources for the Black Church*, 137–138. © 2003, Abingdon Press. Used by permission.

Lord's Supper

The Lord's Supper can be an important occasion for confession and reconciliation in the time of conflict. Preparation for communion can be an intentional time of reconciliation for congregations that have experienced conflict. Participation cannot be required—reconciliation cannot be forced before individuals come to the table. The option of not participating must be allowed. However, pastors and worship leaders should acknowledge that all are imperfect and in need of grace and for that reason invited to the table. They should remember, after all, that even Judas was at the table the first time.

The following prayer of response is appropriate after the Lord's Supper is served:

> O Lord, our God, we give you thanks
> for uniting us by baptism in the body of Christ
> and for filling us with joy in the Eucharist.
> Lead us toward the full visible unity of your church,
> and help us to treasure all the signs of reconciliation you have
>   granted us.
> Now that we have tasted the banquet
> you have prepared for us in the world to come,
> may we all one day share together
> the inheritance of the saints in the life of the heavenly city.
> **Through Jesus Christ, our Lord,**
> **who lives and reigns with you in the unity of the Holy Spirit,**
> **ever one God, world without end. Amen.**

> Eucharistic Liturgy of Lima (Geneva: Faith and Order Commission of the World Council of Churches, 1982).

Songs

Although a great variety of songs could be included in a service at a time of conflict, and be more or less fitting for a particular congregation, a few are listed here with full song text as especially helpful examples of treating conflict. Others are simply listed by title, along with the hymnal in which they were found.

Forgive Our Sins as We Forgive

"Forgive our sins as we forgive," you taught us, Lord, to pray.
But you alone can grant us grace to live the words we say.

How can your pardon reach and bless the unforgiving heart
that broods on wrongs and will not let old bitterness depart?

In blazing light your cross reveals the truth we dimly knew—
what trivial debts are owed to us, how great our debt to you.

Lord, cleanse the depths within our souls and bid resentment cease.
Then, bound to all in bonds of love, our lives will spread your peace.

We Are Members of Christ's Body

We are members of Christ's body, joined by faith in unity;
one in calling, joy, and suffering, wholesome in diversity.
We will work with gifts that differ towards the Kingdom's destiny.

Ear and eye to one another, we have need of every part;
hands and feet belong together, guided by a loyal heart;
tendons, bones, and flesh embody what the Spirit's breath imparts.

When one member suffers hardship, we will shoulder all the pain;
when another part is honored, joys throughout the body reign;
for our common love is pulsing towards the growth of Christ's
     domain.

The Servant Song

Will you let me be your servant, let me be as Christ to you?
Pray that I may have the grace to let you be my servant, too.

We are pilgrims on a journey; we are trav'lers on the road.
We are here to help each other walk the mile and bear the load.

I will hold the Christ-light for you in the night-time of your
     fear.
I will hold my hand out to you, speak the peace you long to
     hear.

I will weep when you are weeping; when you laugh, I'll laugh
     with you.
I will share your joy and sorrow till we've seen this journey
     through.

Text: Richard Gillard
Copyright © 1977, *Scripture in Song* (c/o Integrity Music)/ASCAP
c/o Integrity Media, Inc., 100 Cody Road, Mobile, AL 36695.

A wonderful song from the *African American Heritage Hymnal* is titled "Koinonia"—a word that refers to the fellowship and communion enjoyed by believers who love one another "with the love of my Lord."

Koinonia
How can I say that I love the Lord
whom I've never, ever seen before;
and forget to say that I love the one
whom I walk beside each and ev'ry day?
How can I look upon your face and ignore God's love?
You I must embrace!
You're my brother; you're my sister;
and I love you with the love of my Lord.

Text: Attributed to V. Michael McKay

Sing! A New Creation[36]
   59   Perdón, Señor/Forgive Us, Lord
 205   Healer of Our Every Ill

The United Methodist Hymnal[37]
 130   God Will Take Care of You
 560   Help Us Accept Each Other

Glory & Praise[38]
 298   Come to Set Us Free
 453   One Lord
 646   Christians, Let Us Love One Another

Gather Comprehensive[39]
381   Dust and Ashes
644   Within Our Darkest Night
724   We Shall Overcome
737   The Broken Body
879   Forgive Our Sins

Sending

The sending reinforces the themes of the worship service while calling parishioners to continue in those themes as they go out to serve others.

Call to Service/Discipleship
Lead a life worthy of the calling
to which you have been called,
with all humility and gentleness,
with patience, bearing with one another in love,
making every effort to maintain
the unity of the Spirit in the bond of peace.
There is one body and one Spirit,
just as you were called to the one hope of your calling,
one Lord, one faith, one baptism, one God and Father of all,
who is above all and through all and in all.
—Ephesians 4:1–6

Blessing

It will be important to assure the people of God's blessing as they leave the worship service. The following blessing may be a good choice, and could become a regular blessing throughout the difficult time.

And now may the love of God,
the Creator who brings order out of chaos;
and the grace of Jesus Christ, who prays that we may be one;
and the fellowship of the Spirit, who breathes wisdom and peace
    to all,
be with you, now and forever. **Amen.**

Betty Lynn Schwab, in *Celebrate God's Presence: A Book of Services for The United Church of Canada*, 678. Used by permission.

Another blessing appropriate for the close of worship is this benediction prayer:

O righteous One, our strength and shield, cloak us in your bosom of comfort and forgiving love that we may wear life as a loose garment, that we may release the chips off our shoulders. May we come to know you in an intimate way that we might be totally free. God be with you always; go now in peace. **Amen.**

Cheryl A. Kirk-Duggan, *Soul Pearls: Worship Resources for the Black Church*, 138. © 2003 Abingdon Press. Used by permission.

The goal of worship in a time of conflict is for the congregation truly to experience God's blessing in worship and go out of the worship service reminded of God's call to unity and promise to draw them together through the Holy Spirit.

Chapter Seven

Leadership in Difficult Times

Finding the best resources for worship in difficult times—the most fitting passage, the perfect song, the ideal prayer—will not guarantee the best worship service for a difficult time. Nor will it guarantee that worshiping together will help the congregation though the crisis, transition, or conflict. The best-laid plans sometimes go awry. The leaders may have misjudged the condition and attitude of the congregation. The service's effect may be marred by unrelated problems, like technical difficulties, or by individuals whose presence and anxiety spoils the mood for the rest of the worshipers. Or an event outside worship—such as an incident that escalates a conflict or a new crisis episode—may change the tone and the response required from the church.

In spite of all the uncertainties and possibilities for making the difficulty worse rather than better, leadership that is both thoughtful and nimble will help to make good results more likely. Even then, unpredictable circumstances may affect the situation; but part of good leadership is being aware of what is going on in the congregation, and continually adjusting and responding accordingly. This effort will require good *pastoral* leadership in the crisis, transition, or conflict situation—and not just by pastors, but by all leaders involved in a congregation in a difficult time, from governing board members to worship planners to worship leaders. It will also require the humility of remembering that Christ's church will continue in spite of congregational difficulties and no matter what plans leaders make. Leaders must remember that only God can still the storms in our lives and in our congregations. Effective leadership in turbulent times requires confidence in the grace and peace of Christ, the One who had power to still the storm and stir faith in those first disciples on the Sea of Galilee.

Effective Leadership

Good pastoral leadership in difficult times and good processes for healing from a challenging time are more likely to be present when leaders follow the strategies listed below. This chapter will flesh out these approaches in more detail, to show how leaders can respond successfully to the crisis, transition, or conflict the congregation is facing.

- Know yourself.

    — Understand your predisposition for reactivity.
    — Manage your own anxiety.

- Know the congregation.

    — Pay attention to resistance and anxious congregational reactions.
    — Learn the congregation's history of dealing with difficulty.

- Communicate clearly and appropriately.

    — Use a calm and assuring tone and choose words carefully.
    — Give information as needed without betraying confidences.

- Practice healthy reciprocal leadership with the following factors:

    — Character
    — Conviction
    — Competencies
    — Confluence

- Expect suffering.

- Stay connected with congregational governing leaders and staff.

Know Yourself

Effective leaders know themselves and are able to manage their own feelings in the midst of a difficult time. Wise leaders understand that there is very little they can actually control. Although they can influence and shape people and situations as much as is possible and appropriate, and though they can anticipate events and people's reactions to those events, still they really can control only themselves. Pastor Jim Herrington and counselor Trisha Taylor encourage leaders to realize this limitation and to make it the focus of their leadership efforts. "Most leadership development processes focus on 'leadership techniques,' to be used by the leader on those being led. . . . We go in another direction: helping you understand that as a leader you are part of a living human system of engagement and relationship, and helping you learn to become aware of these systems and navigate them wisely. We offer a focus on managing yourself rather than managing others."[1] In that process of self-management, leaders must take care of themselves, making sure to take time—even in the heat of crisis—to pray and reflect on the situation.

To be effective, leaders must understand their own reactions to difficulty and the reasons behind them. Either alone or in a seminar or group, leaders should explore their own personality traits and tendencies shaped by their upbringing and experiences, and ask questions like these:

- What was my family of origin like, and how did that shape my responses to crisis and conflict?
- How do I handle anxiety? Does it make me nervous or angry or afraid?
- What is my approach to authority, and how do I prefer to develop it and exercise it?
- Do I prefer to work collaboratively or individually? How will that affect my ability to work with others in difficult times?
- At what pace do I tend to work? Am I inclined to procrastinate and need to learn to work ahead, or do I tend

to rush to resolve issues and projects and need to hesitate long enough to allow the process to take its own shape?

When leaders are aware of their own tendencies, they are much more likely to manage the anxiety that accompanies difficult times. And if they are able to manage their own anxiety, and at least be less anxious than others in the situation, their example will influence the entire congregational system. Being less anxious will not be easy; pressures will come from all sides. Some will be legitimate calls to act: to respond to pastoral-care needs of parishioners, to make sure the worship services are planned and the staff and volunteers involved are prepared for their roles, and to address questions that come from within the congregation and from the community, perhaps even the public media. Leaders who understand their own typical reactions are more likely to control them and be able to respond carefully and with discernment.

Leaders may find managing their own anxiety especially challenging when the difficulty affects them personally. Leaders may find themselves grieving a loss as others in the congregation do, but still bear the responsibility to lead. Carol Norén tells leaders that "your authenticity in grief, however you express it, gives your people permission to be equally genuine in their times of sorrow."[2] Even as leaders deal with their own grief, parishioners will want—even demand—the leader's time and attention, so it will take much strength to preserve the solitude the leader needs to manage the situation in as nonanxious a fashion as possible. Norén points out the need for leaders to get away from the crowds, as Jesus did, in part to deal with their own grief.

> The need for downtime and spiritual recharging are part of God's design for human beings. There will always be people and projects clamoring for our attention, but we will serve our Lord best when we keep Sabbath time to be renewed by his Spirit, particularly in times of great stress and change. Personal bereavement is one of those times. Grief cannot be rushed. Part of faithful ministry is equipping others to step in and take leadership when we cannot and should not try.[3]

Leaders may need to get physical distance from the situation and rely on colleagues to fill in for some of their duties. Some leaders have their own retreats or places they like to go to get away and be alone to think and pray. Jesus certainly set an example for withdrawing from the crowds when situations became tense—going up into the mountains or down into the stern of a boat. He drew on the strength of God to renew his ability to manage the conflicts he faced.

Mennonite pastor and professor Arthur Paul Boers recognizes the need to get away; he writes about Jesus's example on the Sea of Galilee:

> Our fears and anxieties often compel us in unhelpful directions. I see this tendency in the curious story of Jesus stilling the storm (Mark 4:35–41). Jesus, you may recall, was sleeping in the stern of the boat when a storm arose and almost swamped the craft. Not surprisingly, the disciples were terrified and thought they were about to perish. In great desperation they awoke Jesus. "Why are you afraid?" Jesus asked.
>
> Metropolitan Anthony, Eastern Orthodox churchman and scholar, has an interesting take on this story. He believes that the disciples' desperate question to Jesus—"Teacher, do you not care that we are perishing?"—was not just a cry for help. First of all, they want him to share their suffering. They want him to be as anxious as they are. They think he will not help them unless he shares their anxiety. While Jesus does in fact help them, he shares neither their anxiety nor their panic. He remains serene and centered. He solves the problem by throwing his own serenity onto the storm: "Peace! Be still."[4]

While Jesus didn't use this tactic in every situation—there were other circumstances that called for raising people's anxiety, such as with the money-changers in the temple—this is a good example of how leaders can remain calm and differentiated from the anxiety of other people in crisis situations. They may not be as perfect as Jesus in discerning when to calm and when to agitate, but they certainly can call on him for help in stormy times. Like the disciples, congregations will pressure leaders to solve their problems and relieve the anxiety they all face in light of the difficulty. But, as noted in chapter 2, wise leaders will resist the pressure to provide a quick fix and will hold out for others to share both the tension of the situation and the opportunity to learn from it.

Family therapist and rabbi Edwin Friedman, expert in applying family systems theory to congregations and leaders, encourages leaders to let go of control. They don't need to know in advance what the results will be, but must "listen to responses, learn, and then move forward." According to Friedman, "leading is less knowing where you're going and more knowing where you are."[5] Leaders who understand themselves and the situation they're in are most likely to weather the storm of a turbulent congregational situation. A self-differentiated leader will be able to give the anxiety back to its rightful owners, helping them to learn and grow as they sort out the difficulty themselves.

Leaders usually assume that they can be most helpful if they empathize with people. Friedman calls that a fallacy and places limits on empathy. He warns against leaders being influenced by the most dependent and anxious parishioners, so that the "energy of the leader is oriented toward weakness, not strength." He advises, "Don't let people invade you. Leaders better serve when they are not overly influenced by the complaints of a group. They help people by setting limits to their invasiveness. . . . The best way to set limits on bad behavior is self-regulation, not chasing after togetherness with trouble makers."[6] Following this counsel will require courage and confidence of leaders. To add to Friedman's advice, good leadership may depend less on knowing where you're going and more on knowing who you are.

Know the Congregation

While knowing yourself is of ultimate importance in difficult leadership situations, knowing the congregation is also extremely important. Leaders can learn much about how congregations will likely respond to such situations by studying resources such as those mentioned in chapter 2. Attending conferences or workshops on these topics can be helpful as well. Joining or organizing a peer learning group with other leaders and pastors may also help leaders apply learning from books and seminars to their own congregations.

In difficult times, leaders have to deal with difficult people, and most congregations have a few of them. One key piece of advice to leaders from those who understand congregational systems is to keep the opposition close—but doing so is not easy. As Ronald Heifetz puts it, "You appear dangerous to people when you question their values, beliefs, and habits of a lifetime. You place yourself on the line when you tell people what they need to hear rather than what they want to hear. Although you may see with clarity and passion a promising future of progress and gain, people will see with equal passion the losses you ask them to sustain."[7] Part of knowing your congregation is being aware of the tension building as you raise the temperature of the situation. You also need to anticipate the reaction of the congregation to avoid getting burned by the steam!

Still, pastoral leaders must love these people—the "rabble" to which Craig Barnes refers in chapter 5. This is a biblical attitude—to love your enemies—but it is difficult to accomplish. That is why differentiation and calm in the face of opposition are crucial for leaders to survive. Those who don't understand this important concept are the most susceptible to being blindsided by the resistance, and hurt in perhaps unrecoverable ways. Or, they may be more likely to make mistakes and worsen the difficulty instead of bringing healing.

Willimon reminds us that signs of resistance in the congregation may actually be good signs. He notes that, just as "'Where there's smoke, there's fire'; where there is resistance, there is sure to be anxiety arising from some inner conflict."[8] Pastoral leaders need to watch for signs of resistance in the congregation and to view it as data about the anxiety level of the congregation. Once leaders are aware of the resistance, they must remember, as Willimon declares in relation to worship issues, that the

resistance is not about you, it's about them—it's not about pastoral failure; it may be about pastoral success! In fact, instead of
trying to mitigate the resistance by either changing the worship
to please the people or trying to change the people to understand
about worship, it may be healthier to *express* the resistance in
worship. When we prematurely reject the people's response, we
cut off the possibilities for meaning in this situation and cut off
the people themselves.[9]

One way to validate the resistance of the congregation as a
healthy sign would be to allow congregants to bring their emotions before God in worship, helping them to express their concerns and frustrations through prayer and the Psalms.

Too often pastors and leaders take the resistance personally,
when it really isn't their problem. As mentioned in chapter 3, Heifetz points out that football players don't chase and tackle the quarterback because they dislike him or are upset with him. They do it
because he has the football![10] Worship leaders need to remember
that because of their visible role in the church in a time of conflict,
they will receive some resistance simply because they are, in effect,
carrying the ball.

How does resistance show itself in worship? One Protestant
church member registered his distaste for the growing liturgical
emphasis in his congregation by focusing on the pastor's clothing.
He objected to the change from a normal business suit to a cleri-
cal collar, and therefore refused to look up and make eye contact
with the pastor during the worship service, even though he continued to attend church regularly. His behavior drew attention to the
problem and raised anxiety in the system for a time, but gradually
the resistance dissipated because the pastor and the congregation
did not allow his behavior to control their responses. They simply
went on with their plans. They weren't going to let one person's
issue bother the whole congregation, and the pastor accepted the
fact that he was simply the target for this man's anxiety about
the transition happening in the congregation. He was carrying
the football. One important way to know your congregation is to
recognize resistance, whether it shows up in worship or in other

aspects of the church's ministry, and to realize why it is being di-
rected toward you at this time.

One other key to knowing the congregation is for leaders to
investigate the history of their church's way of dealing with difficulties, and to learn which members have been most reactive in
the past and are most likely to cause trouble in the future. The
pastor who was criticized for changing his attire discovered that
the objector had transferred from a church embroiled in a serious
conflict that resulted in the release of the minister and the resignation of church officers. The new member brought his anxiety and
objections along to his new congregation and opposed any and all
changes—not just the pastor's collar, on which he was certainly
showing home movies! He opposed the use of a new Bible translation because it was in paperback, as well as a new hymnal version
because it had new songs and liturgical forms. He also objected
to the pastor's new cordless microphone—because he could not
hear as well from it. The pastor visited the cantankerous parishioner but would not cater to his preferences. The only concession
he made concerned the cordless microphone, which had raised a
number of complaints from those who said they could not hear the
sermon well enough. A new gooseneck microphone was installed
in the pulpit and when the people saw it there, they remarked that
they could hear the preacher much better. Little did they know that
the sound technician had never turned it on!

While this incident with what the pastor called "God's peculiar
people" was just one situation, some congregations support a culture of criticism that lives on from generation to generation, and
other congregations simply go through anxious chapters in their
history. Leaders should investigate the history of the congregation
and its predisposition to react to crises, transitions, and conflicts in
inappropriate ways. This can be done by reading old meeting minutes and historical reflections or by talking to long-time members.
Or, as Gil Rendle suggests, a group of church members can create
a timeline of the congregation's history. To deal with the hurts of
the past, they place yellow sticky notes by times of blessing and
blue sticky notes by times of pain. The exercise and the discussions
that surround it will help the leaders understand the congregation

more deeply, and will help the congregation also to see its patterns and perhaps try to change patterns that are not helpful.[11]

Communicate Well

What leaders say in public worship and how they say it will have great influence in a difficult time. Their words are more likely to be remembered because of the heightened awareness of the congregation in this time. Whether or not a leader is the focus of the difficult situation, he or she can be tempted to use the pulpit in destructive ways—by taking sides or making allusions to "problem people." Obviously, such abuse of the pulpit is inappropriate and will not be conducive to the healing of the congregation. The words and tone used in discussing the difficulty will also have a formative effect on the congregation both during the difficult time and long afterward. In public worship, words and tones are extremely important. Tom Long argues that "in the place of worship, we cannot pray or sing faithfully without our words being full of the sorrows and joys of life. Conversely, the words of worship—prayer words, sermon words, hymn words, Bible words, creedal words, words of praise and penitence, protest and pardon—are like stones thrown into the pond; they ripple outward in countless concentric circles, finding ever fresh expression in new places in our lives."[12]

Long also notes the responsibility that leaders have to take great care in choosing their worship words, since they will shape the way the congregation speaks outside of worship as well.

> Christian worship is not only a dialogue, a dramatic conversation, between God and humanity; it is also, as I have been claiming, a kind of dress rehearsal for human speech outside of the sanctuary. To worship is not only to hear and speak truthful and life-changing words inside the sanctuary but also to prepare ourselves for truthful and life-changing speech in the other areas of life. This is why I have called worship God's language school, a place where we are trained to speak in new ways and given the vocabulary to express a new reality.[13]

In worship, therefore, leaders have a great opportunity for modeling the kind of language parishioners should use with one another to explain the difficulty they face and to move toward healing or resolution. In difficult times of transition, even more than usual, worship leaders must be thoughtful, creative, and caring about how they lead people by the words they choose. Even in crisis situations when planning time is short, they must take as much time as possible to think carefully how best to speak to and for the people.

Any announcements or comments about a crisis, transition, or conflict must be thought through carefully before being delivered. Leaders should write out such statements beforehand, since the tension and emotion of the moment may cause them to neglect to say something important, or to communicate something very different from what they intended to say. This reminder applies not only to specific reports about a crisis or transition, but also to all elements of the service and the words between them. Carefully selected transitional phrases in worship can effectively reinforce and communicate the reasons for the selections of songs, readings, and the like. Such phrases should be as concise as possible—just long enough to convey what needs to be communicated.

Knowing what to say and when to say it is just one of the many judgment skills leaders will need in a difficult time, especially when they are on the spot. In *The Spirit of the Disciplines,* Dallas Willard, professor of philosophy at the University of Southern California, explains that leaders cannot prepare for "on the spot" situations when they are on the spot. They have to prepare for them when they are not on the spot—or are "off the spot." He writes that people like *In His Steps* author Charles Sheldon and WWJD ("What Would Jesus Do?") fans make the mistake of assuming that following Jesus "simply means to try to behave as he did when he was 'on the spot,' under pressure or persecution or in the spotlight. There is no realization that what he did in such cases was, in a large and essential measure, the natural outflow of the life he lived when not on the spot." Willard's point for leaders is to "learn from Christ how to live our total lives, how to invest all our time and our energies of mind and body as he did" through the disciplines and habits of the Christian life. Such a life will prepare them for the situations when they are "on the spot."[14]

Practice Reciprocal Leadership

As asserted in previous chapters, good leadership is essential to the process of sustaining a congregation through a difficult time. It will be important for pastors, worship leaders, and worship planners to understand and practice healthy reciprocal leadership, which "is best understood not by focusing upon personality traits in the leader, but upon *the relationship between the leader and those being led.*"[15] According to a study and training tool produced by the Christian Reformed Church in North America, effective congregational leadership can be defined as "the process of helping a congregation embody in its corporate life the practices that shape vital Christian life, community, and witness in ways that are faithful to Jesus Christ and the gospel and appropriate to the particular congregation's setting, resources, and purpose."[16] Worship is one of the key contexts in which this process takes place, making the role of the worship leader extremely important to the process.

According to *Effective Leadership in the Church*, we can expect to see four positive qualities in situations where "effective, reciprocal leadership" is in place. They are called "the four Cs"—"character, conviction, competencies, and confluence."[17] For a full discussion of these qualities see the appendix, which contains that book's chapter 2, "The Shape of Effective Leadership in the Church."

Character

The Christian leader's character is grounded in new life in Jesus Christ—in dying and rising with him. That person's character is also growing as the Holy Spirit produces fruit in him or her. Furthermore, people of character who show "honesty, integrity, compassion, service to others, a life of prayer, and total dependence upon God for strength and guidance" are people others trust.[18]

The reciprocal nature of effective leadership is that character in the leader produces trust in the group, which produces trust in the leader, which produces character in the group. These attributes feed off each other and build each other up. And, as most good leaders know, trust is really the only currency leaders have. Such character and trust are critical to leadership in difficult situations.

Another dimension of character is *emotional intelligence,* which is defined in *Effective Leadership in the Church* as "the ability to manage one's own emotions, motivate oneself, reach out for emotional support in healthy and appropriate ways, recognize emotions in others and respond appropriately, handle relationships, control impulses, demonstrate empathy, listen actively, deal constructively and creatively with conflict, assess one's world in optimistic and hopeful terms, take appropriate risks, patiently persist in the face of anxiety and conflict, and respect differences among people."[19] The various aspects of emotional intelligence, especially being able to manage personal emotions and recognize the emotional atmosphere of the congregation, are essential for planning and leading worship during difficult times. The ability to see beneath the surface of the congregation to the real issues underlying a crisis, transition, or conflict will help pastors and worship leaders to respond meaningfully, both personally and through the services they design.

Conviction

Effective leaders hold certain beliefs deeply and are committed to them; they have strong convictions based on Scripture about what the church should be and do in the practices of worship, fellowship, education, evangelism, and service. With those convictions leaders can foster conversations within the congregation to help them discern where God is leading them, so that the leaders and the followers are jointly discerning the direction they should go. This process of joint discernment is always important but absolutely critical in difficult times. As Anthony Robinson asserts:

> True leadership does not simply influence the community to follow the leader's vision, but also enables the community to face its most critical challenges and to be what God calls and enables it to be. There is too much stress today on the leader as the person

of vision. A vision is not imported from somewhere else, and it is not the idiosyncratic vision of a charismatic woman or man. A vision arises from a careful reading of the context and the work required by God of a particular people with a particular identity."[20]

In a difficult time, discerning the "careful reading of the context and the work required by God" may be the most important task that leaders and congregations do together. Even when anxious and hurting congregations call for strong leadership, good leaders must remember that a joint process of discernment is the best approach, though it takes time that impatient people usually don't want to spend. Such a process definitely takes "strong leadership"; it requires more strength than would be involved in individually casting a vision and trying to impose it on the congregation.

Competencies

The competencies of good leadership can be described as healthy responses to the anxieties of a congregation. Leaders can learn certain skills through training—listening and communication, understanding the congregation as a system, discerning the dynamics of change and levels of conflict, and so forth. When leaders are skilled in these matters, the congregation will benefit and will show healthier responses to the situations it faces. This, then, will benefit the leaders and enhance their competence, which will engender healthier congregational responses—again, a reciprocal process.

In difficult times, leaders will want to supplement their skills by reading about or seeking training in particular areas of ministry. For instance, after a crisis, they may need to increase their understanding of grief and how it affects individuals and communities—with a view to planning more fitting worship services for the congregation. In a transition of location or building, they may want to investigate the impact of space on worshipers and to learn how best to make room for the worship of God. In a conflict, they may want to study typical patterns of conflict in churches or investigate the issue that is the focus of the conflict. Leaders will be motivated to learn because of the circumstances and will find immediate application for their learning. They also should plan for regular learning opportunities to build up their competencies before difficult times come along.

Confluence

Effective leadership happens when there is "a confluence (a convergence, a coming together) of leader, congregation, time, place, ministry opportunity, and resources that is a gift of God's Spirit and that enables a leader and congregation to move forward together in realizing God's purposes."[21] This confluence is important to recognize because every situation is unique, and though the character, convictions, and competencies of leaders may be the same, or may be expanding, the confluence that results is hard to predict. This is where nimble leadership is required—leadership that can quickly adjust and respond to changes in the situation.

Leaders and congregations should find comfort in this reality, knowing that the ultimate flourishing of the congregation is up to God, not them. This knowledge should also produce humility in the leaders when they recognize that many factors were involved in a leadership situation that went well. However, "this reality of confluence cannot be used by leaders as an excuse for passivity."[22] Especially in a difficult time, leaders cannot sit back and expect things to work out if they simply pray for a good confluence. They need to "trust that as they take responsibility for matters of character, convictions, and competence that are within their control, God will work in and through their faithfulness to create this confluence of factors that constitute shalom and blessing."[23]

Expect Suffering

Leaders can enjoy many good things as they lead in good times and bad—the exhilaration of guiding people well, accomplishing tasks and strategies, and fulfilling God's calling in a congregation. But they also are likely to suffer in the process. As Anthony Robinson puts it, "leadership has a cruciform shape."[24] The pain involved in going through a trying time and having to absorb the anxiety of the system can be great. And no matter how differentiated the leader is, the arrows shot by grieving or frustrated parishioners still hurt. One of the realities of leadership is suffering, a truth evident in Scripture. Jesus reflected the suffering servant of Isaiah as he carried out God's plan of redemption. He suffered for articulating his convictions. Often the people projected onto him their frustrations and anger. And he gave his life in the process. Leaders in the church need to understand the sacrificial nature of their work. They need to realize that much will not only go unappreciated, but also may be strongly criticized. Leaders need to develop a thick skin in difficult times. However, they should not become so callous that they cannot feel anymore. Leaders who are out of touch with their congregations can't be hurt by them, but those who love the flock, despite its foibles, are bound to be hurt by it.

"Tall trees get the wind," the saying goes, meaning that the leaders are the ones who really feel the stress of a difficult time. They need to realize that a system will look for a scapegoat when anxiety is high—especially if the system is dysfunctional—and the pastor and other leaders are usually the most likely suspects. As Blackburn puts it, "it's amazing how many churches that crash and burn blame their problems on pilot error!"[25] Leaders need extraordinary strength in difficult times—more than they can produce on their own. They will need the strength that is available only from God in prayer.

Stay Connected

As previous chapters have emphasized, worship services can become a guiding force and a calm island in the storm of conflict or crisis, a place and time in which church members can remember who they are by baptism and find themselves again in the narrative of the gospel. During such a time, careful worship planning becomes more crucial than ever. Not only must services be thoughtfully aware of the delicate situation and the many opinions and questions swirling around, but they must also be designed with the collaboration of the church's governing board or officers. Those who are dealing directly with the conflict, crisis, or transitional situation should be in close contact with those who plan worship services. They should not presume that they can simply take care of business behind the scenes, naively assuming that the difficulty won't affect the worship services. It *will* affect them—one way or another. The challenge is to manage that effect and guide the process in a discerning and healthy way.

Some public acknowledgment of the difficult time will be helpful for a congregation, but it will require great sensitivity and careful planning by the leaders. They may find that simply naming the difficulty will go a long way toward reducing the anxiety in the congregational system. Instead of avoiding the obvious, leaders can help the congregation admit that things are not quite right, not quite the way they're supposed to be. In some difficult situations, this approach may also give congregations permission to admit failure. Amid pressures to be the best church, draw the most people, and have the most inspiring worship services, congregations need to recognize that failures occasionally happen and that challenging times are a normal part of a congregation's life cycle. This attitude may help them to work through the difficulty. In fact, the congregation may also learn that difficult times can be times of great spiritual growth.

Leaders can encourage that growth through collaboration between board members or officers and worship planners. Congregations experiencing difficulty are often characterized by a variety of intense emotions, including an increase in anxiety and a concurrent decrease in creative energy—energy often needed to plan and engage in corporate worship. Leaders should together discuss the impact of the struggle on their congregation and the emotional reactions they have observed to help them plan services that acknowledge the current state of the congregation and work toward decreasing its anxiety level. Sometimes the crisis, transition, or conflict results in a loss of leadership—even a loss of the pastor who is the main worship planner. Other leaders can guide their congregations in these situations by knowing what questions to ask and what aspects of worship are most likely to be affected by the difficulty and the absence of a particular leader.

Stilling the Storm

Leaders of congregations going through difficult times face great opportunities for shaping the congregation by the way they respond to the difficult time, and the way they lead the congregation through it. The process of reciprocal leadership can be very gratifying as trust builds between leaders and followers in the congregation. But leaders must remember that only God can still the storms in our lives and in our congregations. Effective leadership in turbulent times requires confidence in the grace and peace of Christ, the one who had power to still the storm and stir faith in those first disciples on the Sea of Galilee. When tempted to ask God, "Do you not care that we are perishing?" leaders must not be afraid, but be strengthened in their faith by looking to the One the wind and waves obeyed. Then they and their congregations will have the power they need to withstand all storms, whether great or small, as they "grow in the grace and knowledge of our Lord and Savior Jesus Christ. To him be glory both now and forever! Amen." (2 Peter 3:18 [NIV]).

Appendix

The Shape of Effective Leadership in the Church

The following chapter is from *Effective Leadership in the Church,* a publication of the "Sustaining Pastoral Excellence" initiative of the Christian Reformed Church in North America. This training tool is an adaptation of "Leadership: A Working Definition," a paper produced by a cross-agency Leadership Development Team. That team included chairperson and primary author Duane Kelderman (Calvin Theological Seminary), Dan Ackerman (Christian Reformed Home Missions), Richard Hertel (Reformed Bible College), Darlene Meyering (Calvin College), Jim Osterhouse (Christian Reformed Home Missions), Kathy Smith (Calvin Institute of Christian Worship and Calvin Theological Seminary), Norm Thomasma (Christian Reformed Pastor–Church Relations), and Karl Westerhof (Christian Reformed World Relief Committee).

For two years this team worked to arrive at a common understanding of leadership in the church. Their paper was approved by the Ministry Council (MC) of the Christian Reformed Church in North America as "a working statement of MC's understanding of the nature and practice of leadership and a working guide to MC as it implements leadership development initiatives in the denomination." While *Effective Leadership in the Church* was written in the context of one denomination, the principles of this chapter apply to Christian leadership in any congregation or organization. The complete document of *Effective Leadership in the Church* can be downloaded at http://www.crcna.org/site_uploads/uploads/SPE_Effective_Leadership.pdf, including discussion questions and case studies.

The Shape of Effective Leadership in the Church

What does effective leadership look like? How does it work? How do people know whether their congregation is being effectively led? The concept of *reciprocal leadership* helps us to focus on the relationship between follower and leader rather than on certain traits a leader might possess. We can also identify "four Cs"— four factors present in situations where effective leadership is taking place.

What is Christian leadership?

First, a definition:

> Effective Christian leadership is the process of helping a group embody in its corporate life the practices that shape vital Christian life, community, and witness in ways that are faithful to Jesus Christ and the gospel and appropriate to the particular group's setting, resources, and purpose.

The next definition is more specific to leadership in a congregational setting:

> Effective Christian leadership is the process of helping a congregation embody in its corporate life the practices that shape vital Christian life, community, and witness in ways that are faithful to Jesus Christ and the gospel and appropriate to the particular congregation's setting, resources, and purpose.

The church has many leaders

It's important to clarify that the above definitions do not limit the function of leadership to particular individuals or offices. The New Testament teaches and the church affirms that "the task of ministry is shared by all and is not limited to a special, professional class. . . . The ministry of the church is Christ's ministry, shared by all who are in Christ" (from conclusions 1 and 2, "Report on Ecclesiastical Office and Ordination," *Acts of Synod 1973*, p. 714). This point bears repeating, given our strong, historically conditioned tendency to associate leadership with the activity of pastors and other officially designated individuals.

The essence *of leadership vs. the* style *of leadership*

It's also important to clarify that the definitions above address the *essence* of leadership, not the various *styles* in which leadership is expressed. In *essence,* Christian leadership is the same in all times and places. It embodies unchanging principles and values, such as servanthood, morality, respect for all people as divine-image bearers, and so on. But the *style* of leadership varies greatly depending upon the individual leader and the situation in which leadership is exercised. A well-developed and mature leader has the capacity to exercise different styles in different situations. A crisis situation may call for an authoritarian style, a decision-making process among peers may call for a consensus-building style, and a learning situation may call for a prophetic style. Leadership styles are neither linear nor hierarchical; they are best understood as options in a repertoire circle where the situation determines which style will best serve.

The biblical concept of "help"

Finally, it's important to clarify the meaning of the word "help" in the definition. If we don't understand the word "help," we may see this definition as an overly weak concept of leadership. In the Old Testament, the Hebrew word most frequently translated "help" usually refers to God. "I lift up my eyes to the hills—from where will my help come? My help comes from the Lord, who made heaven and earth" (Ps. 121:1–2). When leaders "help" people live the Christian life, they are far from weak. They are agents, albeit humble servants, of the triune God; indeed, they are acting like God.

Why is contextualization so important when it comes to leadership?

Effective leadership takes into account the critical role of the *ministry context* in which leadership is exercised. Every ministry context is unique. It has its own particular history, setting, relationships, and culture.

Leadership takes culture seriously

"Culture" here refers to the common ideas, feelings, and values that guide community and personal behavior, that organize and regulate what a particular group thinks, feels, and does about God, the world, and humanity. Culture is that invisible vault where worldviews, presuppositions, and values are generated and stored.

Effective leaders understand that culture operates most powerfully when it is least visible. Consider these two images: First, culture is like the ocean. The power of the ocean is not in the six-foot waves on top of the water; it's in the massive movement of water underneath the wave, a movement that cannot be seen. Second, as one wag has put it, "Culture is like bad breath: you smell it on everyone else before you smell it on yourself." That is, just like people don't smell their own breath, they often don't see their own cultural values at work. Culture operates most powerfully when it is least visible.

For example, it's easy for Dutch people to assume that thriftiness or cleanliness or deferral of gratification or emotional reserve—cultural characteristics often associated with Dutch—are not merely cultural characteristics of one particular cultural group, but are universal traits. It's even more dangerous when people assume that their own cultural characteristics *should be* true of everyone.

The point here is that effective leaders understand that culture, visible or invisible, functions in powerful ways in any group and must be taken into account as leadership decisions are made.

All ministry is cross-cultural

Effective leaders also understand that virtually all ministry is *cross-cultural*. The cross-cultural nature of ministry and the corresponding need for cultural sensitivity in leadership is most obvious when it involves the meeting of meanings between different races, ethnic groups, nations, regions, and socioeconomic classes. But ministry in a highly secular, post-Christian culture makes virtually all North American ministry cross-cultural and *countercultural*—that is, engaged in the meeting of meanings between cultures that have fundamentally different and opposing worldviews, assumptions, and values. For example, exercising leadership in the church in a racially broken society and racially diverse community will require a keen understanding of racial dynamics (cross-cultural), and a radical commitment to the unity and diversity of the body of Jesus (countercultural).

Every congregation is unique

Effective leaders understand how leadership must be contextualized, or shaped in its expression, in each ministry setting. Leadership must look different in one or another ethnic community; it must be exercised differently in one social structure or another; and it must adapt to the various stages in the development of a church. Knowing the times and the culture of a congregation and knowing how to respond appropriately might be called "cultural intelligence" or "contextual intelligence" and is an important mark of an effective leader.

What are the personality traits of an effective leader?

This is a fairly common question, but the wrong one to ask. One of the most interesting shifts in leadership theory in recent years has been away from the notion of a "leadership personality." Peter Drucker, a leading authority on leadership, has pointed out that a single universal "leadership personality" or set of "leadership traits" simply does not exist. Name a leadership trait that seems "absolutely essential" to being an effective leader, and someone else can name ten situations of effective leadership where the leaders don't have those personality traits.

Effective leadership is best understood not by focusing upon personality traits in the leader, but upon *the relationship between the leader and those being led*. Focusing upon the *situation* and the *relationships* shifts the question from "What are the traits of good leaders?" to "What factors are present in situations where effective leadership is taking place?" and "What do relationships look like in situations where effective leadership is taking place?"

What are the positive things we can expect to see in situations where there is effective, reciprocal leadership?

Four factors (the four "Cs") seem ever-present in situations of effective leadership:

1. *Character* in the leader (which generates *trust* on the part of followers).
2. *Conviction* in the leader (which helps the congregation discern its *purpose and vision*).
3. *Competencies* in the leader (which help a congregation function as a *healthy system*—i.e., deal with the normal anxieties and conflicts of communal life in healthy and productive ways).
4. *Confluence* of leader, congregation, time, place, ministry opportunity, and resources that is *a gift of God's Spirit* and that enables a leader and congregation to work joyfully together in realizing God's purposes.

Three important clarifications must be made before expanding upon each of these factors.

First, notice how all four of these factors involve *both leader and congregation, the relationship between them, and the impact they have on one another.* For example, character in a congregation's leaders helps the congregation trust those leaders, which in turn strengthens the character of the congregation, which in turn helps the leaders trust the congregation. Praise God for such an upward spiral of character and trust!

Second, it's important to distinguish between *personality traits* and *character traits.* The focus in these four factors is not on personality—introvert, extrovert, charismatic, quiet—but on the character of the leaders and those being led. Put another way, a church can be healthy with a leader who's an introvert, but not with a leader who is untrustworthy, arrogant, or sexually promiscuous.

Third, these four factors can be applied to diverse cultural situations. Each cultural situation will define these factors according to norms appropriate to that culture. But these four factors reflect certain realities of human behavior and community that are present and must be reckoned with across all cultural differences.

Effective leaders are people of sound character *who generate trust in their followers.*

For Christian leaders and for all Christians, *the foundation of Christian character* is the believer's union with Jesus Christ. In their death with Christ believers die to the old self, are raised to a new life with Christ (Col. 3:1–17), and are clothed with the character of Christ. As the branch receives its life from the vine, so Christians receive their spiritual life from Christ (John 15:1–17). Christ, by his Holy Spirit, produces in the believer the fruit of the Spirit—love, joy, peace, patience, kindness, goodness, faithfulness, gentleness, and self-control. The foundation of character for all Christians is their new life in Jesus Christ, and Christ's life in them.

The character of Christ in the Christian leader should clearly produce certain moral excellencies that are crucial to the leader's effectiveness—honesty, integrity, fairness, compassion, service to others, a life of prayer, and total dependence upon God for strength and guidance. One of the key evidences of such character in leaders is that people *trust* such leaders, and such leaders trust the people they lead.

Another dimension of character is the life experiences that form a leader. *Who a person is* determines *how that person will lead.* A person's character is determined, in part, by the life experiences that form him or her. Growing up during the Depression, losing a parent as a teenager, experiencing the horror of war, having parents who model generosity and service, growing up in two or three very different cultures—all these life experiences are formative of who we are at the deepest levels.

Another dimension of character is an *emotional intelligence* that is consistent with effective leadership. Emotional intelligence is the ability to manage one's own emotions, motivate oneself, reach out for emotional support in healthy and appropriate ways, recognize emotions in others and respond appropriately, handle relationships, control impulses, demonstrate empathy, listen actively, deal constructively and creatively with conflict, assess one's world in optimistic and hopeful terms, take appropriate risks, patiently persist in the face of anxiety and conflict, and respect differences among people. A key element of emotional intelligence as practiced by leaders is the ability to seek input from people at all levels on how they are performing as a leader, to be non-defensive in response to such input, and to appropriately adapt in light of such input. (See an inspiring and illuminating paper by Craig Dykstra entitled "The Significance of Pastoral Ministry and the Idea of the Pastoral Imagination" in which he develops the concept of "pastoral intelligence" and "pastoral imagination." This paper is unpublished but is available upon request to leadership@calvinseminary.edu.)

Effective leaders operate out of strong conviction, *which helps a congregation discern its* purpose and vision.

Effective leaders believe certain things deeply and commit themselves selflessly to realizing certain ends. Some call this one's "vision" or a "preferred future." For Christian leaders, these convictions must be shaped by the biblical vision of the kingdom of God. Effective Christian leaders must be invigorated by a vision of the kingdom God is establishing in the world. These convictions arise out of the leader's relationship with God in Christ and the Holy Spirit, and God's call to follow God in faith and obedience.

For Christian leaders, such conviction has the greatest potential for long-term good when it arises out of a strong vision of the church's mission and a thorough grasp of the biblical, pastoral, and theological contours of the Christian faith and church. This must be combined with an ability to communicate these contours in meaningful and relevant ways through sound preaching and teaching and imaginative pastoral leadership.

The capacity for *reflexive leadership* (Carroll and Roof, *Bridging Divided Worlds,* Jossey-Bass, 2002) is an important dimension of leading with conviction. Reflexive leadership involves, for example, holding in creative tension the positive value of the tradition and the challenges of the present situation. Effective leaders are capable of informing and guiding an ongoing "argument" between competing convictions. At such points conviction requires a deep grounding in and understanding of the faith tradition, as well as a lively imagination and capacity for thinking creatively. Effective Christian leaders think deeply, theologically, integratively, and creatively.

A note about "conviction" and "vision"

Because the word "vision" is easily misunderstood, we use the word "conviction" in the previous paragraphs. For many, "the leader's vision" conjures up images of fumbled, lone-ranger attempts to introduce major changes in a congregation, painful polarization, and destructive conflict often ending in separation from the pastor and mass exodus of members.

Peter Senge (*The Fifth Discipline,* pp. 205–232) prefers the term "visioning" to avoid some of these pitfalls. "Vision," a noun, connotes an answer, a solution to the problem. Congregations usually want, yet resist, pastors who gladly offer their vision for the church. By contrast, "visioning" refers to "a structured conversation of God's people about what they believe God has called them to be and to do." Effective leaders don't impose their vision but enable a process whereby the congregation develops its vision.

On the other hand, leaders who have no strong convictions and corresponding vision are weak and ineffective leaders in congregations that desperately need leadership. It is difficult to overstate this concern. Many CRC congregations are struggling for direction and desperately need wise, strong leadership. Thus it is important to see the overlap of conviction and vision when both are properly understood.

Effective Christian leaders have strong, biblically shaped convictions that issue forth in a biblically shaped vision. They believe certain things deeply. They have dreams and are passionate about what God's church and kingdom ought to look like. They are bold and courageous. Their strength is in the strength of their convictions and their passion to do the right thing. And they are self-sacrificial and give their lives to turning their biblically shaped vision into reality. They're risk takers. But the difference between an effective leader and a martyr is that the effective leader fosters a process whereby *the congregation as a whole* can discern and own where God is leading the congregation.

One test of whether a leader is "imposing a vision" or "leading with conviction" is to ask this question: Is the leader truly open to where a congregational process of discernment might lead, or does the leader already have a predetermined outcome in mind? At the same time, it would be incorrect to conclude from this test that leaders should never have convictions and a vision that propel them in a certain direction. While effective leaders understand the reciprocal nature of leadership (i.e., the influence of leaders and followers upon one another), they also have biblically shaped convictions regarding the church Christ is building, a church that is called to be engaging in its worship, faithful in its teaching, strong and deep in its fellowship, self-sacrificial in its outreach and service. These biblical convictions rightly propel leaders and the community they lead in a certain direction. Effective leaders make good judgments about the best way to set forth those convictions, set direction, and engage the community in achieving its biblical purpose.

But what if the convictions of the leader and the values of the congregation are at such odds with each other that the leader cannot express his or her most basic convictions without confronting and judging the congregation? In most situations, the leader who thinks this way has already guaranteed conflict and failure. By the very question, the leader has set up a win/lose outcome. He or she would do well to take a different approach: Every Christian Reformed pastor and congregation is on record as believing what the Scriptures and the confessions teach. The convictions and values all members of the CRC share in common are unfathomably great in number. The effective leader accentuates and holds up the best of the congregation's beliefs and values, and then, in a loving and safe environment of mutual trust, helps the congregation confront the gap between its own values and current realities. Effective leaders help people come to the point where they judge themselves. And effective leaders are transparent in confronting the gap between their own values and their own lives! Effective leaders stand *with* a congregation in learning, not *over* a congregation in judgment.

Effective leaders have competencies *that help a congregation function as a* healthy system.

Leaving aside the debate as to whether leadership is a matter of natural talent or learned skills, there are clearly competencies that leaders can learn through training. We should not overstate the distinction between character and competence, or between natural talent and learned skills. However, the attributes discussed above in the section on character tend to be more deeply embedded in who a person is, whereas the competencies listed below tend to be skills that can be learned by a wide variety of persons. These skills include

- listening and encouraging skills
- communication skills
- understanding authority, including the differences between formal and informal authority
- understanding the importance of clear structures and practices of accountability
- understanding dynamics and processes of change
- understanding issues involved in cross-cultural ministry
- understanding the dynamics of conflict and how to lead through conflict
- motivating people to perform at their full potential
- building support for and ownership of a process of change
- using win/win problem solving techniques
- understanding the congregation as a system
- understanding the critical nature of *pace* when it comes to change

- understanding the difference between courage and the temptation to martyrdom
- understanding the pitfalls of charisma
- knowing the difference between solving problems and creating opportunities for learning

Congregations with leaders who possess these specific leadership skills are more likely to deal with the normal anxieties and conflicts of communal life in healthy and productive ways.

A related challenge in leadership development is helping *congregations* to be healthier and more effective in their working relationship with congregational leaders. Some of the features of healthy congregations include

- strong commitment to the church's purpose
- healthy practices of communication within the congregation and between congregation and leaders (communication that, among other things, keeps truth and love, accountability and support together in creative tension)
- deep congregational practices of prayer for leaders and the congregation as a whole
- a congregational culture that takes responsibility for its problems and doesn't blame or scapegoat the pastor or other leaders
- the ability to constructively deal with conflict
- leadership decisions guided first of all by the church's purpose, not by a desire to keep peace at all costs

Situations in which there is effective leadership will be marked by a con-fluence of leader, congregation, ministry opportunities, and resources.

Leadership is exercised not in a vacuum, but in a particular time and place, with a particular group of people who have a particular history, by pastors and other leaders in particular points in their life journeys, in a particular cultural and social situation. The best leaders humbly acknowledge that they were "in the right place at the right time"—that a multitude of factors, some of them beyond their direct control, "came together" to produce relationships and events that resulted in great good. The best leaders will not claim that they could go to the next town and produce the same success story all over again. One of the principles that govern leadership is a unique and unrepeatable confluence of factors that come together in the leader/follower relationship and broader ministry situation. "Synergy," "convergence," and "luck" are words leadership theorists use to describe this phenomenon. "Providence," "gift of God's Spirit," and "answers to prayer" are words Christians use.

Understanding the role of confluence in congregational and institutional life is critical for several reasons. First, it keeps a leader humble. Beware of leaders who think the flourishing of their organization is all their own doing. Second, it keeps leaders flexible. Different circumstances dictate different leadership emphases and strategies. The effective leader constantly adapts to new challenges and opportunities. Third, it explains why the same person is not equally effective in all situations. Some leaders are fabulously successful in one setting and anything but successful in the next. All leaders and followers need to recognize that confluence is not a matter of easy formulas and steps, but of gift, grace, and surprise.

However, this reality of confluence cannot be used by leaders as an excuse for passivity: "Oh, well, things don't seem to be coming together this year. We'll see what happens next year." Effective leaders trust that as they take responsibility for matters of character, convictions, and competence that are within their control, God will work in and through their faithfulness to create this confluence of factors that constitute shalom and blessing.

For Christians, all four of these factors underscore the constant need for fervent prayer and openness to God's leading. But confluence especially underscores how dependent the church is on God's blessing upon the labors of leaders and congregations.

Why do we call this a "reciprocal" understanding of leadership?

"Reciprocal" literally means "back and forth" or "both ways." In any situation involving leadership, influence goes both ways. Leaders shape those they lead, but also are shaped by those they lead. In an extended definition of leadership, Jerry Zandstra points out that leaders both motivate and are motivated by their followers ("What Is Leadership?" unpublished paper, 2002). Leadership is *reciprocal*.

Thus, leadership can be understood only in terms of the leader in relationship to those being led. Such a reciprocal understanding of leadership leads to mutuality and partnership in ministry.

Rev. Rick Williams expressed this mutuality beautifully in a lecture he gave at Calvin Theological Seminary on April 11, 2002, entitled "A Glimpse of Pastoral Leadership in a Multi-Racial Church." When asked about leadership style, Rick answered,

> I know of a number of pastors who articulate for the congregation where the church ought to be going, and their challenge is to bring them along. I'm not that kind of a leader. My strength is to bring people together and say, "OK, this is what I think we should be thinking about; and now let's talk about it and pray about it." I'm always amazed by two things that happen then—how much better the ideas are that they come up with together and how much more responsibility they take for advancing it. I see my responsibility as being a catalyst and making sure we are asking the right questions and facilitating the discussion.

Some might misunderstand this reciprocal approach to leadership as being too weak, as lacking in vision and direction. But such is not the case. Being committed to good congregational process doesn't mean that a leader lacks strong convictions. Rather, he or she has wisdom in "asking the right questions" and strategically guiding the congregation forward.

This reciprocal understanding of leadership has also been called "adaptive leadership."

The concept of "adaptive leadership" is often misunderstood. Adaptive leadership does *not* refer to the pastor adapting to a congregation or a congregation to a pastor. "Adaptive leadership" is leadership that helps the congregation see the gap between its stated values and its current realities, and then adapt in ways that move the congregation closer to its values. Adaptive leadership helps a congregation see the disconnect between what it is and what it ought to be, and then learn and adapt accordingly. For example, a congregation that understands God's call to be a caring, accepting fellowship but is dominated by cliques faces an *adaptive* challenge—adapting *from* what it is (a fellowship dominated by cliques) *to* what it says it wants to be (an accepting, inviting fellowship).

In the leadership literature, "adaptive challenge" is usually contrasted with "technical solution." The congregation that is dominated by cliques and is cold to visitors no doubt desires to have more members join their church. But the temptation is always to reach for a *technical solution*. Examples of technical solutions are better signs on the walls, or more greeters, or a Visitor Center that gives information to visitors. Those may all be fine things to do, but they don't get at the *adaptive challenge*— namely, that the congregation itself must change. They must be more interested in the visitor than in touching base with their best friends.

Adaptive challenges by definition go to the heart of things and involve deep change. One of the biggest mistakes leaders and congregations make is confusing "technical solutions" and "adaptive challenges." Most congregational problems are not problems that have technical solutions. If a congregation's problems were only technical, they would have been solved long ago. Most congregational problems are adaptive challenges: How do we adapt from who we are to who we say we want to be? How do we align our stated values and our current realities? Adaptive leaders don't talk about "solutions" as much as they talk about "learning": What can we learn together? What have we learned through this?

This model of leadership is usually associated with a systems approach to leadership and lies behind much leadership training in North America today. Approaches to and theories of leadership come and go. Our goal is not to endorse a particular theory of leadership, but rather to find ways to talk about leadership that are faithful to biblical and theological principles, transcend past polarities, and give us positive models of leadership.

What are some ways to identify and positively describe effective leaders?

One of the main points of this study has been that leadership is not first of all a set of traits in one or more people designated as "leaders." There is no such thing as a single "leadership personality." Rather, leadership is a reciprocal relationship between leaders and the larger community.

Even so, leaders, no matter what their personality, act in certain ways. There are certain things leaders do, certain habits they practice, certain character strengths they seek to develop. The qualities listed below summarize many of the different points made in this paper. No leader has all of these qualities in equal measure. The list is not meant to make leaders feel more inadequate than they often already feel. This list is meant to be a positive checklist for all of us who want to be the very best leaders we can be.

Effective Christian leaders

- are godly in character, manifesting the life of Christ and the fruit of the Spirit
- pray fervently
- are emotionally healthy and able to function effectively in a variety of relationships
- see the world in optimistic and hopeful terms
- listen carefully
- are trustworthy
- are self-sacrificial
- create ownership of ministry vision
- utilize the giftedness of others
- acknowledge that resistance to effective leadership is normal and unavoidable
- are not afraid of conflict
- are persistent in the face of conflict
- are resilient in the face of setbacks
- are respected by all members of a group even if not always liked or agreed with
- bring people together, building consensus across lines of competing viewpoints

- get people talking about their differences in ways that promote learning, listening, and insight
- understand the importance of clear structures and practices of accountability
- stay in close contact with those who are resisting their leadership
- absorb the normal tensions and anxieties present in any community of people without overreacting and thereby escalating tensions
- understand and manage the process of change
- are humble and take little credit for the good things that happen around them

Adapted from chapter 2, "The Shape of Effective Leadership in the Church," from *Effective Leadership in the Church,* © 2005, Sustaining Pastoral Excellence in the Christian Reformed Church in North America, 2850 Kalamazoo Ave. SE, Grand Rapids, MI 49560. All rights reserved. Used by permission.

Notes

Preface

1. Kathy Smith, "Worship in Difficult Times: Thoughtful Leadership During Crisis, Conflict, or Transition," *Reformed Worship* 72 (June 2004): 3-5.

2. Craig A. Satterlee, *When God Speaks through Change: Preaching in Times of Congregational Transition,* Vital Worship, Healthy Congregations Series (Herndon, Va.: Alban Institute), 2005.

Chapter 2, Congregational Dynamics in Difficult Times

1. "Leadership Surveys Church Conflict," *Leadership* XXV, no. 4 (Fall 2004): 25.

2. John Ortberg, *If You Want to Walk on Water, You've Got to Get Out of the Boat* (Grand Rapids: Zondervan, 2001), 47.

3. Peter Steinke, "The Congregation as an Emotional System," lecture presented at Calvin Theological Seminary, Grand Rapids, Mich. (18 April 2002).

4. Jim Herrington, Robert Creech, and Trisha L. Taylor, *The Leader's Journey: Accepting the Call to Personal and Congregational Transformation* (San Francisco: Jossey-Bass, 2003), 33.

5. William Bridges, *Managing Transitions: Making the Most of Change,* rev. ed. (Cambridge, Mass.: Da Capo Press, 2003), 3-7.

6. Marshall Shelley, "Resolutely Redemptive," *Leadership* XXV, no. 4 (Fall 2004): 3.

7. Speed B. Leas, "Healthy versus Unhealthy Conflict Index," in Gil Rendle, *Behavioral Covenants in Congregations: A Handbook for Honoring Differences* (Herndon, Va.: Alban Institute, 1999), 120-121.

Chapter 3, Worship in Difficult Times

1. Leith Anderson, *Dying for Change* (Minneapolis: Bethany House, 1990).

2. William H. Willimon, *Worship as Pastoral Care* (Nashville: Abingdon, 1979), 16.

3. Michael Lindvall, in a sermon presented at the Music and Worship Conference of the Presbyterian Association of Musicians, Montreat, N.C., 24 June 2003.

4. Ernest Kurtz, *Not God: A History of Alcoholics Anonymous* (Center City, Minn.: Hazelden Educational Services, 1991).

5. Michael Lindvall, *The Christian Life: A Geography of God,* Foundations of Christian Faith Series (Louisville: Geneva Press, 2001), 59.

6. The eight aspects of worship cited are from John D. Witvliet, "Prologue," *The Worship Sourcebook* (Grand Rapids: Calvin Institute of Christian Worship, Faith Alive Christian Resources, and Baker Book House, 2004), 16-17.

7. John D. Witvliet, presentation at the Conference on Liturgy and Music, Denver, 8 July 2004.

8. John D. Witvliet, "A Time to Weep: Liturgical Lament in Times of Crisis," *Reformed Worship* 44 (June 1997): 23.

9. Gilbert Rendle, presentation at the Conference on Liturgy and Music, Denver, 8 July 2004.

10. Tom Brokaw, *The Greatest Generation* (New York: Random House, 1998).

11. Willimon, *Worship as Pastoral Care,* 81.

12. Ronald A. Heifetz, "Exercising Adaptive Leadership," presentation at the Lilly Endowment Forum, Indianapolis, 28 January 2005.

13. Norman Shawchuck, *How to Manage Conflict in the Church: Conflict Interventions and Resources* (Leith, N. Dak.: Spiritual Growth Resources, 1983), 37-39.

Chapter 4, Worship in Times of Crisis

1. Jill M. Hudson, *Congregational Trauma: Caring, Coping, and Learning* (Herndon, Va.: Alban Institute, 1998), 101.

2. Carol M. Norén, *In Times of Crisis and Sorrow: A Minister's Manual Resource Guide* (San Francisco: Jossey-Bass, 2001), 18.

3. Ibid., 59.

4. Ibid., 59–60.

5. Hudson, *Congregational Trauma,* 95.

6. Ibid., 99.

7. J. Frank Henderson, *Liturgies of Lament* (Archdiocese of Chicago: Liturgy Training Publications, 1994), 1.

8. Daniel Migliore and Kathleen Billman, *Rachel's Cry: Prayer of Lament and Rebirth of Hope* (Cleveland: United Church Press, 1999), 14.

9. Roman Crews, *Good Lord, Deliver Us: The Praise of God and the Problem of Evil* (Akron, Ohio: OSL Publications, 2001), 95.

10. Carl J. Bosma and Ronald J. Nydam, "Being Sad in Worship: Lament as Spiritual Muscle," presentation at the Calvin Symposium on Worship, Grand Rapids, 30 January 2004.

11. Witvliet, "A Time to Weep," 22.

12. Ibid., 22–23.

13. Ibid., 23–24.

14. Ibid., 24.

15. Ibid., 26.

16. Ibid., 26.

17. Eugene H. Peterson, *The Message: The Bible in Contemporary Language* (Colorado Springs: NavPress, 2002), 923.

18. Calvin Seerveld, *Voicing God's Psalms* (Grand Rapids: Eerdmans, 2005).

19. Ibid., 85.

20. Norén, *In Times of Crisis and Sorrow,* 63.

21. Ibid., 64.

22. Hudson, *Congregational Trauma,* 95.

23. John W. Cooper, "The Problem of Evil: The Shipwreck of Faith?" *Calvin Theological Seminary Forum* 13, no. 1 (Winter 2006): 7.

24. Norén, *In Times of Crisis and Sorrow,* 223.

25. *Ecumenical Creeds and Reformed Confessions* (Grand Rapids: CRC Publications, 1988), 13.

26. Ibid., 89-90.

27. *The Worship Sourcebook* (Grand Rapids: Calvin Institute of Christian Worship, Faith Alive Christian Resources, and Baker Book House, 2004), 76.

28. Craig A. Satterlee, *When God Speaks through Change,* 61-62.

29. Ronald Byars, "Worship and Theology in Harmony," presentation at the Calvin Symposium on Worship, Grand Rapids, 27 January 2005.

30. Ronald Byars, "Creeds and Prayers = Ecclesiology," in *A More Profound Alleluia: Theology and Worship in Harmony,* ed. Leanne Van Dyk (Grand Rapids: Eerdmans, 2005), 102-103.

31. William H. Willimon, *Worship as Pastoral Care* (Nashville: Abingdon, 1979), 66.

32. Byars, "Creeds and Prayers," 103.

33. Migliore and Billman, *Rachel's Cry,* 19.

34. Carole Cotton Winn, "Turn My Mourning into Joy: Ministry after the Storms," *Sustaining Pastoral Excellence,* electronic newsletter, December 2005–January 2006. http://www.divinity.duke.edu/programs/spe/articles/200512/mourningintojoy.html

35. Henderson, *Liturgies of Lament,* 26.

36. Ibid., 26-27.

37. Thomas Moore, "Come, You Disconsolate," rev. Thomas Hastings, in *Psalter Hymnal* (Grand Rapids: CRC Publications, 1987), 538.

38. John L. Bell and Graham Maule, *When Grief Is Raw: Songs for Times of Sorrow and Bereavement* (Glasgow: Wild Goose Publications; and Chicago: GIA Publications, 1997), 8.

39. *Sing! A New Creation* (Grand Rapids: Calvin Institute of Christian Worship, Faith Alive Christian Resources, and Reformed Church in America, Office of Worship, 2001).

40. *Psalter Hymnal* (Grand Rapids: CRC Publications, 1987).

41. *With One Voice* (Minneapolis: Augsburg Fortress, 1995).

42. *Sing the Faith* (Louisville: Geneva Press, 2003).

43. *Gather Comprehensive* (Chicago: GIA Publications, 2004).

44. *Glory & Praise* (Portland, Ore.: OCP Publications, 1997).

45. *Hymnal: A Worship Book* (Elgin, Ill.: Brethren Press; Newton, Kans.: Faith and Life Press; Scottdale, Pa.: Mennonite Publishing House, 1992).

46. *The United Methodist Hymnal* (Nashville: United Methodist Publishing House, 1989).

47. *African American Heritage Hymnal* (Chicago: GIA Publications, 2001).

48. Crews, *Good Lord, Deliver Us,* 19.

49. Ibid., 61.

50. *The Worship Sourcebook,* 362.

51. Hudson, *Congregational Trauma,* 135.

Chapter 5, Worship in Times of Transition

1. Carolyn Weese and J. Russell Crabtree, *The Elephant in the Boardroom: Speaking the Unspoken about Pastoral Transitions* (San Francisco: Jossey-Bass, 2004), 103.

2. Joyce Zimmerman, seminar on "The Last Thirty Years in Worship: What We've Learned along the Way," Calvin Symposium on Worship, Grand Rapids, 26 January 2006.

3. Loren Mead, *A Change of Pastors . . . and How It Affects Change in the Congregation* (Herndon, Va.: Alban, 2005), 69.

4. Ibid., 70.

5. Satterlee, *When God Speaks through Change,* 118.

6. Anthony B. Robinson, "Step Aside," *Christian Century,* 26 July 2005, 8-9.

7. Edward A. White, *Saying Goodbye: A Time of Growth for Congregations and Pastors* (Herndon, Va.: Alban Institute, 1990), 69-90.

8. Ibid., 71.

9. Duane Kelderman, "Embracing Tensions," *Calvin Theological Seminary Forum* 12, no. 2 (Spring 2005): 4.

10. Terry Foland, "Merger as a New Beginning," in *Ending with Hope: A Resource for Closing Congregations,* ed. Beth Ann Gaede (Herndon, Va.: Alban Institute, 2002), 70.

11. Ibid., 74-76.

12. Robert T. Roberts, "Finding Our Mission: Stages in the Life of an Urban Congregation," in *Size Transitions in Congregations,* ed. Beth Ann Gaede (Herndon, Va.: Alban Institute, 2001), 144.

13. Thomas G. Long, *Beyond the Worship Wars: Building Vital and Faithful Worship* (Herndon, Va.: Alban Institute, 2001), 109.

14. Nancy Beach, seminar on "The Last Thirty Years in Worship: What We've Learned along the Way," Calvin Symposium on Worship, Grand Rapids, 26 January 2006.

15. Michael Bausch, "Multimedia and Worship," *Alban Weekly,* electronic newsletter, 20 February 2006. http://www.alban.org/weekly/2006/060220_Multimedia.asp.

16. Willimon, *Worship as Pastoral Care,* 67.

17. Quentin J. Schultze, *High-Tech Worship? Using Presentational Technologies Wisely* (Grand Rapids: Baker Books, 2004), 65.

18. Ibid., 97-103.

19. Tod Bolsinger, *It Takes a Church to Raise a Christian: How the Community of God Transforms Lives* (Grand Rapids: Brazos Press, 2004), 89.

20. Ibid., 105.

21. Cornelius Plantinga, Jr., and Sue Rozeboom, *Discerning the Spirits: A Guide to Thinking about Christian Worship Today* (Grand Rapids: Eerdmans, 2003), 89-90.

22. Mark Lau Branson, *Memories, Hopes, and Conversations: Appreciative Inquiry and Congregational Change* (Herndon, Va.: Alban Institute, 2004), xiii.

23. Ronald A. Heifetz and Marty Linsky, *Leadership on the Line: Staying Alive through the Dangers of Leading* (Boston: Harvard Business School Press, 2002), 14.

24. Branson, *Memories, Hopes, and Conversations,* 43.

25. Ibid., 64.

26. Ibid., 2, 124.

27. Ibid., 24-27.

28. Ibid., 148.

29. Susan M. Weber, "Appreciative Inquiry: Sustaining the Goodness of Pastoral Excellence," *Sustaining Pastoral Excellence,* electronic newsletter, December 2005–January 2006. http://www.divinity.duke.edu/programs/spe/articles/200512/inquiry.html

30. Ibid.

31. Ibid.

32. Diana Butler Bass, "Pilgrimage Congregations," in *From Nomads to Pilgrims: Stories from Practicing Congregations,* eds. Diana Butler Bass and Joseph Stewart-Sicking (Herndon, Va.: Alban Institute, 2006), 167.

33. Ibid., 168.

34. Joseph Stewart-Sicking, "Christian Practices in the Congregation: The Structure of Vitality," in *From Nomads to Pilgrims: Stories from Practicing Congregations,* eds. Diana Butler Bass and Joseph Stewart-Sicking (Herndon, Va.: Alban Institute, 2006), 2.

35. Eugene Peterson, interview at Calvin Theological Seminary, 25 January 2006.

36. Bass and Stewart-Sicking, *From Nomads to Pilgrims,* 168.

37. Ibid., 169.

38. Heifetz and Linsky, *Leadership on the Line*, 53.

39. Willimon, *Worship as Pastoral Care,* 57-58.

40. An excellent resource for worship evaluation can be found in Norma deWaal Malefyt and Howard Vanderwell, *Designing Worship Together: Models and Strategies for Worship Planning,* Vital Worship, Healthy Congregations Series (Herndon, Va.: Alban Institute, 2005), 153-176.

41. M. Craig Barnes, *When God Interrupts: Finding New Life through Unwanted Change* (Downers Grove, Ill.: InterVarsity Press, 1996), 15.

42. M. Craig Barnes, "Rabble Roused," *Leadership* XXV, no. 4 (Fall 2004): 114.

43. Ibid.

Chapter 6, Worship in Times of Conflict

1. Larry W. Osborne, "Making Changes without Getting People Steamed," *Leadership* (Spring 1998): 42-48.

2. Ibid., 47.

3. Gilbert R. Rendle, *Leading Change in the Congregation: Spiritual and Organizational Tools for Leaders* (Herndon, Va.: Alban Institute, 1998), 21.

4. *The Worship Sourcebook,* 166.

5. Speed B. Leas, *Moving Your Church through Conflict* (Herndon, Va.: Alban Institute, 1985, 2002), online only at http://www.alban.org/OnLineReports.asp

6. Speed B. Leas, presentation in a workshop on "Healthy Congregations," Peoria, Ill. (June 2002).

7. Congregational Resource Guide (Indianapolis: Indianapolis Center for Congregations, and Alban Institute), www.congregationalresources.org

8. Leas, workshop on "Healthy Congregations."

9. Debra Rienstra, *So Much More: An Invitation to Christian Spirituality* (San Francisco: Jossey-Bass, 2005), 167-168.

10. Richard Blackburn, workshop on "Facilitating Healthy Pastor-Congregation Relations," Grand Rapids, May 2002.

11. Richard Blackburn, *Mediation Skills Training Institute* (Lombard, Ill.: Lombard Mennonite Peace Center, 2004), E-1.

12. Thomas G. Long, presentation at the Calvin Symposium on Worship, Grand Rapids, 26 January 2006.

13. Thomas G. Long, *Testimony: Talking Ourselves into Being Christian* (San Francisco: Jossey-Bass, 2004), 34.

14. Ibid., 35.

15. Marshall Shelley, "Resolutely Redemptive," *Leadership* XXV, no. 4 (Fall 2004): 3.

16. Loren Mead, foreword to *The Practicing Congregation: Imagining a New Old Church,* by Diana Butler Bass (Herndon, Va.: Alban Institute, 2004), x.

17. Bass, *The Practicing Congregation,* 21.

18. Ibid., 22.

19. Ibid., 35-36.

20. Ibid., 48.

21. Rienstra, *So Much More,* 171-172.

22. Ibid., 176.

23. Cornelius Plantinga, Jr, "Hypocrisy and Grace," *The Banner,* February 2004, 40-42.

24. Long, *Testimony,* 61.

25. Lewis B. Smedes, *The Art of Forgiving: When You Need to Forgive and Don't Know How* (New York: Ballantine Books, 1996), 135, 137.

26. Steven Chase, *The Tree of Life: Models of Christian Prayer* (Grand Rapids: Baker Academic, 2005), 107.

27. Ibid., 198.

28. Leas, *Moving Your Church through Conflict,* 7-8.

29. Willimon, *Worship as Pastoral Care,* 68.

30. *The Worship Sourcebook,* 734.

31. Ibid., 394-395.

32. *Sing! A New Creation,* 240.

33. Arthur Paul Boers, *Never Call Them Jerks: Healthy Responses to Difficult Behavior* (Herndon, Va.: Alban Institute, 1999), 73-75.

34. Shawchuck, *How to Manage Conflict in the Church,* 44.

35. *Celebrate God's Presence,* 690.

36. *Sing! A New Creation* (Grand Rapids: Calvin Institute of Christian Worship, Faith Alive Christian Resources, and Reformed Church in America, Office of Worship, 2001).

37. *The United Methodist Hymnal* (Nashville: United Methodist Publishing House, 1989).

38. *Glory & Praise* (Portland, Ore.: OCP Publications, 1997).

39. *Gather Comprehensive* (Chicago: GIA Publications, 2004).

Chapter 7, Leadership in Difficult Times

1. Herrington, Creech, and Taylor, *The Leader's Journey,* xiv.

2. Norén, *In Times of Crisis and Sorrow,* 94.

3. Ibid.

4. Boers, *Never Call Them Jerks,* 30.

5. Edwin H. Friedman, *Reinventing Leadership* (New York: Guilford Publications, 1996), videocassette, 42 min.

6. Ibid.

7. Ronald Heifetz quoted in Anthony B. Robinson, "Give and Take: Leadership as a Spiritual Practice," *Christian Century,* 4 October 2005, 28.

8. Willimon, *Worship as Pastoral Care,* 80-81.

9. Ibid., 84.

10. Heifetz, presentation on "Exercising Adaptive Leadership."

11. Rendle, presentation at the Conference on Liturgy and Music.

12. Long, *Testimony,* 47.

13. Ibid., 54.

14. Dallas Willard, *The Spirit of the Disciplines: Understanding How God Changes Lives* (San Francisco: Harper Collins, 1998), 9.

15. *Effective Leadership in the Church* (Grand Rapids: Sustaining Pastoral Excellence in the Christian Reformed Church in North America, 2005), 20.

16. Ibid., 17.

17. Ibid., 20.

18. Ibid., 21.

19. Ibid.

20. Robinson, "Give and Take," 28.

21. *Effective Leadership in the Church,* 25.

22. Ibid.

23. Ibid., 25-26.

24. Robinson, "Give and Take," 28.

25. Blackburn, workshop on "Facilitating Healthy Pastor-Congregation Relations."

Bibliography

African American Heritage Hymnal. Chicago: GIA Publications, Inc., 2001.

Anderson, Leith. *Dying for Change.* Minneapolis: Bethany House Publishers, 1990.

Authentic Worship in a Changing Culture. Grand Rapids, Mich.: CRC Publications, 1997.

Barnes, M. Craig. "Rabble Roused." *Leadership* XXV, no. 4 (2004): 114.

———. *When God Interrupts: Finding New Life through Unwanted Change.* Downers Grove, Ill.: InterVarsity Press, 1996.

Bass, Diana Butler. "Pilgrimage Congregations." In *From Nomads to Pilgrims: Stories from Practicing Congregations,* eds. Diana Butler Bass and Joseph Stewart-Sicking, 167-178. Herndon, Va.: Alban Institute, 2006.

———. *The Practicing Congregation: Imagining a New Old Church.* Herndon, Va.: Alban Institute, 2004.

Bass, Diana Butler, and Joseph Stewart-Sicking, eds. *From Nomads to Pilgrims: Stories from Practicing Congregations.* Herndon, Va.: Alban Institute, 2006.

Bausch, Michael. "Multimedia and Worship," *Alban Weekly,* electronic newsletter, 20 February 2006.

Beach, Nancy. "The Last Thirty Years in Worship: What We've Learned along the Way." Seminar at the Calvin Symposium on Worship, Grand Rapids, Mich., 26 January 2006.

Bell, John L., and Graham Maule. *When Grief Is Raw: Songs for Times of Sorrow and Bereavement.* Glasgow: Wild Goose Publications, and Chicago: GIA Publications, 1997.

Blackburn, Richard. *Mediation Skills Training Institute.* Lombard, Ill.: Lombard Mennonite Peace Center, 2004. www.LMPeaceCenter.org.

————. Workshop on "Facilitating Healthy Pastor-Congregation Relations." Grand Rapids, Mich., May 2002.

Boers, Arthur P. *Never Call Them Jerks: Healthy Responses to Difficult
Behavior.* Herndon, Va.: Alban Institute, 1999.

Bolsinger, Tod. *It Takes a Church to Raise a Christian: How the Community of God Transforms Lives.* Grand Rapids, Mich.: Brazos Press,
2004.

The Book of Alternative Services of the Anglican Church of Canada.
Toronto: Anglican Book Centre, 1985.

Book of Common Worship. Louisville, Ky.: Westminster/John Knox
Press, 1993.

*Book of Occasional Services: A Liturgical Resource Supplementing the Book
of Common Worship,* 1993. Louisville, Ky.: Geneva Press, 1999.

Book of Worship, United Church of Christ. New York: United Church
of Christ, Office for Church Life and Leadership, 1986; Cleveland:
United Church of Christ, Local Church Ministries, Worship and Education Ministry Team, 2002.

Bosma, Carl J., and Ronald J. Nydam. "Being Sad in Worship: Lament
as Spiritual Muscle." Presentation at the Calvin Symposium on Worship, Grand Rapids, Mich., 30 January 2004.

Branson, Mark Lau. *Memories, Hopes, and Conversations: Appreciative
Inquiry and Congregational Change.* Herndon, Va.: Alban Institute,
2004.

Bridges, William. *Managing Transitions: Making the Most of Change,*
rev. ed. Cambridge, Mass.: Da Capo Press, 2003.

Brokaw, Tom. *The Greatest Generation.* New York: Random House, 1998.

Byars, Ronald. "Creeds and Prayers = Ecclesiology." *In A More Pro-
found Alleluia: Theology and Worship in Harmony,* ed. Leanne Van
Dyk, 83-108. Grand Rapids, Mich.: William B. Eerdmans Publishing
Co., 2005.

————. "Worship and Theology in Harmony." Presentation at the Calvin
Symposium on Worship. Grand Rapids, Mich., 27 January 2005.

*Celebrate God's Presence: A Book of Services for The United Church
of Canada.* Etobicoke, Ontario: United Church Publishing House,
2000.

Chase, Steven. *The Tree of Life: Models of Christian Prayer.* Grand Rapids, Mich.: Baker Academic, 2005.

The Complete Book of Christian Prayer. New York: Continuum, 2000.

Congregational Resource Guide. Herndon, Va.: Alban Institute and Indianapolis Center for Congregations. www.congregational resources.org.

Cooper, John W. "The Problem of Evil: The Shipwreck of Faith?" *Calvin Theological Seminary Forum* 13, no. 1 (Winter 2006): 6–7.

Crawford, Janet, et al. *Celebrating Community: Prayers and Songs of Unity.* Geneva, Switzerland: World Council of Churches, 1993.

Crews, Roman. *Good Lord, Deliver Us: The Praise of God and the Problem of Evil.* Akron, Ohio: OSL Publications, 2001.

deWaal Malefyt, Norma, and Howard Vanderwell. *Designing Worship Together: Models and Strategies for Worship Planning.* Vital Worship, Healthy Congregations Series. Herndon, Va.: Alban Institute, 2005.

Ecumenical Creeds and Reformed Confessions. Grand Rapids, Mich.: CRC Publications, 1988.

Effective Leadership in the Church. Grand Rapids, Mich.: Sustaining Pastoral Excellence in the Christian Reformed Church in North America, 2005.

Engle, Paul E. *Baker's Worship Handbook.* Grand Rapids, Mich.: Baker Books, 1998.

Eucharistic Liturgy of Lima. Geneva, Switzerland: Faith and Order Commission of the World Council of Churches, 1982.

Foland, Terry. "Merger as a New Beginning." In *Ending with Hope: A Resource for Closing Congregations,* ed. Beth Ann Gaede, 70-76. Herndon, Va.: Alban Institute, 2002.

Friedman, Edwin H. *Reinventing Leadership.* Guilford Publications, Inc., 1996. Videocassette, 42 min.

Galloway, Kathy, ed. *The Pattern of Our Days: Worship in the Celtic Tradition from the Iona Community.* New York: Paulist Press, 1996.

Gather Comprehensive. Chicago: GIA Publications, Inc., 2004.

Glory & Praise. Portland, Ore.: OCP Publications, 1997.

Heifetz, Ronald A. "Exercising Adaptive Leadership." Presentation at the Lilly Endowment Forum, Indianapolis, Ind., 28 January 2005.

Heifetz, Ronald A. and Marty Linsky. *Leadership on the Line: Staying Alive through the Dangers of Leading.* Boston: Harvard Business School Press, 2002.

Henderson, J. Frank. *Liturgies of Lament.* Archdiocese of Chicago: Liturgy Training Publications, 1994.

Herrington, Jim, Robert Creech, and Trisha L. Taylor. *The Leader's Journey: Accepting the Call to Personal and Congregational Transformation.* San Francisco: Jossey-Bass, 2003.

Hudson, Jill M. *Congregational Trauma: Caring, Coping, and Learning.* Herndon, Va.: Alban Institute, 1998.

Hymnal: A Worship Book. Elgin, Ill.: Brethren Press; Newton, Kans.: Faith and Life Press; Scottdale, Pa.: Mennonite Publishing House, 1992.

Jesus Christ—the Life of the World: A Worship Book for the Sixth Assembly of the World Council of Churches. Geneva, Switzerland: World Council of Churches, 1983.

Kelderman, Duane. "Embracing Tensions." *Calvin Theological Seminary Forum* 12, no. 2 (Spring 2005): 3-4.

Kirk-Duggan, Cheryl A. *Soul Pearls: Worship Resources for the Black Church.* Nashville, Tenn.: Abingdon Press, 2003.

Kurtz, Ernest. *Not God: A History of Alcoholics Anonymous.* Center City, Minn.: Hazelden Educational Services, 1991.

"Leadership Surveys Church Conflict," *Leadership* XXV, no. 4 (Fall 2004): 25.

Leas, Speed B. "Healthy versus Unhealthy Conflict Index." In *Behavioral Covenants in Congregations: A Handbook for Honoring Differences,* Gil Rendle, 120-121. Herndon, Va.: Alban Institute, 1999.

———. *Moving Your Church through Conflict.* Herndon, Va.: Alban Institute, 1985, 2002), online only at http://www.alban.org/OnLineReports.asp (accessed 11 November 2005).

———. Presentation at Workshop on "Healthy Congregations." Peoria, Ill., June 2002.

Lindvall, Michael. *The Christian Life: A Geography of God.* Foundations of Christian Faith Series. Louisville, Ky.: Geneva Press, 2001.

———. Sermon at the Music and Worship Conference of the Presbyterian Association of Musicians. Montreat, N.C., 24 June 2003.

Long, Thomas G. *Beyond the Worship Wars: Building Vital and Faithful Worship.* Herndon, Va.: Alban Institute, 2001.

———. Presentation at the Calvin Symposium on Worship. Grand Rapids, Mich., 26 January 2006.

———. *Testimony: Talking Ourselves into Being Christian.* San Francisco: Jossey-Bass, 2004.

Mead, Loren. *A Change of Pastors . . . and How It Affects Change in the Congregation.* Herndon, Va.: Alban Institute, 2005.

Migliore, Daniel and Kathleen Billman. *Rachel's Cry: Prayer of Lament and Rebirth of Hope*. Cleveland: United Church Press, 1999.

Network. London: United Society for the Propagation of the Gospel, 1976–1990.

Norén, Carol M. *In Times of Crisis and Sorrow: A Minister's Manual Resource Guide*. San Francisco: Jossey-Bass, 2001.

Ortberg, John. *If You Want to Walk on Water, You've Got to Get Out of the Boat*. Grand Rapids, Mich.: Zondervan, 2001.

Osborne, Larry W. "Making Changes without Getting People Steamed." *Leadership* (Spring 1998): 42-48.

Peterson, Eugene H. Interview at Calvin Theological Seminary. Grand Rapids, Mich., 25 January 2006.

———. *The Message: The Bible in Contemporary Language*. Colorado Springs, Colo.: NavPress, 2002.

Plantinga, Cornelius, Jr. "Hypocrisy and Grace." *The Banner*, February 2004, 40-42.

Plantinga, Cornelius, Jr., and Sue A. Rozeboom. *Discerning the Spirits: A Guide to Thinking about Christian Worship Today*. Grand Rapids, Mich.: William B. Eerdmans Publishing Co., 2003.

Psalter Hymnal. Grand Rapids, Mich.: CRC Publications, 1987.

Rendle, Gilbert R. *Behavioral Covenants in Congregations: A Handbook for Honoring Differences*. Herndon, Va.: Alban Institute, 1999.

———. *Leading Change in the Congregation: Spiritual and Organizational Tools for Leaders*. Herndon, Va.: Alban Institute, 1998.

———. Presentation at the Conference on Liturgy and Music. Denver, Colo., 8 July 2004.

Rienstra, Debra. *So Much More: An Invitation to Christian Spirituality*. San Francisco: Jossey-Bass, 2005.

Roberts, Robert T. "Finding Our Mission: Stages in the Life of an Urban Congregation." In *Size Transitions in Congregations,* ed. Beth Ann Gaede, 143-149. Herndon, Va.: Alban Institute, 2001.

Robinson, Anthony B. "Give and Take: Leadership as a Spiritual Practice." *The Christian Century,* 4 October 2005, 28-32.

———. "Step Aside." *The Christian Century,* 26 July 2005, 8-9.

Satterlee, Craig A. *When God Speaks through Change: Preaching in Times of Congregational Transition*. Vital Worship, Healthy Congregations Series. Herndon, Va.: Alban Institute, 2005.

Schultze, Quentin J. *High-Tech Worship? Using Presentational Technologies Wisely*. Grand Rapids, Mich.: Baker Books, 2004.

Seerveld, Calvin. *Voicing God's Psalms.* Grand Rapids, Mich.: William B. Eerdmans Publishing Co., 2005.

Shawchuck, Norman. *How to Manage Conflict in the Church: Conflict Interventions and Resources.* Leith, N. Dak.: Spiritual Growth Resources, 1983. Call 800-359-7363 for further information.

Shelley, Marshall. "Resolutely Redemptive." *Leadership* XXV, no. 4 (Fall 2004): 3.

Sing! A New Creation. Grand Rapids: Calvin Institute of Christian Worship, Faith Alive Christian Resources; and New York: Reformed Church Press, 2001.

Sing the Faith. Louisville, Ky.: Geneva Press, 2003.

Smedes, Lewis B. *The Art of Forgiving: When You Need to Forgive and Don't Know How.* New York: Ballantine Books, 1996.

Smith, Kathy. "Worship in Difficult Times: Thoughtful Leadership During Crisis, Conflict, or Transition," *Reformed Worship* 72 (June 2004): 3-5.

Steinke, Peter. "The Congregation as an Emotional System." Lecture presented at Calvin Theological Seminary, Grand Rapids, Mich., 18 April 2002.

Stewart-Sicking, Joseph. "Christian Practices in the Congregation: The Structure of Vitality." In *From Nomads to Pilgrims: Stories from Practicing Congregations,* eds. Diana Butler Bass and Joseph Stewart-Sicking, 1-6. Herndon, Va.: Alban Institute, 2006.

The United Methodist Hymnal. Nashville, Tenn.: United Methodist Publishing House, 1989.

Van Dyk, Leanne, ed. *A More Profound Alleluia: Theology and Worship in Harmony.* Grand Rapids, Mich.: William B. Eerdmans Publishing Co., 2004.

Weber, Susan M. "Appreciative Inquiry: Sustaining the Goodness of Pastoral Excellence," *Sustaining Pastoral Excellence,* electronic newsletter, December 2005–January 2006. http://www.divinity.duke.edu/programs/spe/articles/200512/inquiry.html (accessed January 13, 2006).

Weese, Carolyn and J. Russell Crabtree. *The Elephant in the Boardroom: Speaking the Unspoken about Pastoral Transitions.* San Francisco: Jossey-Bass, 2004.

White, Edward A. *Saying Goodbye: A Time of Growth for Congregations and Pastors.* Herndon, Va.: Alban Institute, 1990.

Wild Goose Worship Group. *A Wee Worship Book;* fourth incarnation. Chicago: GIA Publications, Inc., 1999.

Willard, Dallas. *The Spirit of the Disciplines: Understanding How God Changes Lives.* San Francisco: Harper Collins, 1998.

Williams, Dick, ed. *Prayers for Today's Church.* Minneapolis: Augsburg Publishing House, 1977.

Willimon, William H. *Worship as Pastoral Care.* Nashville, Tenn.: Abingdon, 1979.

Winn, Carole Cotton. "Turn My Mourning into Joy: Ministry after the Storms." *Sustaining Pastoral Excellence,* electronic newsletter, December 2005–January 2006. http://www.divinity.duke.edu/programs/spe/articles/200512/mourningintojoy.html (accessed January 13, 2006).

With One Voice. Minneapolis, Minn.: Augsburg Fortress, 1995.

Witvliet, John D. "A Time to Weep: Liturgical Lament in Times of Crisis." *Reformed Worship* 44 (June 1997): 22-26.

———. Presentation at the Conference on Liturgy and Music. Denver, Colo., 8 July 2004.

———. "Prologue." In *The Worship Sourcebook,* 15-39. Grand Rapids, Mich.: Calvin Institute of Christian Worship, Faith Alive Christian Resources, and Baker Book House, 2004.

The Worship Sourcebook. Grand Rapids, Mich.: Calvin Institute of Christian Worship, Faith Alive Christian Resources, and Baker Book House, 2004.

Zimmerman, Joyce. "The Last Thirty Years in Worship: What We've Learned along the Way." Seminar at the Calvin Symposium on Worship. Grand Rapids, Mich., 26 January 2006.